D1129040

The Gifts of Interpretation

Fifteen Guiding Principles for
Interpreting Nature and Culture

Third Edition

Larry Beck

Ted T. Cable

SAGAMORE
PUBLISHING

©2011 Larry Beck and Ted T. Cable
All rights reserved. No part of this book may be reproduced in any form
or by any electronic or mechanical means including information storage
and retrieval systems without permission in writing from the publisher,
except by a reviewer who may quote brief passages in a review.

Chapter illustrations and cover drawing © Tsuyoshi Matsumoto
Pine cone illustration © Helen Kagan
All artwork is published courtesy of Tsuyoshi Matsumoto and Helen
Kagan. The artists' work is strictly protected by copyright law. Images of
the artwork may not be reproduced without the express written consent
of the artist.

Publishers: Joseph J. Bannon and Peter L. Bannon
Director of Sales and Marketing: M. Douglas Sanders
Director of Development and Production: Susan M. Davis
Technology Manager: Christopher Thompson

ISBN print edition: 978-1-57167-636-8
ISBN ebook: 978-1-57167-637-5
LCCN: 2011930870

Sagamore Publishing LLC
1807 N. Federal Dr.
Urbana, IL 61801
www.sagamorepub.com

For our sons:

Spencer and Benjamin
—L.B.

Tim, Eric, and Scott
—T.C.

Aye, starry-eyed did I rejoice
With marvel of a child
And there were those who heard my voice
Although my words were wild:
So as I go my wistful way,
With worship let me sing,
And treasure to my farewell day
God's Gift of Wondering.

—Robert Service

Contents

Foreword

to the Third Edition

By Sam H. Ham, Ph.D.

A person engages in a communication event unaware that it's something that someone else, somewhere, has called an "interpretive this or that." So now what happens? What's in store for the person? Who are the people behind the "this or that," and what are they trying to achieve with it? What principles guided their planning, development and delivery of it? How did they even know where to start? What was their thinking?

These are the questions awaiting the reader of *The Gifts of Interpretation—Fifteen Guiding Principles for Interpreting Nature and Culture*. What my colleagues, Larry Beck and Ted Cable, have produced here is certainly a how-to book; but it is not so much a how-to-do book (as they point out, many other good ones are available today), but rather this is a how-to-think book. It is a scholar's view of interpretation, rooted in seminal literatures, not only about interpretation itself, but about knowledge, philosophy, science, and human behavior. Such books are rare in the interpretation field, notwithstanding the classics given us by the likes of Freeman Tilden, Enos Mills, and others. Indeed, in the contemporary literature on interpretation, this volume stands alone.

The Gifts of Interpretation is a masterful collection of the authors' thoughts, views, and guiding philosophies about the act and process of interpretation. It is written as well for the university classroom as it is for the interpreter lying awake at night contemplating the value and potential of her work. It addresses itself to the real world, the one in which the interpreter on the other end of the "this or that" actually inhabits, and it speaks powerful ideas in plain and engaging language that will potentially transform one's thinking. All told, I cannot help but feel that this work is itself destined to be a classic in the interpretation literature.

As did its two previous editions, *The Gifts of Interpretation* will make you think! And that is perhaps its single greatest contribution. Many texts tell interpreters what to think, but only rarely do they provoke their readers to do their own thinking—to struggle with inconsistencies, to challenge dogma, and to question what might previously have been their own philosophical comfort zones. Toward this end, Larry and Ted engage their readers in thought, where questions rather than answers are often the outcome.

I am especially pleased to see the essays on "meaning making" and the important recognition that Tilden was correct in advancing his famous dichotomy, "not instruction, but provocation." Although Tilden was writing about the interface between an interpreter and a visitor, he might well have been writing about books like this one. Interpreters who turn these pages will be motivated to achieve their own brand of excellence, not because of what Larry and Ted tell them, but because of the thinking Larry and Ted provoke them to do for themselves. According to decades of research (and many hundreds of published studies), this quality destines *The Gifts of Interpretation* to become a landmark achievement in the interpretation literature. I believe its impact will be felt for generations.

So what's with the "gifts" metaphor? Or is it even a metaphor? Admittedly, when I first read the title of this new edition, I wondered whether Ted and Larry would be able to make a case that each of the chapters truly treats something "gift-like" that interpreters bear and give to others (the spark, the revelation, the story, and so forth). Is there something literal in their claim, or is the "gift" link just another warm and fuzzy idea?

Whatever doubts I might have harbored had vanished by the end of the first chapter (The Gift of a Spark). Yes, the spark an interpreter might ignite in someone else is nothing short of a gift. It is given not only freely by the interpreter, but it is the potential to catalyze the spark that validates the interpreter's role in the first place. It is given of the interpreter's best quality—love, and its value grows with time in the lives of those who received it.

So went my thinking through each and every one of the fifteen chapters. "Yes," I thought. "Larry and Ted are right. This too is a gift." What remains is for interpreters everywhere to realize that they possess these gifts and that the greatest satisfaction any of us ever receives from professional success manifests itself in knowing (truly knowing) at the end of a career that these gifts have been handed off to others countless times. There is little that is tangible or material in the rewards an interpreter hopes will result from a life of work. But, of course, that was never the point of it in the first place. As Larry and Ted remind us in their brilliant concluding chapter (The Gift of Hope):

Many interpreters ... are in their profession for reasons other than financial gain. The challenge and joy of the work itself is rewarding, along with the knowledge that one is giving a gift that cannot be measured monetarily.

I began this foreword with a premise and a fair question about it: A person engages in a communication event unaware that it's something that someone else, somewhere, has called an "interpretive this or that." So now what happens?

In a perfect world, the answer is, "something important." Potentially, many gifts are given in the form of sparks, revelations, and deeply personal connections with things that matter to the recipients; and yes, there is the gift of hope itself. Such gifts can go a long way toward defining and enhancing the human spirit. What better gift could there be, save one? That would be this book itself. Indeed, Larry and Ted have given us yet another gift of seeing interpretation through their eyes. It's a view worth having in my opinion.

Sam H. Ham, Ph.D.
Professor and Director
Center for International Training and Outreach
Department of Conservation Social Sciences
University of Idaho

Foreword

to the Second Edition

By John C. F. Luzader

"Passion!"

The word resounded throughout the room. "Passion! Love! A deep, emotional feeling for the subject!" Like an evangelical minister, the speaker had jolted us out of our early-morning drowsiness with this emotional outburst. I was sitting in a classroom listening in awe to the impassioned teachings of an "old man" wearing a bolo tie telling all of us what was required to be an outstanding interpreter.

"Do you know what it takes to be a great interpreter? Passion! Passion! Love! A deep emotional feeling for the subject."

Thus began my journey in the field of interpretation. The "old man" was Freeman Tilden and for the next few days, he took the class through his six principles of interpretation which he published as *Interpreting Our Heritage*. It was an exhausting and exhilarating passage into the field and an awakening to the realization that I had much to learn before I could consider myself a professional.

On the last day of the training, Freeman Tilden did a brief wrap-up of our experience, and as he gathered his notes and put on his hat, he turned one last time to the class. "And now it is up to all of you to come up with the seventh, eighth, ninth, and 10th principles of interpretation. Good luck, and have fun!" And with a quick exit out the door, he was gone.

For the next 30 years, I traveled throughout the United States, Canada, and Europe participating in costumed historical events, encampments, and training sessions covering historic themes from the beginnings of European settlements in the New World to post-WWI farms. Through all of these endeavors I regularly returned to Tilden's principles as a guide.

But I kept wondering why no one had pursued his challenge. Where were the additional principles of interpretation?

The years passed, and I had come to believe that there wouldn't be a new set of principles for interpretation. I felt that Tilden's challenge would go unanswered and we would bog down in a rut of non-experimentation and little growth.

Then in 1998, a friend told me that I needed to look at a new book titled *Interpretation for the 21st Century*. I picked up a copy and opened to the chapter listings, and there it was—Chapter 15: Passion! Not only had the authors gone beyond the boundaries of Tilden's principles, they had brought the teachings full circle with that powerful word: *Passion!*

Since the day I was made aware of the first edition of this book, I have digested, used, and trained with both texts, *Interpreting Our Heritage* and *Interpretation for the 21st Century*. I have had the pleasure of knowing all three authors. And now I regularly challenge my students with: "It is up to you to come up with the 16th, 17th, and 18th principles of interpretation. The groundwork has been laid by these men."

John C. F. Luzader
Living Museums of the West

Foreword

to the First Edition

By Tim Merriman, Ph.D.

One sunny Saturday, years ago, I led the weekly guided trail hike up into the narrow canyons of sandstone, the Giant City Nature Trail, 10 miles south of Carbondale, Illinois. My group was the usual—25 or so adults and children—all clustered around me for Stop Three, one of my favorites.

"What does this look like to you?" I asked.

"A face," someone answered. "An Indian face!" another offered.

"Yes, a petroglyph. A face carved by native people who lived here. Do you see the feathers carved above the face?"

They did. I explained that an archaeologist told me that the carving of the face was about 1,000 years old, but the feathers were recent. Someone who knew Indians only from television added the feathers—an act of vandalism. The people were transfixed by the stone face which hovered in time and space within their minds. Physically it was just above waist height to an adult, on a square corner of Mississippi sandstone, an ancient river sandbar.

Then a young girl asked. "Where are the others?"

"What others?" I answered, a little too quickly.

"There must be others."

"In my five years of walking this trail," I said confidently, "I've never seen others."

She was sure I was wrong, and asked my permission to look for them. I might have thought she was a pest for being so insistent that day. I hope I didn't, but I might have.

Much to her delight and my surprise, she found four more before we finished the one-mile hike. She believed there were more. She made important discoveries that I had missed in my hundreds of trips on the very same trail. In the years that followed I found three more, after she had opened my eyes. As I led people on that same trail each week, I began seeing and feeling new things among the familiar.

You have just opened a book that takes us to familiar places in the field of interpretation. And it asks us to see it all differently with a look into the 21st century. Freeman Tilden's book, *Interpreting Our Heritage*, established a firm foundation with six principles of interpretation. Larry Beck and Ted Cable remind us that many others, including Enos Mills, have also written about the principles of interpretation. Their influence on the profession has been significant.

Beck and Cable relate the parallels between Tilden's words and those of Mills. Mills left us incredible stories of his time and all times as he wrote of his experiences on Long's Peak in the Rockies and of his travels. A little more than a decade ago, Enda Mills Kiley, the daughter of Enos Mills, gave me a copy of his book, *The Story of a Thousand Year Old Pine*. Reading it caused me to look at every tree differently, with more interest in its personal story.

The authors have taken on an awesome task and have done it very well. Those of us who have studied, practiced, and taught interpretive principles over the past 30 years have rightfully paid regular homage to Tilden. He spoke to the profession so clearly and eloquently that it became the standard, almost unquestioned. We say "Tilden's six principles of interpretation" as if there could be no more. Who would dare look for more of them?

The authors even find Tilden's principles in need of a tune-up. It seems like a sacrilege. It is not. Like the girl looking for carved faces from the past, we must continue probing our profession for deeper understandings, principles learned from practice, and new challenges. We must provoke ourselves to learn more in both familiar and unfamiliar settings.

It is time to take a different look at the conceptual landscape of interpretation. The extension of the six principles into 15 is interesting. I can almost hear the discussions among "lumpers" and "splitters" about the rightness of the "15." I silently applauded the work of Beck and Cable while reading each chapter. They document very well the many contributors to our knowledge and beliefs about the art and science of interpretation. I find no argument with the number of principles they chose. Their reasons are very well stated. They have created a new teaching and training aid of great value.

Cable and Beck frame their guiding principles around the work of Mills and Tilden, but they also take them into critical new areas for the 21st century. From basic communication techniques to high technology, they have addressed the importance of all forms of communication.

They even point out the political realities of our profession in Chapter 12. Interpretive programs must find relevance to organizational goals, build essential income sources, and seek advocates who will throw their political might behind the program. In this new century and millennium, our business and political skills will be tested along with our interpretive abilities.

Beck and Cable have been good interpreters as well. They will lead you through their thought processes with knowledge, challenges, and thought-provoking stories and ideas. They have studied diverse scholars and interpreters before them (including Bill Lewis, Grant Sharpe, Sam Ham, Terry Tempest Williams, Doug Knudson, and many others) in developing the foundation of their principles. *Interpretation for the 21st Century* will provoke you to think in new ways about this very ancient profession. May we never think we have found the only truths, the one set of principles about our profession. There will always be more to know, and change is one of several immutable rules of life. One day in the future, someone else will build from their ideas to reframe the principles of interpretation again. That is as it should be.

When I was a park interpreter, I experimented with my work with naivete, foolish courage, and passion. I remember first reading Tilden's book and feeling like I had discovered the Holy Grail. It gave this young interpreter with limited experience six general guidelines that helped me to improve. I encourage all interpreters who love to learn and grow to read this book and study Beck and Cable's guiding principles. We must all search the trails ahead. There are many more faces to find and stories to tell.

Tim Merriman, Ph.D.
Executive Director
National Association for Interpretation

Prologue

―――――――――

We walked along the narrow beach between the Pacific surf and high cliffs rising up to Torrey Pines State Reserve near San Diego, California. Our conversation about our work would be interrupted by the pleasant distraction of sandpipers hurrying ahead of us. When tired of being driven down the beach, the birds would burst off the sand and whirl out over the breakers. The flock would flash past, suddenly alight behind us, and resume feeding in our footprints. Gulls floated overhead, motionless, like kites.

Ahead in the distance, high above the cliff, we saw a black bird with a strange object in its beak. Through the binoculars we could see that it was a raven. It flew closer at a leisurely pace. Occasionally, the raven perched on top of a rare Torrey Pine, or on a branch overhanging the cliff, and we could see that the object the raven was holding was a pine cone the size of a softball. What would a raven be doing with a pine cone?

The raven landed on a branch jutting out from the cliff face. Holding the cone in its beak, it looked down at us. After pausing on that perch for a few moments, the raven flew yet closer toward us to a branch extending over the top of the cliff, more than a hundred feet above the beach. After looking directly at us, the raven tossed the cone in our direction. The cone tumbled down, down, down the steep cliff bouncing off rocks, and gaining momentum in the channels of near-vertical gullies, until it came to the bottom of the ridge and skittered a good distance across the sand on the beach to rest at our feet.

> Interpreters are fortunate to have work that can so profoundly impact others, that is so rewarding and meaningful to conduct, and that lends itself to making the world a better place.

We had each witnessed the unlikely prospect of the cone, somehow, careening down the cliff to ultimately land directly in front of us. We were both speechless. After leaning over to pick up the cone we passed it back and forth between us. The raven clearly did not accidently drop the cone. It did not slip from its beak. The bird was not struggling to hold on to it. Nor did it flush after dropping the cone as if it had been startled.

We could never prove it, but we were convinced the raven gave us the pine cone. When we spoke again it was in quiet tones, seeking meaning in what had just happened. We had been talking about our writing projects and the upcoming new edition of this book. Was this an omen, a blessing, an avian endorsement that held some sort of meaning? It was certainly a gift.

Sometimes nature surprises us with tangible gifts—gifts like a cone from a rare Torrey Pine, delivered airmail by a raven. At times, nature's gift-giving is more subtle and less tangible. In fact, sometimes we might not even notice a gift. But the purpose of this gift was clear, so much so that we have changed the title of this edition of the book and associated each of the 15 principles of interpretation with a gift. These gifts include revelation, provocation, illumination, beauty, joy, passion, hope. We believe these gifts, in sum, are what interpretation is all about.

The *Gifts of Interpretation* suggests principles to use when passing on to others the gifts that nature and culture have bestowed upon us. Interpreters are fortunate to have work that can so profoundly impact others, that is so rewarding and meaningful to conduct, and that lends itself to making the world a better place.

Preface

Interpretation is an educational activity that aims to reveal meanings about our cultural and natural resources. Through various media—including talks, guided tours, and exhibits—interpretation enhances our understanding, appreciation, and, therefore, protection of historic sites and natural wonders. Interpretation is an informational and inspirational process that occurs in our nation's parks, forests, wildlife refuges, zoos, museums, and cultural sites—places like the Grand Canyon, Yellowstone, Gettysburg National Military Park, the Smithsonian Museums, Yosemite, Mt. Rushmore, Colonial Williamsburg, and Thomas Jefferson's Monticello in the United States. Well-known international sites include Canada's Banff National Park, the Great Barrier Reef, the Egyptian pyramids, the Tower of London, and the Great Wall of China. Although such places are inspirational in and of themselves, interpretation can add to a fuller understanding of their beauty and meaning, as well as protect their integrity. This book is intended to contribute to an evolving philosophy of interpretation.

> Interpretation is an informational and inspirational process that occurs in our nation's parks, forests, wildlife refuges, zoos, museums, and cultural sites.

Enos Mills was an interpretive guide in what is now Rocky Mountain National Park from the late 1880s to the early 1920s. He wrote *Adventures of a Nature Guide and Essays in Interpretation*, which was published in 1920. Mills devised a number of principles that laid a philosophical foundation for effective interpretation. He wrote, "A nature guide [i.e., interpreter] is a naturalist who can guide others to the secrets of nature."[1] He believed in the importance of first-hand, experiential learning. Mills observed, "He who feels the spell of the wild, the rhythmic melody of falling water, the echoes among the crags, the bird songs, the winds in the pines, and the endless beat of waves upon the shore, is in tune with the universe."[2]

Mills presented a poetic interpretation of the facts of nature. He sought to make his topics meaningful by compiling material from "nature's storybook" in the form of its "manners and customs, its neighbors and its biography."[3] Mills developed his principles based upon his own professional experience as an interpreter.

The next landmark contribution to a philosophy of interpretation was Freeman Tilden's *Interpreting Our Heritage*, initially published in 1957.[4] Tilden's six "principles of interpretation" are parallel to those principles championed by Mills. Yet Tilden is far better known and is often credited with first formulating a philosophy of interpretation. The wisdom of Tilden's principles continues to be useful, but we need to relate his work to the present and engage the issues of the future.

Many have since contributed to the body of knowledge about interpretation. For example, the 1980s saw publication of an introductory handbook designed primarily for national park interpreters titled *Interpreting for Park Visitors* by William Lewis.[5] The early 1990s brought Sam Ham's practical sourcebook for "people with big ideas and small budgets" titled *Environmental Interpretation*,[6] which has since been updated. More recent is a comprehensive book designed to cross the boundaries between theory and practice—*Interpretation of Cultural and Natural Resources*.[7] Finally, the National Association for Interpretation is publishing a series of books specifically related to the interpretive field that includes volumes focused on personal interpretation,[8] interpretive writing,[9] interpretive planning,[10] interpretive management,[11] interpretive design,[12] and applied interpretive research.[13]

Tilden's *Interpreting Our Heritage* has remained the standard in terms of an interpretive philosophy. Aspects of Tilden's interpretive principles are timeless, but some elements of his philosophy can benefit from a current perspective. For example, Tilden's third principle of interpretation suggests that interpretation is an art—knowledge treated imaginatively. We agree. However, Tilden continued by noting that interpreters should not "read poems, give a dramatic performance, deliver an oration...or anything as horribly out of place as these." Yet such delivery methods have become increasingly popular in a broad array of interpretive settings because they have proven to be appealing and effective. A second example lies in Tilden's discussion of "gadgetry," which obviously contains no mention of today's advancing technologies and their applications in interpretive venues.

In this book, we restructure Tilden's treatment of interpretation to fit today's world. We update and build upon his well-established six interpretive principles. Then we add nine principles, many of which are grounded in the work of Mills, Tilden, and other pioneering champions of our heritage such as John Muir and Robert Marshall, and more current spokespersons such as Barry Lopez and Terry Tempest Williams. What we present is intended to be a stepping-stone in an evolving philosophy of interpretation.

In addition, in this third edition of the book, we will expand on our notion that interpretation is a gift. Our Conclusion has previously taken this into account in a broad sense. Now, for each of the 15 principles, we title each chapter to highlight how that particular principle is a gift.

This book is written for a broad audience. Students and educators may find it valuable as a supplement to traditional, more comprehensive interpretive textbooks. The book should also be useful to field interpreters and managers at parks, forests, wildlife refuges, museums, zoos, aquariums, historic areas, nature centers, and other tourism sites.

Finally, this book is meant to guide the general reader who wants to explore and learn more about our cultural and natural legacy. For those who enjoy visiting places that commemorate our heritage, an understanding of interpretation offers the means for evaluating interpretive services and interpreting resources personally. We hope all readers find our treatment of an interpretive philosophy useful in their own lives.

Introduction

The legacy of any nation is encompassed by its natural landscapes, its wild-life, its historic sites, its people, its culture. As Aldo Leopold stressed, we are members of a community that includes the whole environment.[1] Pride in a place—an understanding of the past, a concern for the present, and a vision for the future—stems from a close attachment to the land and our cultural roots.

In the Preface we acknowledged the contributions of Enos Mills and Free-man Tilden to an evolving interpretive philosophy, and we want to continue with their impact on the broad field of interpretation.

Enos Mills (1870-1922) grew up on a farm in Kansas. In 1884, at the age of 14, he began building a log cabin at the base of Long's Peak in Colorado. In his career he led more than 250 parties of "flatlanders" up the 14,255-foot Long's Peak. He developed a lifelong friendship with John Muir, who helped him broaden his commitment as a crusader for parks and wilderness. Mills was a naturalist, mountain guide, author, and lecturer. He served on the committee that wrote the guiding mandate of the National Park Service Act of 1916: "To conserve the scenery and the natural and historic objects and the wildlife therein ... as will leave them unimpaired for the enjoyment of future generations." Perhaps the accomplishment in which Mills took the greatest pride was the establishment of Rocky Mountain National Park. In addition to establishing standards of nature guiding and principles of interpretation, Mills developed a vision of the world in which people might live in harmony with their environment and with each other.

> ... interpretation gives meaning to a "foreign" landscape or event from the past.

Freeman Tilden (1883-1980) was a native of Massachusetts. He quit a successful career as a writer of fiction and plays to devote himself to conservation, with particular emphasis on the symbolism of national parks in American culture. His best-known work, in interpretive circles, is the classic *Interpreting Our Heritage*. He also wrote *The National Parks* (a comprehensive book that covered the natural, historical, and recreational areas of our national park system) and *The Fifth Essence* (an eloquent book about the important role of private donations in protecting our national parks). Freeman Tilden served as a consultant to four directors of the National Park Service.

In the Preface we also addressed interpretation as an informational and inspirational process designed to enhance understanding, appreciation, and protection of our cultural and natural legacy. However, other more familiar meanings of the word interpretation confuse the general public and create controversy within the profession. Tilden observed that the word interpretation has several special implications—translation of a foreign language, for example.[2] For our purposes, interpretation gives meaning to a "foreign" landscape or event from the past. What is being translated (such as, glaciation of Yosemite Valley, ecosystem dynamics at Yellowstone, or events surrounding the battle at Gettysburg) may well be "foreign" to substantial numbers of visitors. The interpreter elucidates technical information about the geology, ecology, or history of an area in a straightforward, understandable, and engaging manner. Mills observed that the effective interpreter has "the faculty of being entertaining, instructive, watchful, and commanding, all without his party realizing it."[3]

Others have provided great insight into this activity as well. Tilden stated the role of interpretation in a small book titled *The Fifth Essence*:

> Vital to any administrative program that envisages the fullest and finest use of [our] Parks—whether areas of solacing wilderness or historic shrines—is the work of creating understanding. It is true that each preserved monument "speaks for itself." But unfortunately it speaks partly in a language that the average visitor cannot comprehend. Beauty and the majesty of natural forces need no interlocutor. They constitute a personal spiritual experience. But when the question is "why?" or "what?" or "how did this come to be?" [interpretive] people must have the answers. And this requires both patient research and the development of a program fitted to a great variety of needs.[4]

Each interpreter should strive to communicate a sense of place or a sense of historic meaning in a personal, individualized manner.[5] The many facets of interpretation are part of what makes it so fascinating. The most effective interpreters orchestrate their interpretation to elicit a response from the audience: astonishment, wonder, inspiration, action, sometimes tears.

Interpretation is a process, a rendering, by which visitors see, learn, experience, and are inspired firsthand. Interpreters must be skilled in communication and knowledgeable in natural and cultural history consistent with their site's mission.

> The most effective interpreters orchestrate their interpretation to elicit a response from the audience: astonishment, wonder, inspiration, action, sometimes tears.

At best, interpreters promote enriched recreational experiences that turn to magic, where everything comes together, where participants feel unencumbered delight in knowledge and experience—a greater joy in living, a better understanding of one's place in the overall scheme, a positive hope for the future. Interpretation may provoke visitors to initiate a long-term path of exploration and learning related to cultural or natural history, or both.

Interpretation is important to federal agencies such as the National Park Service, U.S. Forest Service, U.S. Fish and Wildlife Service, U.S. Army Corps of Engineers, and the Bureau of Land Management. Through interpretation of the landscape comes better visitor understanding of agency policies. Similarly, state, regional, and county natural resource agencies employ interpretation to explain their policies and to protect their sites.

Visitors may learn through interpretation about wise use of our natural resources and ways to minimize our impact on the environment. Good interpretation encourages greater sensitivity to one's surroundings, heightened ecological and cultural awareness, and meaningful links to the past and future.

> Interpreters help convey a fuller appreciation and understanding of a place.

Interpretation tells the story behind the scenery or history of an area. It is a process that can help people see beyond their capabilities. Mills wrote, "A day with a nature guide may help to train the eyes and all of the senses."[6] Interpreters, in sum, help convey a fuller appreciation and understanding of a place.

Interpretation is offered in many forms. Personal interpretation refers to programs in the form of talks, demonstrations, puppet shows, living history, storytelling, nature walks, and tours. These may occur in auditoriums, outdoor arenas (as with the traditional national park campfire program), along a trail, or following a route inside a historic building. Nonpersonal interpretation encompasses everything from self-guided trails, to exhibits, to websites, to interactive computers, to smartphone apps.

Evolution of an Interpretive Philosophy

Mills was among the first to use the term interpret to describe his nature guiding at Long's Peak, Colorado. He presented various philosophical principles in *Adventures of a Nature Guide and Essays in Interpretation* in 1920. Tilden wrote the first edition of *Interpreting Our Heritage* in 1957. The guiding principles of Mills and Tilden are strikingly similar to each other and to the progressivism education principles of John Dewey, a contemporary of Mills.[7] To track, and credit, the evolution of an interpretive philosophy, we present Tilden's six principles of interpretation along with consistent observations from Mills.

Tilden's First Principle is, "Any interpretation that does not somehow relate what is being displayed or described to something within the personality or experience of the visitor will be sterile."[8] And Enos Mills observed, "The nature guide is at his best when he discusses facts so that they appeal to the imagination and reason."[9] He continued, "The nature guide who understands human nature and possesses tact and ingenuity is able to hold divergent interests. ..."[10] This focus on the needs and desires of the visitor is appropriately the first element to be considered by the interpreter.

Tilden's Second Principle is, "Information, as such, is not interpretation. Interpretation is revelation based upon information. But they are entirely different things. However, all interpretation includes information."[11] And Enos Mills determined, "A nature guide ... has been rightfully associated with information and some form of education. But nature guiding, as we see it, is more inspirational than informational. The nature guide arouses interest by dealing in big principles—not with detached and colorless information."[12] Mills continued, "The aim is to illuminate and reveal the alluring world."[13] The purpose of interpretation goes beyond providing information to reveal deeper meaning and truth.

Tilden's Third Principle is, "Interpretation is an art, which combines many arts, whether the materials presented are scientific, historical or architectural. Any art is in some degree teachable."[14] Similarly, Mills described a colleague as having "a purpose—a vision. Daily she accumulated experience and information. These she handled like an artist. ... Our [interpreter] had the art and the vision which enabled her to make these outings permanent, purposeful, growth-compelling experiences."[15] This principle challenges all interpreters to treat interpretation as a creative activity.

Tilden's Fourth Principle is, "The chief aim of interpretation is not instruction, but provocation."[16] And Mills observed, "This new occupation [interpretation] is likely to be far-reaching in its influences; it is inspirational and educational ... and possess[es] astounding possibilities for arousing the feelings and developing the unlimited resources of the mind."[17] Thus, interpreters are challenged to inspire intellectual and emotional responses.

Tilden's Fifth Principle is, "Interpretation should aim to present a whole rather than a part, and must address itself to the whole man rather than any phase."[18] And Mills quoted Liberty H. Bailey as follows: "This [recipient of good interpretation] will see first the large and significant events; he will grasp relationships; he will correlate; later, he will consider the details."[19] Interpreters must be aware of the entire sphere of their interpretation and communicate that whole as an overriding theme or thesis.

Tilden's Sixth Principle is, "Interpretation addressed to children (say, up to the age of 12) should not be a dilution of the presentation to adults, but should follow a fundamentally different approach. To be at its best it will require a separate program."[20] And Mills suggested, "This childish desire to know, to learn, will assure mental development if information be given in a way that appeals. ... The experiences these children have and their reflections concerning the things seen give them the ability to reason, and develop their observation and imagination."[21] Interpreters must be aware that different life stages present different needs and interests, and therefore different approaches to interpretation.

Out of respect for the work of Tilden and Mills, and particularly because of the familiarity so many interpreters have with Tilden's six principles, our framework of principles begins with a re-statement of Tilden's. Note that the principles have been re-worded to better reflect their treatment in the chapters that follow. In addition to these six principles, we offer nine new principles that provide a more elaborate interpretive philosophy.

Here, then, are the 15 principles, which are presented in detail in the following chapters:

1. To spark an interest, interpreters must relate the subject to the lives of the people in their audience.
2. The purpose of interpretation goes beyond providing information to reveal deeper meaning and truth.
3. The interpretive presentation—as a work of art—should be designed as a story that informs, entertains, and enlightens.
4. The purpose of the interpretive story is to inspire and to provoke people to broaden their horizons.
5. Interpretation should present a complete theme or thesis and address the whole person.
6. Interpretation for children, teenagers, and seniors—when these comprise uniform groups—should follow fundamentally different approaches.
7. Every place has a history. Interpreters can bring the past alive to make the present more enjoyable and the future more meaningful.
8. Technology can reveal the world in exciting new ways. However, incorporating this technology into the interpretive program must be done with foresight and thoughtful care.
9. Interpreters must concern themselves with the quantity and quality (selection and accuracy) of information presented. Focused, well-researched interpretation will be more powerful than a longer discourse.
10. Before applying the arts in interpretation, the interpreter must be familiar with basic communication techniques. Quality interpretation depends on the interpreter's knowledge and skills, which must be continually developed over time.
11. Interpretive writing should address what readers would like to know, with the authority of wisdom and its accompanying humility and care.
12. The overall interpretive program must be capable of attracting support—financial, volunteer, political, administrative—whatever support is needed for the program to flourish.
13. Interpretation should instill in people the ability, and the desire, to sense the beauty in their surroundings—to provide spiritual uplift and to encourage resource preservation.

14. Interpreters can promote optimal experiences through intentional and thoughtful program and facility design.
15. Passion is the essential ingredient for powerful and effective interpretation—passion for the resource and for those people who come to be inspired by it.

Benefits of Interpretation

To *individuals* who are attracted to our programs, we offer an engaging activity that can be recreational, educational, and deeply meaningful. At the most basic level, the program may be a diversion for someone—an antidote to despair. But interpretation offers much more.[22]

At historic sites, the program may offer a chance to better understand our history and to reflect on such universal concepts as liberty, justice, and civic responsibility. Many of our cultural sites celebrate the drama of human conduct. The story of any nation includes men and women who have exhibited great courage and integrity in the face of adversity. What of our past helps us to better understand the present? What are we called to do, as individuals, in light of our past? Answers can be found as interpreters find meaning in events and help people to personalize that meaning.

> To *individuals* who are attracted to our programs, we offer an engaging activity that can be recreational, educational, and deeply meaningful.

Likewise, a natural history program offers the opportunity to connect with the beauty found in nature. It may offer moments for contemplation and reflection. We can celebrate the stability and resilience of nature. Rachel Carson wrote:

> There is symbolic as well as actual beauty in the migration of the birds … There is something infinitely healing in the repeated refrains of nature—the assurance that dawn comes after night, and spring after the winter.[23]

The splendor of nature and a greater understanding of its wonders can comfort and inspire us. Individuals can find solace, direction, and hope through interpretation.

Furthermore, identification with our land and culture helps to sustain us as a *society*. Historian Roderick Nash indicated that the landscape shaped our national character—one of independence, freedom, perseverance, and tenacity.[24]

Democracy requires an informed public, and interpreters are a source of knowledge and inspiration in this regard. Thomas Jefferson wrote:

I know of no safe depository of the ultimate powers of society but the people themselves, and if we think them not enlightened enough to exercise that control with a wholesome discretion, the remedy is not to take it from them, but to inform their discretion.[25]

As interpreters we help to inform the discretion of our audience members. Through interpretation we enhance understanding and appreciation of our cultural and natural legacy—that which defines us as a democracy. Society has much to gain from our interpretive efforts.

> **Interpreters have daily opportunities to influence lives. Our privilege, and our obligation, is to help others enjoy, reflect upon, and find meaning in the places we work.**

Finally, challenging circumstances provide each of us an opportunity to give more of ourselves, and through giving we receive blessings in return. Love for a culture and landscape allows interpreters chances to share their inspirational enjoyment with others.

Interpreters have daily opportunities to influence lives. Our privilege, and our obligation, is to help others enjoy, reflect upon, and find meaning in the places we work.

Our commitment to the profession of interpretation will enhance our own sense of purpose and well-being. We need to be connected and support each other in a reaffirmation of civilized values. Our profession is a noble one.

An Interpreter Is ...

To sum up this introductory chapter and the principles put forth, we suggest an interpreter is someone who works with people to convey the meaning of our cultural and natural landscapes and the features that comprise these landscapes. An interpreter is invested in a lifelong quest for learning and experience, and in sharing that accumulated wisdom. He or she is familiar with and practices effective communication techniques and strives to create meaningful and provocative stories. An interpreter has a grounding in the liberal arts and stays current with the news (local, regional, national, international) to better relate to a vast consortium of visitors.

An interpreter can communicate excitement for the resource and inspire a response. An interpreter is deeply concerned with the welfare of visitors—their safety, their dignity, and the quality of their experiences. He or she interprets imaginatively by knowledge and personal example.

An interpreter acts out of authority and humility, confidence and compassion, integrity and respect for others, stability and enthusiasm, and joy.

An interpreter respects the moral worth of visitors and their potential for growth. The interpreter is enthused and energetic about the place, the visitors who come there, and the work at hand. An interpreter strives to embrace the wonder and beauty of life.

S.P 122
Of the Graceful Third
Sunday, 4 Aug. '68

at

© Tsuyoshi Matsumoto

CHAPTER

1

The Gift of a Spark

To spark an interest, interpreters must relate the subject to the lives of the people in their audience.

> *No man can reveal to you aught but that which already lies half asleep in the dawning of your knowledge. The teacher who walks in the shadow of the temple, among his followers, gives not of his wisdom but rather of his faith and his lovingness. If he is indeed wise he does not bid you enter the house of his wisdom, but rather leads you to the threshold of your own mind.*
>
> **—Kahlil Gibran**

As Kahlil Gibran reflected, receiving information is a deep and personal matter. The knowledge and experiences we gain constitute who we are. Interpreters must relate to the people to whom they interpret if they wish to lead them to the "thresholds" of their minds.

People choose when, where, what, and how to learn based on their interests. Richard Saul Wurman wrote, "Learning can be seen as the acquisition of information, but before it can take place, there must be interest; interest permeates all endeavors and precedes learning . . . .Learning can be defined as the process of remembering what you are interested in."[1]

Freeman Tilden suggested the "chief" interests of visitors to sites of natural beauty and cultural significance are in whatever touches their personalities, experiences, or ideals.[2] This is the backbone of effective interpretation; taking information about cultural and natural resources and making it relevant to the audience.[3] This is the gift of a spark; finding common ground with your visitors to draw them into the wonders of your site.

> **This is the gift of a spark; finding common ground with your visitors to draw them into the wonders of your site.**

Interpretive messages must be interesting to capture attention, meaningful so people care, and compelling so people no longer think or act the same after hearing them. By identifying key interests of particular audiences, the interpreter has, at least, a broad target at which to aim.

The First Principle in Theory

Tilden's dictum to relate information to the visitors' "chief" interests may have been intuitive, but it is grounded in solid theory. For years, educational psychologists and theorists have been suggesting that people learn by integrating and storing information in the context of their past experience.

Cognitive Map Theory

William Hammitt analyzed Tilden's interpretive principles in the context of cognitive map theory, a widely adopted view of how people process information.[4] This theory suggests that people receive information, code it into simplified units, and then store it in relationship to other existing information. As information continues to be stored in this way, a network of informational units form and are linked by pathways of commonality. These units and pathways collectively form cognitive maps—a person's structure of storage and organization of information. Subsequent stimuli "spark" the internal model that best matches them.

Effective interpretation produces external stimuli that trigger existing maps, thereby allowing the audience to "get it" and store the information in relation to other information they already possess. If the interpreter expresses irrelevant or completely unfamiliar information, then existing maps will not be triggered. We should, ideally, be aware of the common knowledge and experiences held by an audience relative to the topic of interpretation. With this awareness, we may target messages to trigger existing maps and to build on that scaffolding.[5]

Another important factor with implications for interpreters is that when a map is triggered, people can perceive more than what actually exists in the immediate environment. Hammitt suggested that "few individuals who have caught trout and cooked them over a campfire cannot view a photograph of such a scene without visualizing the landscape, smelling the smoke and feeling the warmth of the fire, and even tasting the fish."[6]

The External-Internal Shift

Consistent with cognitive map theory, brain researchers have delved into how our brains determine which stimuli are attended to and which are ignored. Scientists have identified a process called the external-internal shift that explains how people attend to communication by relating to their experiences.[7]

Before focusing attention, the brain stem passively receives many sensory stimuli from our sense organs. The brain cannot process all the information, so it actively scans the stimuli, searching for anything that requires immediate attention. It ignores or merely monitors other stimuli. During this search the brain is constantly switching its focus between external events and internal memories and interests.

For example, while an interpreter is telling the audience how to react if they encounter a bear, a listener may recall a childhood observation of a bear. The listener's attention shifts to the personal bear story, and he or she merely monitors the presentation while processing the personal story. In fact, because we can think six to seven times faster than people can talk, most of the time we are "talking" (that is, thinking) to ourselves. This explains the ease in tuning a speaker out, especially if the information is not relevant to one's interests or past experiences.

Such mental shifts between external and internal events seem to be an important factor in maintaining and updating long-term memory. Recalling memories strengthens neural networks that contain and process them.

> Relating the message to the knowledge and experiences of the audience teaches new information, reinforces old information and memories, and gives the audience satisfying personal experiences.

Most important for interpreters is the knowledge that people tend to seek out stimuli and situations (e.g., movies, books, trips, conversations) that will trigger these memories and build on them. Educators Robert Sylwester and Joo-Yun Cho observed, "When we consciously seek such specific information, our attention system primes itself in anticipation. It increases the response levels of the networks that process that information, and it inhibits other networks."[8] Relating the message to the knowledge and experiences of the audience teaches new information, reinforces old information and memories, and gives the audience satisfying personal experiences.

Meaning-Making

Another communication paradigm has been developed called meaning-making. In essence, this model redefines communication. No longer is communication considered merely a linear sender-receiver process. Rather, meaning-making conceptualizes communication as a negotiation process between parties whereby information is created rather than transmitted. Individuals receiving the information shape the meaning based on their store of past knowledge and experiences.[9] Because visitors actively create meaning through the contexts they bring to the interpretive site, being aware of their perspectives, knowledge, and past experiences is useful for successful interpretation.

Research conducted at two nationally significant interpretive sites (National Museum of American History of the Smithsonian Institution and Old Faithful of Yellowstone National Park) applied the meaning-making paradigm. Results indicated that "personal interest was the most frequent reason given for selecting an interpretive experience as most meaningful."[10]

A Review of the Theoretical Literature

In an article that appeared in the *Journal of Interpretation Research*, Sam Ham draws on recent advances in cognitive and behavioral psychology. He notes "hundreds of published studies" in the past three decades that offer application to the cause-and-effect relationships of good interpretation. In this definitive article Ham concludes, "… the only caring any of us is capable of doing will be that which is based on the meanings we, ourselves, make. Interpretation that provokes visitors to think in positive ways about a thing can make that thing matter to them. When things matter to us, we are likely to act in their behalf if confronted with the opportunity to do so."[11] Ham provided evidence, rooted in cognitive science, to support the National Park Service adage: Through interpretation, understanding; through understanding, appreciation; through appreciation, protection.

The First Principle in Practice

With respect for theory used to conceptualize effective communication, interpreters must know about their visitors. Knowing the audience is important in any communication, whether by a preacher, professor, or politician. Many interpretive agencies now realize the importance of knowing the needs and wants of their customers. They conduct visitor surveys to assess the characteristics of their clientele in an attempt to determine what is meaningful to them. By finding what is meaningful to visitors, interpreters may provoke them to further think for themselves in making emotional and intellectual connections with the resource.

Demographics

Most visitor surveys have focused on identifying the visitors' demographic characteristics. Whether the audience is local or transient, rural or urban, foreign or domestic—all have ramifications for targeting interpretive messages. To the interpreter, this means carefully considering these characteristics and choosing approaches, metaphors, anecdotes, and stories that will match visitor interests.

If a site has many repeat visitors, interpreters must change interpretive offerings more frequently or schedule special events to recapture interest continually. With repeat visitors, interpreters can offer a sequence of programs with increasing sophistication, thereby allowing visitors to advance to progressively higher levels of understanding. If a site has mostly first-time, non-repeat visitors, programs do not have to be changed as frequently. Then program offerings should be broad and meaningful in presenting the compelling story of the site.

Most adult visitors have some level of rural and urban experiences, regardless of where they live. With children, however, this may not be as likely. For example, those who interpret to school groups need to know whether they are coming from rural or inner-city school systems. Using subways and high-rise apartments as metaphors for burrows and nesting colonies would miss the mark for farm kids. On the other hand, city kids might not know the source of their water or food. Many, for example, think that bread originates from the grocery store.

Foreign audiences may require language translations or background information to provide frameworks that already exist in the minds of domestic visitors. Furthermore, history is understood differently by Americans and many foreigners. Mexicans may have a different view of Texas settlement, and Europeans may view "new world" colonization differently. The Japanese have a different perspective than Americans on events leading to the end of World War II.

Still other visitor characteristics that might affect the interpretive approach include gender, race, and educational levels. Sometimes the ethnic or religious background of the audience is important, particularly in developing countries where ethnic and religious beliefs strongly affect how people perceive the use of natural and cultural resources. Interpreting to different ages—children, teenagers, and older persons—is the focus of Chapter 6.

Beyond Demographics

A study conducted at the Ronald V. Jensen Living Historical Farm, in Utah, found that the staff intuitively knew the demographics of their visitors. However, despite high levels of staff-visitor contact, interpreters did not understand visitors' motivations and satisfactions.[12]

Most visitor studies have merely documented visitor characteristics and participation patterns. According to the Jensen Farm research, in cases where the staff is in regular contact with visitors, such studies may not be necessary. Interpreters seem to grasp quickly general audience demographics.[13]

Understanding who is interested in what subjects is important, but understanding why they are interested in those subjects is also vital.

However, to respond to visitors fully, research should concentrate on visitors' values, motivations, attitudes, and satisfactions. Indeed, knowing these traits allows us to predict the demographics that likely accompany them—although we usually assume that only the reverse is true.[14]

Targeting Motivations and Learning Styles

Research designed to assess the visitors' motivations allows interpreters to more successfully apply this first principle. Understanding what audience members already know, and what motivates them, permits interpreters to present more interesting, pertinent, and challenging information.

Understanding who is interested in what subjects is important, but understanding why they are interested in those subjects is also vital. The reasons may be surprising and provide clues for presenting information in interesting ways. For example, visitors could be interested in an old locomotive because their fathers or grandfathers worked for the railroad. Or they may be interested because they are fascinated by how steam-powered machines work. Or they could have a passion for American history and westward expansion. Or they may have been enamored with trains as kids.

If we know the reason for the interest in a particular subject, then we can structure the content of the interpretation to fit that interest. This means we must ask visitors why they are interested in various interpretive possibilities. Such research may be conducted formally (questionnaires or structured interviews) or informally (in conversation).

We should also be aware of whether visitors want to learn and, if so, how they want to learn. Ross Loomis reviewed social psychological studies that suggested visitors vary in their "need for cognition" and in how they process information.[15]

Different preferences for learning may include those who like to read material, those who like to hear a presentation, those who want to see first-hand what is being interpreted, and those who want to be physically involved. Some people learn best through reflection and others through social interaction.

To enhance interest and effectiveness, some interpretation researchers identify visitors' learning styles and then match exhibits to these specific learning preferences. A study at the Milwaukee Public Museum used the popular Myers-

Briggs Type Indicator as an instrument to identify learning styles of visitors. As a consequence of this research, the museum modified a rainforest exhibit and determined that matching learning styles with exhibit presentation can result in increased learning.[16]

Barriers to Participation

Interpreters also should know why people do not visit interpretive sites so barriers may be eliminated. Knowing who is absent, and why, may be as pertinent as knowing who attends. Fear and negative perceptions are two widespread and powerful barriers to visitation to, and interest in, natural areas. Researchers have found that many people find wildland settings to be scary, disgusting, and uncomfortable.[17] Likewise, many people hold images of museums as being formal, stuffy, and elitist. We can strive to correct misconceptions and structure interpretive possibilities so they are accessible to those who are otherwise inhibited. For example, personal comfort, esteem, and security are key interests of these potential visitors and interpretation can be adjusted accordingly.

> Knowing who is absent, and why, may be as pertinent as knowing who attends.

Knowing and addressing visitors' interests does not mean pandering to any desire of the audience. For example, part of what makes natural settings attractive is the contrast they provide to civilization. Such aspects of the setting should not be compromised. But, when the interests of the audience are appropriate for the site and consistent with management objectives, interpreters are wise to attend to those interests.

How to Capture Interests

Even if the visitors' interests are correctly identified, poor delivery will cause attention to wane. Effective interpretive delivery must be mastered and applied (see Chapter 10). The following is a discussion of some general considerations for delivering messages to capture and maintain interest.

Interpreters can capture attention by using movement, noise, bright colors, unusual objects, or with startling statements, either written or spoken. Attention is limited, and many stimuli are constantly competing for it. Mihalyi Csikszentmihalyi and Kim Hermanson wrote, "Even though we are surrounded by increasing waves of information, the amount of it that any person actually notices and then retains in memory may be less than it was in the days of our cave-dwelling ancestors, and it certainly cannot be much more."[18]

After attention is captured, the task becomes one of maintaining interest. Poor mechanics can derail the interpretation. Can the speaker be clearly heard? Is the exhibit text easily read? Are visuals comprehensible? If not, interest vaporizes and audiences escape—mentally, if not physically.

We can make interpretation more interesting by using personal language. The word *you* immediately makes the audience members think of themselves. This is a key component in implementing this first principle because self-referencing quickly engages and involves the audience—it creates an inviting opportunity for them to relate to the material. Other personal words such as *your*, *we*, and *our* can be similarly effective when used in a positive context.

> After attention is captured, the task becomes one of maintaining interest. Poor mechanics can derail the interpretation.

Posing relevant questions is a good technique for maintaining interest. People will try to answer questions, even rhetorical ones. Asking personalized questions such as "What would you have done?" with reference to a historical event connects the person with the subject. Visitors immediately imagine what their own conduct would have been under the historical circumstances. The gift of a spark brings visitors into the historic mindset.

Visitor interests can be tapped in histories, personal and otherwise. We are all historians.[19] Although far removed from the dates, famous names, and places taught in history classes, people engage in history-related activities all the time. We make photographic records of our personal and family histories through snapshots and videos. Our homes become museums filled with baby books, scrapbooks, and yearbooks. Diaries and journals provide a personal historical record. We are also history makers.[20] History is the composite of innumerable personal biographies.

Although we are all historians and history makers, people generally consider history to be dry, impersonal, and serious—something remote and distant from their lives.[21] Yet, people consider the past to be relevant and personal. People connect with the past, whereas history conjures images of obscure presidents and wars. The challenge for interpreters is to capture interests in such a way so that people may "personalize the past."[22]

Another approach to stimulating interest is leading the visitor through personal discovery. Most people enjoy the sense of accomplishment that comes from making discoveries. Discovery-oriented programs in interpretive settings allow people to gain new insights and to see previously known facts in new ways.

Discovery approaches have been popular in formal science education settings for many years. One science educator noted, "Discovery has become a big word in science education ... discovery and rediscovery appear more and more to be essential elements of learning experiences. ..."[23] Discovery lends itself to the application of this first principle because information is personally revealed to the individual investigator. Discovery carries with it elements of suspense and surprise. Interactive exhibits increase personal involvement and can provide mental challenges through puzzles or games that lead people to discover new facts or relationships. By providing discovery situations, interpreters provoke interest and connect the subject matter with the audience.

> **Enthusiasm reveals the interest of the interpreter and sparks the interest of the audience.**

Humor and novelty may also contribute to capturing and maintaining interest, but the most powerful force is enthusiasm. As enthusiasm is contagious, so is interest. William Everhart, former director of the National Park Service, when asked what it took to become an interpreter, replied, "There [are] few essentials. You have to be a genuine enthusiast, almost impelled to share your knowledge with others."[24] Enthusiasm reveals the interest of the interpreter and sparks the interest of the audience.

Interpreters should not only stimulate curiosity and capture interest for the duration of someone's visit to an interpretive site, but also strive to provoke continued interest. This can be accomplished initially by relating to the visitor's chief interests. From there, visitors may be self-motivated to new horizons. Anatole France wrote, "Do not try to satisfy your vanity by teaching a great many things. Awaken people's curiosity. It is enough to open minds; do not overload them. Put there just a spark. If there is some good inflammable stuff, it will catch fire."[25]

Interpreters must know the visitor's key interests to determine where and how to place the spark. We must strive to understand the "inflammable stuff." Delivering the message effectively ensures that the inflammable stuff will ignite. When fires of curiosity burn, the interpreter has successfully applied this first principle and has led visitors to the thresholds of their own minds, where learning and inspiration occur. This is the gift of a spark.

Saturday, June 19, 1998
Parry Grove Trail
SP 789

2

The Gift of Revelation

The purpose of interpretation goes beyond providing information to reveal deeper meaning and truth.

When I Heard the Learn'd Astronomer

When I heard the learn'd astronomer,
When the proofs, the figures,
were ranged in columns before me,
When I was shown the charts and diagrams,
to add, divide, and measure them,
When I sitting heard the astronomer where he lectured with much applause in the lecture room,
How soon unaccountable I became tired and sick,
Till rising and gliding out I wandered off by myself,
In the mystical moist night air, and from time to time,
Looked up in perfect silence at the stars.

—Walt Whitman

Some interpreters are like the "learn'd astronomer." They possess and present detailed information that misses the larger point. Enos Mills understood this: "From personal experience I would say that the chief errors likely to be made by a nature guide are: to become too booky, to follow academic methods, to compel, like the school teacher, the learning of lessons. There has been altogether too much of this dulling lesson business."[1]

This second principle speaks to using information properly and distinguishing between information and interpretation. Mills suggested the interpreter "is at his best when he discusses facts so that they appeal to the imagination and to the reason."[2] Of course, all interpretation includes information.[3] But the gift is in providing revelation.

If no information is imparted, then the program is, at best, entertainment. For example, some interpreters show cartoons, on occasion, in campground amphitheaters. Others entertain with magic or games. The appropriateness of such activities is not in question here—this could be great entertainment. However, without information these activities do not qualify as interpretation.

Furthermore, providing information does not automatically mean interpretation is taking place. Interpreters on "information duty" at visitor centers and entrance stations efficiently communicate considerable amounts of information to large numbers of people. They give weather reports, communicate road conditions, and direct people to restrooms, trailheads, and lodges. Although the information is important to those who receive it, none of this qualifies as interpretation. Interpretation must be more than information. The gift is revelation, based upon information.

Those on "information duty" have an opportunity to interpret. A question about a recent forest fire provides a chance not only to give a straight answer, but also to explain the role of fire in the ecosystem. A question about poisonous snakes offers a chance not only to give appropriate warnings, but also to do some public relations work on behalf of all snakes. A question about regulations provides an opportunity to interpret the reason for the rule, thereby enhancing the probability of compliance.

Discretion is necessary when interjecting interpretation into "information duty." A harried visitor who wants to know the time does not want to know how to build a clock. Interpreters will try visitors' patience and increase their anxiety by launching into an impromptu interpretive program. Yet, if we sense the state of mind and receptiveness of the visitor, then we should seize opportunities to interpret requested information.

The charge for interpreters, here, is to reveal information about our cultural and natural history in meaningful ways. Revealing information about the subject may be accomplished in formal programs, exhibits, or interpretive publications.

At Sandridge Nature Center, near Chicago, the visitors are almost exclusively local. Audiences are asked by interpreters to think about major intersections in the surrounding area. When approaching intersections with major east-west highways, travelers go up a gentle hill. Audience members can easily visualize these specific intersections. Interpreters then explain that each of these roads, running parallel to the southern shore of Lake Michigan, traverse the tops of ancient sand dunes formed as the lake receded after the last glaciation. Interpreters relate that bison, Native Americans, fur trappers, and others used these high and dry ridges as their highways, too. These roads, driven daily, take on new meaning as people learn about local geology, ecology, and history.

At the Stephen Birch Aquarium and Museum at the Scripps Institution of Oceanography in La Jolla, California, exhibits interpret the migration of gray whales. The annual gray whale migration route of approximately 10,000 miles is the longest of any mammal. The distance traveled over the lifespan of a gray whale is equivalent to the distance from the Earth to the moon and back. Nine 32-gallon trash cans represent the quantity of shrimp-like organisms called amphipods an adult gray whale eats in a day. A baby gray whale drinks 50 gallons of milk and, consequently, gains 60 to 70 pounds—a day. Such an interpretive approach offers a revelatory moment to those at the aquarium.

Tangibles and Intangibles

Deriving and communicating meaning in interpretation is to connect the physical aspects of a site or object with associated concepts. Freeman Tilden stated, "Information, as such, is not interpretation. Interpretation is revelation based upon information."[4] The National Park Service has elaborated on this to indicate that interpretation makes a connection between the tangible and intangible dimensions associated with an interpretive site.[5]

The tangible elements are those items that are concrete, that can be touched or seen, such as plants, animals, rock formations, and historic buildings. Intangible dimensions associated with the interpretive site cannot be perceived by the senses. These are broad meanings that are related to the place, such as ideas, processes, systems, and values. The tangible elements lend themselves to these broader meanings.

An entire group of intangibles can be labeled "universal concepts" (beauty, freedom, community, courage, responsibility) because almost everyone can relate to them, but not in the same way.[6] For instance, everyone has his or her own individual concept of God. Many universal concepts also include their opposites: life/death, creation/destruction, elation/despair and good/evil.[7]

> The charge of the interpreter, then, is to help make the connection between the tangible and intangible meanings of the resource in the hearts and minds of visitors. This is the gift of revelation.

The key to revealing meanings is to find connections between the tangible aspects of the site (artifacts, structures, wildlife, trees) and the intangible ideas associated with those resources. For example, the Liberty Bell is a tangible product. Yet when people see the bell they make personal connections to intangible ideas such as courage, freedom, and democracy.[8] The cliffs of Yosemite tell the story of glaciation and yet also hold meanings concerning beauty, mystery, adventure, and conservation. The tangible resource of wilderness also represents intangible concepts such as harmony, self-sufficiency, wholeness, and spirituality.

The power of the resources we interpret comes from their capacity to reveal meanings, those things that move our souls.[9] The charge of the interpreter, then, is to help make the connection between the tangible and intangible meanings of the resource in the hearts and minds of visitors.[10] This is the gift of revelation.

This approach to interpretation is fully consistent with the National Association for Interpretation definition: "Interpretation is a mission-based communication process that forges emotional and intellectual connections between the interests of the audience and the inherent meanings in the resource."[11] To craft worthy interpretation, the interpreter should consider the tangibles at the interpretive site. Information about the tangibles lays the foundation for adding the intangibles, revealing the meanings of the site, and addressing one or more universal concepts. In sum, the interpreter creates separate lists of tangibles, intangibles, and universal concepts. The next step is to consider the audience at hand and weave a relevant interpretation of the place.[12] A balanced approach is essential—too much focus on the tangibles could get boring, whereas too much emphasis on the intangibles could be perceived as patronizing or irrelevant.[13]

The Raw Material

Information is the raw material of interpretation.[14] Like all raw materials, information must be found and collected. Unlike other raw materials, information is an inexhaustible resource. New information about every conceivable topic is being produced at unprecedented rates.

What does this exploding body of information mean to interpreters? It means that we have a daunting task of keeping up. A *Dilbert* comic, by Scott Adams, vividly captures the challenge. As they walk, Dogbert tells Dilbert:

People are getting stupider every day, relatively speaking. The complexity of the world is increasing geometrically. But your ability to learn is at the same slow trickle it has always been. Information is gushing toward your brain like a firehose aimed at a teacup. You're at a crossroads in history. Even the smartest among you has become "functionally stupid." Your only hope is to choose a leader whose vision can penetrate the thick fog of human incompetence. Dogbert concludes, "Dogbert for supreme ruler of Earth!!"[15]

For our purposes, Adams provided vivid imagery. Because people are constantly being bombarded with more and more information, we must be diligent in providing quality opportunities to compete for their attention. We must ensure that our information is among that which ends up in the "teacup."

Staying abreast of new information may be especially challenging for interpreters because so many of us are generalists. Furthermore, we often interpret many facets of a park or historic site. At Cabrillo National Monument in California, park interpretive topics include the voyage and discoveries of Juan Rodriguez Cabrillo, the history of the Old Point Loma Lighthouse, the migration of gray whales, tidepool ecology, coastal sage scrub ecology, and military history of the San Diego harbor. All of this on 160 acres!

> We must ensure that our information is among that which ends up in the "teacup."

Some interpreters respond to the swelling body of information by exhibiting what Richard Saul Wurman calls "information bulimia."[16] Like the diet disorder characterized by binge eating, those who fear being uninformed begin "manic subscribing" to information sources. Then comes the purge—we delete everything or throw it away. The Internet offers a limitless outlet for gaining information, and it will only continue to expand with explosions in technology and communications.[17]

Unfortunately, instead of assisting people to broaden themselves, the information boom may cause some people to narrow their interests. This becomes the classic case, as some pundits have noted, of people learning more and more about less and less until they know everything about nothing. The other hazard is that some people may simply give up. According to Hal Kane, the difficulty of assimilating all this information "and forming it into a coherent analysis of our time—and then applying that analysis in ways that can improve our politics and our communities—may be so large as to have prevented it from happening."[18]

How can we prevent becoming overwhelmed when faced with trying to keep up? A challenge here is to be certain that our sources are accurate. We can eliminate junk information, just as we try to eliminate junk food. By subscribing to only the best journals and news groups, we can consume information with little waste of time. We might ask, "Will the information enrich my life? Is it necessary for excellence in my work?" We also need to strive for balance between "book" learning and "experiential" learning concerning the resources we interpret. Personal experience with the resource is essential for quality interpretation.

Another challenge faced by interpreters from the information explosion is the task of getting a message through to the audience without it being deflected or buried by other stimuli. Interpreters provide only a tiny segment of the public's total information intake. The way in which information is delivered will determine whether it will break through the competing stimuli.

As noted in the previous chapter, the brain constantly selects its focus, attending to the important and ignoring the unimportant. Our brains have a built-in bias for noticing high-contrast stimuli, novelty, and emotion. Interpreters may respond to this insight by using catchy and provocative titles for programs, by composing attractive publications, by designing colorful and dynamic exhibits, by offering unusual presentations, and by appealing at the level of the visitor's emotion.

Other factors influence the brain's selection process as it affects our attention. Cyclical fluctuations in the efficacy of neurotransmitter molecules chemically regulate attention.[19] These fluctuations occur about every 90 minutes throughout the day. At about 6 a.m., many people experience a rise in these attention molecules, causing them to wake up. The average level of molecules remains high in the morning and tends to decline during the afternoon. This means it is easiest to maintain attention in the morning and more difficult to maintain it later in the day. Typically, if we have a choice, we do what is most demanding in the morning when attention is greatest. This implies that interpreters might be wise to schedule programs that teach skills, identification techniques, and other tasks requiring rapt concentration in the morning and schedule less demanding, more socially engaging programs in the afternoon.

Scientists have also determined that our brains are designed to respond to immediate dangers. Yet, interpreters attempt to communicate gradual processes that over time may reach crisis proportions such as deforestation and species extinction.[20] Educators suggest that the most challenging aspect of teaching is to help people consciously manage aspects of their attentional system that aren't preprogrammed to enhance survival. Robert Sylwester and Joo-Yun Cho wrote:

> In the modern era, human life is more than attending to immediate survival. It is now vital to attend to the quality of our lives and to the potential gradual erosion of that quality. It's important we teach … how to appreciate a fine work of art without asking how much it costs, how to simply observe a sunset. The energy released by the plants that surround a rocket launch site is at least as socially meaningful as the energy used to launch the rocket. Although we attend to the televised blast-off, we now have to learn how to attend to the equally important gentle growth of the plants in the background of the televised sequence.[21]

To reveal this deeper meaning is one of the gifts that interpreters provide.

The Finished Product

If information is the raw material, then interpretation is the finished product. Interpreters equipped with good information can produce a finished product that transcends merely informing people of facts, instead revealing deeper meanings and truth.

What is involved in this process? Interpreters must make sure the collected raw material is accurate and that sufficient quantity has been collected. Tremendous damage can be done to the credibility of the individual and organization if misinformation is given to the public. Misinformation can also be confusing or harmful to those who have received it. Interpreters who respect their audiences and themselves will readily admit not knowing the answer to a question. We should thank visitors for their questions and assure them we will try to find the answers. Speculation and guesses should be clearly identified as such. When working with the media, the distinction between facts, opinions, and editorial comments becomes especially important.

> Interpreters equipped with good information can produce a finished product that transcends merely informing people of facts.

When convinced the raw material is suitable, the interpreter can begin to shape it into interpretation: revealing meanings associated with the site by making connections between the tangibles, intangibles, and universal concepts. This is a creative and personal process that we will continue to describe in the next chapter.

We can touch people not only by revealing information about the subject, but also by having the courage (and humility) to reveal something of ourselves. Interpreters can and should share personal perspectives, insights, and testimonies related to the subject matter. Audiences generally appreciate these personal touches. These efforts make us seem more human as we bridge the gap between "expert" and audience. A saying in the field of education suggests that students don't care what the teacher knows; they just want to know that the teacher cares.

To Enjoy Understandingly

The joy of knowing can be stimulating. Mihalyi Csikszentmihalyi stated, "Great thinkers have always been motivated by the enjoyment of thinking rather than by the material rewards that could be gained by it."[22] Cognitive learning can produce positive outcomes for our visitors.

John Burroughs, in an essay titled "The Gospel of Nature," struck a balance between the importance of the cognitive and emotional dimensions of enjoyment. Both are important, and the end result is to "enjoy understandingly:"

All that science has to tell me is welcome, is indeed, eagerly sought for. I must know as well as feel. I am not merely contented, like Wordsworth's poet, to enjoy what others understand. I must understand also; but above all things, I must enjoy. How much of my enjoyment springs from my knowledge I do not know. The joy of knowing is very great; the delight of picking up the threads of meaning here and there, and following them through the maze of confusing facts, I know well. When I hear the woodpecker drumming in the woods, and know what it is all for, why, that knowledge, I suppose, is part of my enjoyment. The other part is the associations that those sounds call up as voicing the arrival of spring; they are the drums that lead the joyous procession. To enjoy understandingly, that, I fancy, is the great thing to be desired.[23]

We can encourage visitors to "enjoy understandingly" through interpretation that reveals deeper meanings. Enos Mills concluded, "People are out for recreation and need restful, intellectual visions, and not dull, dry facts."[24]

Facilitating Memory of the Experience

Extensive research by Doug Knapp is rooted in the theory of Endel Tulving, a Canadian neuroscientist.[25] Tulving's theory distinguished between semantic memory that encompasses facts and knowledge of the world, and episodic memory that has to do with remembering experiences.[26] Sam Ham notes, in the Foreword of Knapp's *Applied Interpretation*, "perhaps the best indicator of an interpreter's success wasn't whether visitors could remember the facts the interpreter presented, but whether the interpreter had orchestrated a memorable experience that, in turn, could lead them to make their own conceptual associations."[27]

> We can encourage visitors to "enjoy understandingly" through interpretation that reveals deeper meanings.

Based on his research, Knapp determined three variables that can aid in episodic memory: repeated exposure, relevance to the individual, and active engagement with the content.[28] These are all elements that can be ingrained in interpretive programs. As Ham observed, the more an interpreter succeeds in getting people to think on their own and generate their own meanings, "the less likely those people are to do well on a test of the facts that were actually presented."[29] Think about it. What would you rather have? Someone who can regurgitate the facts of the program? Or someone who has developed profound personal meanings derived from an experience you conducted?

Emily Dickinson wrote of one who "has the facts but not the phosphorescence of learning."[30] The interpreter's aim is to use the raw material of information to produce interpretation that will instill in people not only the facts, but the "phosphorescence of learning," that lends itself to deeply meaningful visitor experiences that become embedded in memory. We must strive to construct our interpretation so it has the potential for people to "enjoy understandingly." Thoughtful and well-designed interpretation can lead to exhilarating visitor experiences in which one may exclaim, "Ah-ha! Suddenly I see everything in a different light!" This is the gift of revelation.

mat 6/30/78

CHAPTER

3

The Gift of Story

The interpretive presentation—as a work of art—should be designed as a story that informs, entertains, and enlightens.

After the listening you become accountable for the sacred knowledge that has been shared.
Shared knowledge equals power. Energy. Strength.
Story is an affirmation of our ties to one another.

—Terry Tempest Williams

Enos Mills wrote about the "poetic interpretation" of nature and compared the nature guide to an artist. Mills himself was an accomplished storyteller. Through the encouragement of John Muir, Enos Mills began writing and "lecturing," but storytelling is a more appropriate term to describe Mill's presentation style. He did not use a lectern or notes. Newspaper reviews of his talks consistently stressed that he was animated, exciting, and spellbinding. Indeed, during a private presentation at the White House, President William Howard Taft refused to leave for an official appointment until Mills finished his story about bears. Mills was a master at creating suspense and drama, and then adding just the right amount of humor. He walked around as his stories unfolded

and his hands were constantly in motion. Although he spoke frequently to prestigious groups, he believed his most important audiences were children.[1]

Freeman Tilden identified interpretation as "an art, which combines many
arts."[2] The use of "art" in defining interpretation refers to the creative process of
putting together the interpretive story. In addition, interpretation employs various arts from drama to music to dance.

As stated in the first principle, the story must somehow relate to something
within the personality or experience of the visitor. Furthermore, information,
as such, is not interpretation. The story offers revelation based upon information, as noted in the second principle. Within this principle is also the seed of
the fourth principle; the purpose of the interpretive story is to inspire, to provoke people to broaden their horizons.

The Meaning of Story

A meaningful story makes interpretation provocative. To assemble an effective story requires a great deal of research, thought, organization, and care. This
is a gift to your audience.

At one level, presenting an interpretive story encompasses orchestration of
an introduction, body, and conclusion. The interpreter tells the audience what
he or she is going to do, does it, and then tells the audience what he or she
has done. This is the standard format of an oral
presentation. Various strategies, such as the use of
examples or anecdotes, are incorporated to add interest. The story, even at this basic level, is an act
of creativity.

> To assemble an
> effective story requires
> a great deal of research,
> thought, organization,
> and care. This is a gift to
> your audience.

At another level is story as myth, legend, tale,
historic event, or elaborate personal experience.
Depending upon the circumstances and intent, the
story may be fiction or nonfiction. One full histori-
cal account or Native American story of nature may constitute the entire presentation. Or perhaps shorter vignettes may be woven into the larger whole of
a program. Or the interpretive presentation may be like Matriochka dolls, with
stories inside stories.

The interpretive storyteller may speak to an audience or interact with people
who both listen and participate as the story unfolds. Responsive participation is
especially effective with children. This method demands the listener's presence
and fully reveals the intimacy, immediacy, and excitement of storytelling.

Keeping the Story Pertinent and On Track

Consider the tale of a traveler passing through and spending the night in a small Midwest town. He joined a group of men sitting on the porch of the general store. After several futile attempts to initiate a conversation he asked, in exasperation, "Is there a law against talking in this town?"

"No law against it," said one old-timer. "We just like to make sure it's an improvement on silence."

Interpreters, first of all, must be certain that their interpretation is an improvement on silence. Furthermore, they must eliminate unnecessary details and sidetracks that detract from the message. Tilden stated, "The artist ruthlessly cuts away all the material that is not vital to his story."[3]

We are all familiar with well-meaning accounts that drag on with various unimportant tangents until the narrative finally bogs down in an abundance of details that are no longer remotely related to the start of the tale. The reader's own experiences are sufficient, here, to make the point.

> The artist ruthlessly cuts away all the material that is not vital to his story.
>
> —FREEMAN TILDEN

The skilled and considerate interpreter knows precisely where he or she is going. Any divergence is an integral slice of the overall story. A book title from several years ago stated the situation clearly: *If You Don't Know Where You're Going, You'll Probably End Up Somewhere Else.*

Note that we are not suggesting that interpretation be inflexible. On the contrary, the very command of the material and structure advocated here allows for flexibility—a thoughtful reaction to an unusual occurrence or an intelligent and appropriate response to the particular nuances of the audience.

Treating Knowledge Imaginatively

Tilden suggested that interpreters treat knowledge imaginatively, and Mills admonished them to reveal the "biography" of the place.[4] A number of strategies may be employed to make the story more personal, meaningful, and interesting. These tactics can be used to bridge the familiar with the unfamiliar or to vary the presentation for more impact. Here are some possibilities: [5]

Examples: Use concrete illustrations to assist the audience to understand and relate to the message.

Cause and Effect: Show relationships—people are interested in what things cause other things to happen.

Analogies: Explain a point by making a comparison to something similar that is more familiar to the audience.

Exaggerate the Time Scale: Make information more meaningful by exaggerating the scale of time (e.g., the history of the Earth condensed into a 24-hour day to explain geological features).

Similies: Use the words like or as to relate characteristics of two things.

Metaphors: Provide a word or phrase that is usually used to describe something very different to capture the meaning of a new idea and to fuel interest.

Anecdotes: Use concise personal sketches that relate to the theme of the presentation to lend interest.

Quotations: Quote others to add color to the message. People are interested in the observations of others.

Humor: Use appropriate humor to engage an audience. Humor may be especially useful in the early stages of the presentation to loosen up the audience. As the old adage states: if they are laughing, they are listening.

Repetition: Repeat key phrases to create memorable messages.

Current News Events: Incorporate current events into the presentation to make a related point.

These strategies can be purposefully used in various combinations to orchestrate meaningful and effective interpretation.

Stories in Our Lives

Stories are omnipresent in our lives. "Man lives surrounded by his stories and the stories of others," Sartre told us. "He sees everything that happens to him through them."[6] Indeed, we are encircled by stories. Yet the interpretive contribution of storytelling is anything but mundane. Unlike many of the stories that we meet elsewhere, those that are offered in interpretive settings are designed to inform and enlighten us.

As noted in the previous chapter, we are bombarded by a constant stream of information from the advertising industry and other forms of mass media that offer little substance. The telling of an interpretive story can change people in beneficial and enduring ways. We seldom expect the same from most of the stories that we casually encounter elsewhere.[7]

A broken connection with landscape and our history has been a compelling factor in the modern mindset in which detachment seems to dominate over collective and meaningful interaction. Jeremy Rifkin notes that in oral cultures closely tied to the land most language is stored in the mind, wisdom is cherished above all else, and that by their very nature these cultures are intimate and sensual.[8] Information is not retrieved; it is recalled for the good of the community.

Interpreters can benefit from an understanding of the intricacies of oral cultures. For example, one function of a story is to entertain people. Another, the epistemological function of a story, is to serve an educational purpose—to equip people with knowledge. A third possibility is the transformative function of a story whereby people are motivated to form a more balanced relationship to the Earth and other people.[9]

According to storyteller Susan Strauss, Native American folklore is useful because the stories are indigenous to the landscape, they weave in natural history, and they often embody totemic qualities such as courage and endurance.[10]

Story and the Proper Use of the Arts

The many avenues for treating knowledge imaginatively constitute one aspect of creating story as an art form. In addition, every interpreter is capable of some level of artistic talent. Tilden exclaimed, "You have been so frustrated by the curatorship of unimportant details that you have forgotten your inborn talent."[11] Furthermore, when interpreters use art to create story, they will find that they are among people who have the capacity to appreciate and understand their efforts. Interpreters, therefore, must be bold in seeking, practicing, and using the arts in interpretation.

According to Tilden, the effective telling of an interpretive story implies the use of art. However, he goes on to apparently contradict the original premise:

> I am sure that what I am saying will not be misconstrued to mean that the interpreter should be any sort of practicing artist: that he should read poems, give a dramatic performance, deliver an oration, become a tragic or comic thespian, or anything as horribly out of place as these. Nothing could be worse, except perhaps to indulge in an evangelical homily.[12]

Tilden would likely be surprised to see the incorporation of many of these techniques into effective interpretation today. In the past three decades, the field of interpretation has witnessed an elaborate expression of story through poetry, dramatic performance, storytelling, puppetry, music, dance, and visual art. This mode of interpretive programming has been tremendously effective in its power to attract and move people. It offers broad appeal to visitors who might otherwise forego more traditional interpretive opportunities.

> Interpretation has witnessed an elaborate expression of story through poetry, dramatic performance, storytelling, puppetry, music, dance, and visual art.

Furthermore, this type of programming may attract members of the local community who may have previously shown minimal interest in interpretation.

The actor Lee Stetson, who portrays John Muir at Yosemite National Park, notes that dramatic performances offer a vitality to the listener, provide a sharing of one another's truth, and "reaffirm the possibility of Creation."[13] Stetson explained:

> I am passionately convinced that art can serve to enhance our moral sensibilities and to promote in many a sense of environmental integrity. It used to be that our place on this planet was well claimed by the feelings of the people who lived here. Indigenous peoples, once naturally contained and nourished by the environment, integrated and celebrated that environment in their art, dance, music, community rituals. Their daily art evoked their values, aspirations, understanding, and their thoughts. The things we still need to learn are very old things we once knew well.[14]

As for evangelistic interpretation, it is telling that Guy Kawasaki was the keynote speaker at a past National Association for Interpretation conference. He wrote *Selling the Dream: How to Promote Your Product, Company, or Ideas*—and *Make a Difference—Using Everyday Evangelism*. Kawasaki defines evangelism as the process of convincing people to become as passionate about your cause as you are. The book is written for people who, like interpreters, want to make a difference.

> ... the final product is a function of the individual interpreter's knowledge, talents, experiences, imagination, organizational care, and presentation skills.

According to Kawasaki, evangelism "is the purest form of selling because it involves sharing ideas, insights, and hope in contrast to exchanging goods or services for money."[15] The goal of evangelism is sharing, not promotion for personal gain. Is this not what interpretation is all about—sharing a story that is revealing, penetrating, and affirming?

Indeed, interpretation is an art that combines many arts. The basic principles for creating and presenting an effective story also apply to any of the arts used wholly or in combination: drama, poetry, puppetry, storytelling, music, and dance.[16] The possibilities are endless and the final product is a function of the individual interpreter's knowledge, talents, experiences, imagination, organizational care, and presentation skills.

The Power of Story

Stories can hold tremendous power. The following discussion is a brief, philosophical overview that considers story, in its broadest meaning, as an integral and prominent component of our lives. Story, as discussed here, is an ideal for which to strive in interpretation.

We are proposing what Robert Coles suggested as "a respect for narrative as everyone's rock-bottom capacity, but also as the universal gift."[17] Terry Tempest Williams wrote, "We have all been nurtured on stories. Story is the umbilical cord that connects us to the past, present, and future."[18] In a live performance, a visceral and intimate connection between the teller and the listeners can be far more powerful than the intervention of electronic media. Yet we live in a culture that is increasingly dominated by impersonal communication.[19]

Interpretation, along with education and religion, retains the tradition of oral communication. People most often learn in settings where instructors speak to them and are available to answer questions. Similarly, people prefer to worship in settings where a message is preached and where they participate in the service. Oral communication has traditionally been, and can continue to be, a distinguishing feature of natural and cultural history interpretation. Although interpretation need not be entirely dependent on live performance, it should be a prominent and critical dimension of the overall interpretive mix.

Scott Russell Sanders provided a summary of the power of stories as follows:

Of all our reasons for telling and hearing stories, I want to focus here on ten: Stories entertain us. They create community. They help us to see through the eyes of other people. They show us the consequences of our actions.
They educate our desires. Stories help us to dwell in place. They help us to dwell in time. They help us to deal with suffering, loss, and death. They teach us how to be human. And stories acknowledge the wonder and mystery of Creation.[20]

Barry Lopez suggested that listening to stories may be exhilarating and can renew a sense of purpose in one's life:

> This feeling, an inexplicable renewal of enthusiasm after storytelling, is familiar to many people. ... I think intimacy is indispensable—a feeling that derives from the listener's trust and a storyteller's certain knowledge of his subject and regard for his audience. This intimacy deepens if the storyteller tempers his authority with humility, or when terms of idiomatic expression, or at least the physical setting for the story, are shared.[21]

Story, then, entertains, enlightens, and enriches our existence through a better understanding of the shadow side of life, as well as the reverence we experience as awe.[22] Story is structured and offered with the hope that the listener will find something of personal value. Knowing our subject is essential; otherwise, a tentative tone may be detected. Furthermore, our authority must be tempered by humility; otherwise, the message, however valuable, may be thwarted, lost in the arrogant atmosphere of the presentation.

... the interpreter's story becomes that of his or her listeners as well. They will carry it with them. This is the exemplar for which we strive; the gift of story.

The depth of what is being interpreted is made vivid through story. The story must be relevant to the visitor, and it must reveal the deeper meanings the subject holds. The interpreter creates a whole, yet focused message that is provocative, an inspirational message designed for the audience at hand. With these ingredients considered and fulfilled, the interpreter's story becomes that of his or her listeners as well. They will carry it with them. This is the exemplar for which we strive; the gift of story.

Stories that instruct, renew, and heal provide a vital nourishment to the psyche that cannot be obtained in any other way. Stories ... provide all the vital instructions we need to live a useful, necessary, and unbounded life— a life of meaning, a life worth remembering.

—Clarissa Pinkola Estes

CHAPTER

4

The Gift of Provocation

The purpose of the interpretive story is to inspire and to provoke people to broaden their horizons.

Let us probe the silent places,
let us seek what luck betide us;
Let us journey to a lonely land I know.
There's a whisper on the night-wind,
there's a star agleam to guide us,
And the Wild is calling, calling . . . let us go.

—Robert Service

The purpose of the interpretive story, whether oral or written, is to prompt the listener or reader to broaden his or her horizons and then act on that new-found breadth. Most visitors to interpretive settings are interested and eager to learn the deeper truths of the places they have selected to experience.

One task of the art of interpretation is to peel away layer after layer of mystery from the natural and cultural world. Of course, diminishing the mystery need not limit the sense of wonder. Certainly, enjoyment, knowledge, and inspiration can increase together. Anyone can rejoice in a spectacular vista and this, in and of itself, is worthy. However, interpretation can add an intellectual spice to a basic emotion and motivate further experiences, knowledge, and action. This is the gift of provocation.

> … interpretation can add an intellectual spice to a basic emotion and motivate further experiences, knowledge, and action. This is the gift of provocation.

Provocation through interpretation spans a broad spectrum, as we will see in this chapter. At its highest level, interpretation can result in changed perspectives and behavior. As Sallie McFague concluded in a book subtitled *Rethinking Theology and Economy for a Planet in Peril,* "We are called to see differently—and then to live differently…"[1]

Inspiration by Example

Interpreters entice visitors to learn more about the cultural and natural history of an area through their own passion for the place. Messages presented by example are highly motivational.

People are inspired by representative aspects of those they admire. As role models, interpreters present their quality of life as a consequence of staying close to the landscape—the physical landscape for natural history interpreters and the landscape of human conduct for those who interpret cultural history.

The relationship of the interpreter to his or her subject, marked by a depth of knowledge and a sense of wonder, serenity, and fulfillment, is something that visitors will notice. They may inquire, on a personal level, how the interpreter can achieve these qualities in life, and they may ultimately try to emulate them.[2]

Promoting the Place

As noted in previous chapters, many people are swamped by information yet removed from meaningful stories. Likewise, many are removed from their natural and cultural roots. We are becoming, more and more, a society that appreciates history and nature from secondary sources: television, books, magazines, videos, the Internet, apps, and theme parks.

Even when people plan trips to places of natural or cultural significance, they often isolate themselves from the resource itself. Terry Tempest Williams bemoans "a society of individuals who only observe a landscape from behind the lens of a camera or the window of an automobile without ever entering in."[3]

The first challenge may well be to get people out of their cars. Edward Abbey asked, "What can I tell them? Sealed in their metallic shells like molluscs on wheels, how can I pry the people free? The auto as tin can, the park ranger as opener."[4]

Visitors must be made aware of the possibilities, and this orientation can be accomplished in several ways. Visitors may be given information about what to do at an entrance station. Usually, visitors are charged an entry fee, provided with a map or brochure, and hustled along. However, the booth attendant should find out how much time the visitors have and what their specific interests are (the first principle), then make recommendations accordingly. Too often, visitors are left to their own devices, and it is no surprise that they wind up following the road to a developed area where they see more cars, a clue that they have arrived at their destination, perhaps a gift shop.

> What can I tell them?
> Sealed in their metallic shells
> like molluscs on wheels, how
> can I pry the people free?
>
> —EDWARD ABBEY

If traffic volume precludes this level of personal interpretation, groups of visitors could be addressed on the quarter hour at a gathering place near the entrance station or further along at a visitor center. The overall objective is to give visitors an overview of rewarding activities and provoke them to get involved.

Visitors who are motivated to seek experiences on their own (in contrast to interpreter-led services) should be adequately prepared for such adventures. Sending them out without proper knowledge about potential dangers would be a disservice. For example, all visitors to Yellowstone National Park should be provided basic interpretation of park highlights including the history and symbolism of the park, thermal features, current resource issues, and wildlife. Visitors who choose to venture beyond the parking lots and guided walks should then be provided the following additional information: 1) recommended action in case of confrontation with bears, bison, moose, or other wildlife, 2) hazards present in the geyser basins, and 3) hazards associated with restricted areas (such as grizzly closures or unstable cliffs).

Preservation of the Treasure

Based on the interpreter's intimate knowledge, the soul of the setting may be revealed. Why has this place been set aside for past, present, and future generations? What is the genius loci: the unique and representative values, the distinctive atmosphere, the pervading character of the place? What should everyone know about this remarkable setting?

As an interpreter, it may be useful to ask yourself about the most striking aspect of the place you interpret. What did you find most enchanting, most enthralling about the place during your first experiences? How has that changed, if at all, as you have matured in your tenure at the site? This firsthand perspective can be fascinating to visitors who will relate to your initial experiences.

When diplomats and missionaries arrive in a foreign country, they are often encouraged to take many photographs right away because after a short time things become too familiar. The uniqueness of people and places fades. Scenes that were exciting soon become mundane. Photographs taken early on provide a record of what was initially inspiring. Similarly, newly hired interpreters should be encouraged to record their first impressions in words and pictures. Later, such a record could be used to bring the veteran interpreter back to a clearer understanding of visitor perceptions.

> At best, interpretation should encourage in visitors a sense of self-love, self-respect, and self-worth because it is out of these emotions that responsible behavior originates.

Soliciting the opinions of visitors about what they find most resplendent about the place could also be useful and/or surprising. These insights could then be used to target and bolster future interpretive programming.

Just as solid interpretation helps the visitor begin to value the place, another benefit is preservation of the area: parks, forests, wildlife preserves, historic homes, battlefields, or other monuments dedicated to our culture. Most visitors are truly concerned and responsive to calls for the preservation of a place of natural beauty or cultural significance.

Furthermore, this type of interpretation may be effective for those who, out of ignorance or selfishness, might do the resource harm. Provocative interpretation speaks to those who may purposefully deface something rare and precious. According to Freeman Tilden, "If you vandalize a beautiful thing, you vandalize yourself. And this is what true interpretation can inject into the consciousness."[5] As a result of such interpretation, unthinking visitors may be less inclined to vandalize the resource and more motivated to respect it. At best, interpretation should encourage in visitors a sense of self-love, self-respect, and self-worth because it is out of these emotions that responsible behavior originates.[6]

Producing Behavior Change

Interpreters often attempt to affect the visitor's attitudes and behaviors toward the resource. Most interpreters believe that the role of the interpreter is to challenge the visitors' belief systems. [7] Interpreters trust that changed beliefs will lead to changed behaviors (such as enhanced compliance and stewardship of the site). Interpretation has been applied to provoke behavior changes to decrease depreciative behaviors, as well as to provoke positive behaviors such as public support for policies or funding. Indeed, interpretation has become a key tool in changing behaviors to address management issues and interpreters are becoming important members of the management team (see Chapter 12).

If interpreters are seeking to change attitudes and behavior, they must offer experiences that accomplish that objective.

If interpreters are seeking to change attitudes and behavior, they must offer experiences that accomplish that objective. Research by Doug Knapp provides a framework of goals to assist interpreters in producing programs that attempt to affect attitudes and behavior. The following account is a synthesis of literature related to environmental interpretation and curriculum development in environmental education conducted by Knapp. [8] The three levels of goals for program development in environmental interpretation are entry-level goals, ownership goals, and empowerment goals.

Entry-Level Goals

Entry-level goals are broken down into various components that promote basic site information. These goals, in sum, provide the visitor with 1) overview information (layout, visitor amenities, and other pertinent site characteristics) and general awareness of the ecology and cultural history, 2) opportunities to comprehend the ecological and cultural relationships between the resource site and the surrounding area, 3) an awareness of management policies and objectives and the effect these policies have on the resource, and 4) experiences that inspire environmental sensitivity through greater appreciation and enhanced enjoyment of the site—"an empathetic perspective toward the resource site." [9]

Ownership Goals

Ownership goals are separated into two components in which interpretation seeks to 1) foster an awareness of the collective actions of visitors on the quality of the site and 2) encourage investigation and evaluation of these resource issues. [10]

The skills associated with pursuing the ecological and cultural implications of human impact could also be used to investigate broader environmental issues.

Empowerment Goals

Empowerment goals are structured to encourage visitors to embrace responsible actions. Interpretive programming with these goals would promote experiences that develop visitors' abilities to differentiate the types of actions available for solving resource issues and to choose responsible courses of action.[11] The most powerful use of the above framework is to offer interpretive experiences that represent all three levels in a sequential order. However, several research studies by Knapp and his colleagues indicate that although stewardship goals may be attained after interpretive programs, this is certainly not guaranteed.[12]

To promote stewardship goals further, Knapp suggests a stronger focus on the entry-level variables, and, especially, to encourage children to have positive contact with the outdoors. He also recommends a connection of the environmental message with the visitor's own life. Finally, he notes that interpreters should be pragmatic about expectations and impact basic awareness of an interpretive site, and this may form the foundation for the ultimate goal of environmental stewardship.[13]

Empowerment goals are consistent with Aldo Leopold's concept of ecological consciousness and the development of a land ethic. "It is inconceivable to me," Leopold wrote, "that an ethical relation to land can exist without love, respect, and admiration ...." Or more to the point, "A thing is right when it tends to preserve the integrity, stability, and beauty of the biotic community. It is wrong when it tends otherwise."[14]

Knapp's model provides a framework to stimulate attitude and behavior change in visitors. But how interpreters can more effectively achieve empowerment outcomes is an important question to answer.

Sharing the Vision

A shared vision becomes a force in people's hearts. At its most basic level, a shared vision is the answer to the question, "What is it that we want to do?" A shared vision is one that many visitors commit to because it reflects their own personal vision. In other instances visitors may shift their existing attitudes and behaviors.

The role of the interpreter is to provide meaning and revelation, to generate a context that relates to visitors' lives. By sharing a vision the interpreter can spark a flame that creates a common identity among diverse people. Interpreters who seek to build shared visions must be willing to share their personal visions. They must also be prepared to ask, in essence, "Will you follow my lead?"

To expect enrollment or commitment to a cause from others, the interpreter must be committed. To be otherwise, of course, would be hypocritical. We must also be honest. The vision must be presented without inflating the benefits or neglecting the costs. Two distinct strategies can motivate people: fear and aspiration.[15] The response motivated by fear (reacting to change) is at the root of negative visions. The source of energy behind aspiration (generating change) drives positive visions. Although appealing to people's fear may foster changes in the short term, only appealing to aspiration generates long-term change. A vision comes alive only when people feel they can shape their futures. Visitors to our treasures of natural and cultural history will commit to a cause over the long term not because they must, but because they want to commit.

> A shared vision becomes a force in people's hearts.

To be most effective in sharing a vision, we should know and relate to the audience. This is the first principle of interpretation, for knowing the audience allows us to make the presentation interesting and relevant. Moreover, the interpreter must know the vision. A broad and deep knowledge of the cause provides the confidence to explain and defend it.

Guy Kawasaki suggested the following elements for effective presentation of your vision: 1) Foster the tone of the presentation to be upbeat, optimistic, and bold. 2) Communicate ambitious goals. Large goals will not scare off those committed to the vision, and even small ones will scare off those who are doubters. 3) Highlight personal benefits. How will what you propose translate into changes in an individual's life? 4) Reach a peak. As the presentation progresses, it should nudge the audience's emotions higher and higher until it reaches a summit. This approach makes the presentation vivid and exciting.[16]

The Courage to Look for Trouble

We have moved from relatively safe modes of provoking visitors (inspiration by example, promoting the place, and preserving the treasure) to a framework for producing behavior change and the principles for sharing vision. Indeed, these persuasive approaches overlap in some ways.

Now we're going to take a step further, recognizing that this last level of provocation may not be appropriate in all instances. It conflicts with many instincts of a bureaucracy and may cause discomfort in some interpreters. In essence, we are presenting the concept of facing conflict in support of our convictions. This takes courage, which Sigurd Olson has characterized as a multi-faceted virtue. There is courage to withstand adversity without complaint, to show humility in the midst of success, or to stand and be counted for deep personal convictions.[17]

Conflict is painful, but it is also educational, and it leads us to the crux of our environmental problems. According to Bill McKibben, for example, if people can acknowledge that a grizzly bear habitat is as important as sheep ranches, then they have taken a giant step toward realizing that their own way of life or job may require change for the upper atmosphere to remain intact. McKibben continues:

> ... Martin Luther King, Jr. and the civil rights movement did not concentrate as much on winning over the rednecks who were burning crosses as they did on converting the great mute majority of Americans to a new way of thinking. They created a series of confrontations that served to educate ... those of us who simply had never given the issue enough attention.[18]

Of course, complex environmental issues are not as straightforward as civil rights crusades. But the same kind of shifts in attitude—toward understanding, appreciation, unselfishness, compassion, and enlightenment—are as necessary and perhaps as possible. McKibben concluded:

> In any event, those who run our parks should remember that every decision that involves a choice between people on the one hand and trees and animals and rivers on the other is an opportunity for education in humility. It will not be easy. ...But if your goal is to teach the public about the natural world, your work can't stop with the nature trail and the diorama.[19]

An interpreter who has the "courage to look for trouble" does so in an intelligent way. Focus on what it is about your program that might cause someone to say, 10, 20, or 30 years later, "I heard an interpreter say this a long time ago. It made sense to me, and I changed. I'll never forget it."

I heard an interpreter say this a long time ago. It made sense to me, and I changed.

If the audience mostly favors your view on a controversial issue, then your presentation should reinforce existing beliefs and be motivational in nature. Bring the listeners beyond complacency to a level of firm commitment with specific recommendations for action.

If the audience mostly opposes your position, guide listeners to basic principles and establish common agreement, even if it is only harmony of opinion that an existing problem needs to be solved. Structure the presentation to minimize the differences between you and the audience by focusing on facts that are irrefutable and basic strands of perception that are common to each view.

Whatever the makeup of the audience, when the goal is to persuade others on a controversial topic, we must phrase our appeal in terms of the higher principles of the listeners. For example, we can show the audience how the issue coincides with noble motives such as compassion, justice, civic responsibility, and concern for future generations.

Interpreters are obligated to present the truth. They must acknowledge issues that have not yet been resolved and those with conflicting evidence. Yet when it is clear that, as Leopold admonished, "a thing is right" or "it is wrong," then it must be logically and forcefully presented as such.

As a broad example, consider the importance of protecting the diversity of life on this planet. Edward Wilson demands that the ethical imperative be, first of all, prudence: we should not knowingly allow any species to go extinct. The responsible stewardship of our Earth preserves not only the well-being and freedom of other species, but also the health and spiritual uplift of our own. This is uncontestable, something on which we should all be able to agree. As Wilson suggested, "Those committed by religion to believe that life was put on earth in one divine stroke will recognize that we are destroying the Creation, and those who perceive biodiversity to be the product of blind evolution will agree."[20]

The Galapagos Conservation Fund

An exciting area in the realm of interpretive provocation comes from the concept of travel philanthropy. Leading the way in this arena is Sam Ham, who served as a consultant to Lindblad Expeditions, an international travel company. The communication campaign actually begins before guests leave home through information provided on the Internet and then continues throughout the experience. Travelers on the cruise are informed of the special qualities of the Galapagos Islands including the plants and animals, and the local community. They are provided a "sense of obligation to improve the beautiful locations they visit."[21] Then, on the second-to-last night of the cruise, the participants are given information about the Galapagos Conservation Fund and are informed on how to contribute if they choose.

In less than 10 years, Lindblad Expeditions raised more than $3.6 million. This funding has enabled eradication of feral pigs and goats from the Galapagos island of Santiago and the re-establishment of native plant species, as well as other conservation projects. The various project allocations require joint proposals and agreement by the Galapagos National Park and Charles Darwin Research Station.

> If you find something people can care about, help them to care about it, and then give them the opportunity to act on it— they'll do it.
>
> —SAM HAM

According to Ham, "If you find something people can care about, help them to care about it, and then give them the opportunity to act on it—they'll do it."[22]

Promoting Conservation Around the World

Tourism played an important role in the justification and establishment of the early national parks in America, the first in the world, and continues to be used as a tool of conservation today. Among the fastest-growing sectors of the tourism industry are ecotourism and voluntourism (volunteer travel), often to developing countries. Highly threatened biological resources and local poverty often characterize these countries. Ecotourism and voluntourism support protecting the natural resources and welfare of the local people. These modes of travel benefit the host nation through payment of fees and the purchase of local goods and services. This, in turn, results in the generation of jobs.[23] Significant donations from altruistic travelers may occur as they are exposed to the conservation needs of the areas they visit, as discussed above.

In the case of voluntourism, travelers volunteer some or all of their time onsite to assist with conservation efforts (such as a wildlife census or constructing trails) and local infrastructure (such as building schools or clinics). Voluntourism offers opportunities to connect with and help host cultures while simultaneously seeing the sights of new and exotic places. Research indicates that host cultures prefer to be involved with the assistance they receive. Rather than having assistance imposed on a community, local residents become players in the decision-making process. That is, the local culture is able to determine the projects that are designed to help them. Unlike traditional tourism, where contact with the host culture is limited to monetary exchanges for goods and services, travelers are able to interact directly with local residents through the work projects. This powerful approach to tourism allows us to transform ourselves through helping others.[24]

Interpreters have a responsibility to broaden horizons and provoke a more sensitive, caring attitude toward our cultural and natural resources. This may occur anywhere from the local nature center to international tourism sites. Through interpretive programs, visitors learn the compelling stories of the places they visit. This heightened understanding lends itself to a greater appreciation of the cultural and natural heritage of the interpretive site. Finally, visitors are prompted to act in ways that make them feel they are making a difference in the world, which lends to their sense of hope and esteem, and indeed, through their actions, makes the world a better place. This is the gift of provocation.

Whatever you can do, or dream you can, begin it.
Boldness has genius, power and magic in it.

—Johann Wolfgang von Goethe

Our own Torrey pine
in the front yard — about 20 years old
at   March 3, 1981

5

The Gift of Wholeness

Interpretation should present a complete theme or thesis and address the whole person.

Wholeness is the sum total ... it is the ephemeral essence,
the ultimate that puts one in tune
with cosmic values.

—Sigurd Olson

Sigurd Olson suggested that to explain wholeness we must return to the very depths of being, for it entails all that has gone before us. "It is harmony and oneness, the very antithesis of fragmentation, emptiness, and frustration. It means being alive and aware of all about you and all that has ever been. It is being in tune with waters and rocks, with vistas and horizons, with constellations and the infinity of time and space."[1] Two major issues are addressed by this principle: presenting a whole picture and interpreting to the whole person. We will address each separately. In addition, we will consider regional and global interpretation as important factors in interpreting a whole.

Presenting A Whole

It is important not to misconstrue this principle to mean that interpreters should present the whole—should not leave anything out. Telling the whole story of any site would be impossible. Barry Commoner's First Law of Ecology succinctly stated, "Everything is connected to everything else."[2] If we were to attempt to communicate everything known about a topic, we would find ourselves facing an infinite web of information. But, even if the whole story of an event or place could be presented, visitors could not receive the whole message. People are limited by their short-term memories and attention spans. Psychologist George Miller found that people can concentrate on or hold only about seven "chunks" of information (plus or minus two) in their short-term memory.[3] For example, when going to the store for more than seven items, one usually resorts to making a list rather than relying on memory. By grouping facts into chunks we can condense several items that are similar and thereby remember more information. Remembering a nine-digit social security number is easier if we divide the numbers into three chunks.

Freeman Tilden stated, "A cardinal purpose of interpretation, it seems to me, is to present a whole, rather than a part, no matter how interesting the specific part may be."[4] Whether planning a battlefield tour or a nature trail, interpreters must be selective in deciding which "parts" to present to make a whole. Given the limited capacity of human memory, interpreters should not present more than a few important concepts; however, interpreters often present large numbers of miscellaneous facts to the public.

> As tempting as it may be to include everything, the interpretation should support a *focused* whole.

For example, from battlefields where thousands fell, to local sites memorializing those who fought in an almost forgotten skirmish, interpretive media often focus on technical descriptions of the weapons and the numbers and affiliation of dead and wounded. The statistics are often presented, and read, like a baseball box score. Self-guiding nature trails often offer 20+ stops with an abundance of information on topics ranging from geology to wildflowers, history to ecology. When the stops offer no linkage or continuity, the information will exceed short-term memory capabilities. As tempting as it may be to include everything, the interpretation should support a *focused* whole.

Interpretation of Meaningful Themes

The possession of facts is knowledge; the use of them wisdom;
the choice of them education.

–Thomas Jefferson

Interpretation toward a whole makes visitors more knowledgeable by communicating facts, makes visitors wise by attaching meaning to the facts, and educates visitors by guiding them through mountains of information, presenting only the most salient and rewarding material. The key to making this selection lies in theme-based interpretation.

All interpretation, whether written or spoken, should have a theme—a specific message to communicate. Themes are statements of what the interpreter wants the audience members to understand and remember. In the context of this principle, a theme is a "whole."

Thematic interpretation eliminates the tendency to present a collection of unrelated facts. Focusing on a single "whole" directs interpreters only to those facts that must be presented to develop and support the theme. This not only avoids overloading the audience, but also saves time for the interpreter preparing the presentation.

According to Sam Ham, another important advantage of thematic interpretation is that "people remember themes ... but forget facts."[5] Ham argued that when people know the theme at the beginning of the presentation, exhibition, or trail, attention is enhanced and they comprehend and remember more of the information. When no theme is identified, attention, comprehension, and retention are weaker. Drawing upon experiments by P.W. Thorndyke, Ham concluded that when a theme isn't given, comprehension and recall is no better than when the audience is presented with "a completely jumbled story comprised of unrelated sentences."[6]

Themes are not the same as topics or subject matter. At a historic site such as the Little Bighorn Battlefield National Monument the topic could be broad, such as "the battle," or as narrow as "the Colt Single Action Army model 1873 revolver." Countless facts about the battle or firearm could be presented to the visitor, but presenting these facts would not be thematic. Interpretive planners at the Little Bighorn Battlefield have identified six themes. All interpretation at the Battlefield must address one of these themes, each of which represents a whole. The first theme is that the battle of the Little Bighorn has a symbolic dimension

In selecting themes, interpreters should consider the special characteristics of the place.

that far exceeds its military significance. This first theme is further broken into two sub-themes as follows: 1) The battlefield name change and the Indian monument create symbols of inclusion, rather than exclusion; it is no longer Custer's or Sitting Bull's battlefield, but the nation's. 2) All of the participants saw themselves as patriots—fighting for their country, land, and way of life.[7] At battlefields, meaningful stories abound among the statistics—stories about bravery, cowardice, intelligence, suffering, honor, terror, heroism, and pain. Abraham Lincoln attached meaning to the statistics at the Gettysburg battlefield and gave his Gettysburg Address, a history-changing interpretation of events. The lasting results of warfare can have a meaning to present-day visitors.

Some human conditions and situations seem to have universal meaning. People from all ages and cultures are drawn to certain concepts with universal significance, as discussed in Chapter 2. These concepts may involve human conflict: conflict within a person, conflict among people, or conflict between humans and their environment.

In selecting themes, interpreters should consider the special characteristics of the place. Interpreters should focus on concepts derived from the site's genius loci—special meaning—and directed at the visitors' interests. This is one aspect of the gift of wholeness.

Thesis-Based Interpretation

Ann Lundberg argued that a thesis (as opposed to a theme) goes beyond subject content to challenge visitors' attitudes or perspectives. A thesis is an expression of an opinion—something with which someone might disagree. Lundberg said, "The inclusion of an opposing point of view inherent to a thesis statement adds a dynamic tension to what is being said, an element of suspense which interests the audience in how you will prove your case. Suddenly their own point of view matters; they will have to choose sides."[8]

Lundberg provided two examples of turning a theme into a thesis.

Theme: Native American rock art has been interpreted in many different ways.
Thesis: The ways in which prehistoric Native American rock art has been interpreted tells us more about the desires of those who do the interpreting than about what the ancients meant.
Theme: Geyser function is dependent upon three variables.
Thesis: Changes in the three variables that determine geyser function suggest that Old Faithful may not be faithful for long.[9]

Lundberg concluded that thesis-based interpretation seeks to have an effect in the world: "By disturbing and unsettling an audience, we can wake them from complacency to responsibility and to action."[10]

In the last chapter, we discussed a spectrum of interpretive modes to provoke visitors, including "the courage to look for trouble." Thesis-based interpretation likewise involves risks to the interpreter because the thesis is a statement with which people may disagree. However, at issue here is the notion of themes versus theses, and the argument is partly rooted in semantics.

We believe that good theme statements have the potential to provoke an audience. Nonetheless, not all themes argue a single thesis or point of view. This should be acceptable. For example, an interpretive program may be provocative by enlightening people to see something in a new way without introducing an overriding point of view, by arguing a point of view, or by presenting multiple points of view with an argument for each. Differing circumstances may define which approach is used. Some interpreters are limited in their expression of personal opinions if they don't represent the official position of the agency for which they work. Some interpreters, as a matter of style, may prefer less confrontational—but perhaps no less effective—approaches. Finally, some statements, traditionally classified as themes, may argue a point of view and fall into the thesis category as well.

Meeting the Needs of the Whole Person

Interpretation must address itself to the whole [person]
rather than any phase.

—Freeman Tilden

As detailed in Chapter 1, we must know our audiences to target messages effectively. To apply this principle fully, interpreters must know the needs and motivations of those they address. Psychologist Abraham Maslow developed a theoretical model of motivation based on human needs.[11] He combined Freudianism (which focused only on internal and intrinsic determinants of behavior) and behaviorism (which focused on extrinsic or environmental determinants of behavior) to study the whole person. Maslow's model is built upon a hierarchy of motivations leading from physiological needs, to safety, to social connectedness, to esteem, to self-actualization.

People with unmet physiological needs (such as thirst or hunger) still require the higher needs, but their attention is focused on satisfying immediate requirements first. As individuals meet lower-level needs, they can then satisfy the higher-level needs.

In industrialized countries, Maslow found that few people are motivated by basic physiological needs because these have already been met. Interpreters can expect to encounter people primarily in the mid-levels of the hierarchy. Visi tors often are motivated by safety, belonging, and esteem needs. As we assist people in meeting lower-level needs, they can be lifted to realizing higher needs. Self-actualization, the apex of Maslow's model, consists of moments of highest happiness.

Working upward in Maslow's hierarchy, interpreters should strive to understand visitors' fears and safety concerns. After these concerns are identified and understood, then they may be countered to assure that visitors are not preoccupied with them.

Understanding visitors' needs is another aspect of the gift of wholeness.

Tilden observed that it is "easy to put the visitor down as a moron."[12] Responding kindly to exasperating questions tests the patience of some interpreters. Yet an impatient or harsh rejoinder will exacerbate the needs visitors have for security, acceptance, and esteem. The interpreter may have heard the question a thousand times, but each particular visitor asks it, and hears the answer to it, only once.

Minda Borun, at the Franklin Institute in Philadelphia, found that "naive notions" about science are held not only by children, but are widespread in adults. Borun and her research associates found that regardless of age, most visitors did not fully comprehend the concept of gravity. Correcting misconceptions and changing tightly held but naive beliefs requires a different approach than merely teaching new information. By applying this insight, Borun and her associates found that a "corrective" interpretive exhibit changed many of the visitors' misconceptions about gravity.[13]

Interpreters also encounter people who seek to fulfill needs for belonging. We live in a time of increasing mobility and scattered families. Many people don't know their neighbors. People with unmet belonging needs may exhibit feelings of loneliness and alienation. Interpreters have the opportunity to welcome such people and make them feel like they belong to the broad "family" of visitors to the site. One particularly effective strategy is to call visitors by their names.

Often, visitors are welcomed to a visitor center or interpretive program. A further personal touch is to acknowledge them as they leave, thanking them for coming. We can give all visitors our attention and our respect to encourage them to feel welcome and to come again. This approach has the potential to lift people above their self-consciousness and contribute to their sense of esteem. We might also recognize individuals for their special abilities or valuable characteristics. Understanding visitors' needs is another aspect of the gift of wholeness.

Presenting a Multi-sensory Whole

Engaging as many of the visitor's senses as possible allows the interpreter to go beyond meeting intellectual needs alone. Touching, seeing, smelling, tasting, and listening all help communicate a whole. This approach can be accomplished creatively in both natural and cultural settings. For example, in distinguishing between trees, people can feel the different textures or smell of bark. Historic sites can use aromas from bygone eras to engage visitors' sense of smell or tools to bring back sounds from the past. Recipes from the past can allow people to taste food of that era, as has successfully been done with baked cookies at the Old Point Loma Lighthouse in California.

Activating the senses creates a holistic experience. Diane Ackerman observed, "There is no way in which to understand the world without first detecting it through the radar-net of our senses. . . . The senses feed shards of information to the brain like microscopic pieces of a jigsaw puzzle."[14]

Interpreting Regional Wholes and Global Wholes

At historic sites, to present a whole, it may be necessary to give an overview of an entire trail, such as the Oregon Trail of westward expansion, which stretched between the Missouri and Columbia rivers. As another example, visitors to a specific "Underground Railroad" hiding place would need to understand the full extent of the "Railroad" to gain the full meaning of the site.

At nature sites, interpreting a whole may mean going beyond park boundaries that were set using economic or political criteria rather than ecological or historical criteria. For example, interpreting natural history themes may involve an entire watershed. A park's wetland in the upper reaches of a watershed may provide benefits such as flood control, sediment trapping, removal of heavy metals, and groundwater recharge for those who live downstream. Similarly, interpreters at Grand Canyon National Park address the theme of air quality. That is, air pollution from coal burning power plants hundreds of miles away has obscured the view from rim to rim of the canyon.

> ... interpreting a whole may mean going beyond park boundaries that were set using economic or political criteria rather than ecological or historical criteria.

Interpretive sites in the same region sometimes coordinate efforts when interpreting similar broad regional topics. This can prevent undue redundancy among these sites. Planners can collaborate in deciding which themes will be presented at each particular site. For example, at two nearby parks, each with a similar restored farmstead, one may interpret 1890s family life emphasizing themes involving the role of the farm wife and what it was like to be a child on the farm, whereas the farm equipment of the period will be interpreted at the other site.

Interpreters within a region can also coordinate state-of-the-art interpretation of the same themes at several related sites. The Great Lakes Lighthouse

Keepers Association, in conjunction with interpretation faculty and students at the University of Michigan, Dearborn, developed an innovative interpretive program that uses music, video, written materials, and youth involvement to interpret and preserve historic lighthouses at locations throughout Michigan.[15]

On a larger scale, cumulative individual and local actions may have global ramifications. Bumper stickers call for us to "Think Globally—Act Locally." Consider themes involving migratory species, international trade in plants and animals, and issues dealing with the global atmosphere. To what degree should interpreters challenge the visitor to take local action? Michael Frome asked the tough question, "What should interpreters really be interpreting?" He answered, "If you ask me, interpretation as a profession and interpreters as individuals are failing in their stewardship responsibility. Of course, there are good interpreters with conscience and courage, but they are the minority."[16]

We face grave environmental problems: species extinction, climate change, disposal of toxic waste, desertification, food and water shortages, infectious diseases, human overpopulation. These global environmental concerns permeate various interpretive themes. Consequently, we should be able to weave pertinent information into our interpretation. Abraham Lincoln said, "To sin by silence when they should cry out makes cowards out of men."[17] Ideally, we can help visitors feel they can be a part of the larger solution.

If you treat an individual as he is, he will stay that way,
but if you treat him as if he were what he could be,
he will become what he could be.

—**Johann Wolfgang von Goethe**

The dictionary offers the words healed and restored as synonyms of whole. Interpretation should focus on presenting a whole picture through a thematic approach. In addition, interpretation toward a whole seeks to encompass the whole person. By meeting personal needs, interpretation can enhance the visitor's well-being. Finally, regional and global interpretation can lend itself to the cause of restoring our planet to environmental health. Tilden wrote, "Of all the words in our English language, none is more beautiful and significant than the word 'whole.'"[18] By knowing our visitors and our interpretive place (both in its immediate and larger context), we may best interpret a whole that will be meaningful and enduring. Overall, this is the multi-faceted gift of wholeness.

© Tsuyoshi Matsumoto

CHAPTER

6

The Gift of Targeted Programs

Interpretation for children, teenagers, and seniors—when these comprise uniform groups—should follow fundamentally different approaches.

> *If I had influence with the good fairy who is supposed*
> *to preside over the christening of all children I should*
> *ask that her gift to each child in the world be a sense*
> *of wonder so indestructible that it would last throughout*
> *life, as an unfailing antidote against the boredom and*
> *disenchantments of later years, the sterile preoccupation*
> *with things that are artificial, the alienation from the*
> *sources of our strength.*

> **—Rachel Carson**

Enos Mills devoted considerable attention to interpretation for children. He wrote, "No other school [as Nature] is likely so to inspire children, so to give them vision and fire their imagination."[1] He continued by suggesting that this "unrivaled" outdoor school and playground is always open as a library, a museum, a zoological garden, and as a type of wilderness frontier. Mills allowed that interpreters may enter "a little more intimately" into the experiences of children and that "slight re-adjustments" would be necessary in interpretation to meet their needs.[2] He was adamant, however, in his refusal to talk down to children. Freeman Tilden also felt children should have special focus.

Tilden's sixth principle of interpretation stated: "Interpretation addressed to children (say, up to the age of twelve) should not be a dilution of the presentation to adults, but should follow a fundamentally different approach. To be at its best, it will require a separate program."[3]

We agree with Mills and Tilden but expand the concept to include two other unique age groups—teenagers and seniors. We recognize, too, the tremendous diversity within these groups as well as the commonalities among all people. At some level, we'd like to believe we are all children. Nevertheless, we propose that each of the aforementioned groups—if uniform in age—gain from deviations from, and enhancements to, standard mass-oriented interpretive programs.

According to Gary Machlis and Donald Field, matching an interpretive approach to the appropriate audience is perhaps the most difficult challenge facing interpreters. They suggested, "The bases for assessing differences are numerous. ... Perhaps the most obvious difference among visitors is their age."[4] And they concluded, "Yet an assessment of programs offered reveals a low number of interpretive options specifically designed for either the young or the old."[5]

This chapter will address interpretation that can be thoughtfully designed and presented for uniform groups of children, teenagers, and seniors. Our emphasis will be on children because, as we shall see, more is at stake. Also, a much broader and deeper literature addresses children's interpretation (primarily in the area of children and nature). Specifically programmed interpretation for teenagers and seniors is a relatively new frontier.[6]

Children

Nothing you do for children is ever wasted. They seem not to notice us, hovering, averting our eyes, and they seldom offer thanks, but what we do for them is never wasted.

—Garrison Keillor

Children can be simultaneously exasperating and the greatest earthly delight imaginable. Part of what is so engaging (and unnerving) about children is their unpredictability. They are also distinguished by their innocence, trust, raw enthusiasm, spontaneity, vitality, and curiosity. This section of the chapter explores the concern that children are not bonding with nature and the reasons why. It then focuses on efforts designed to attract children to nature and to interpret effectively for them after they arrive.

Kids Are Not Bonding With Nature

In a book titled *Childhood's Future*, columnist Richard Louv observed that just as children need meaningful adult contact and a sense of connection to the broader human community, they also need independence, solitude, adventure, and a sense of wonder.[7] These latter needs, in the past, have been met through contact with nature. Although children have so much to gain from experiences in nature, these opportunities are increasingly limited. This thesis became the topic of a subsequent book by Louv, titled *Last Child in the Woods*, which was a synthesis of extensive research in this field by academics such as Louise Chawla.[8] Richard Louv coined the term nature-deficit disorder to describe the condition of children being removed from nature in the past few decades and the toll this takes on their development physically, mentally, emotionally, socially, and even spiritually.

> Richard Louv coined the term nature-deficit disorder to describe the condition of children being removed from nature in the past few decades and the toll this takes on their development physically, mentally, emotionally, socially, and even spiritually.

Children in the inner city are not bonding with nature because it is so overwhelmed by human factors. René Dubos warned about "the wholesale and constant exposure of children to noise, ugliness, and garbage in the street, thereby conditioning [children] to accept public squalor as the normal state of affairs."[9] Furthermore, although suburban tracts may be less noisy, less ugly, and less filthy, they are often "sterile and restrictive in their own way."[10] In intensely farmed areas, children are also isolated from nature as natural biotic communities have been replaced with expansive monocultures of corn, wheat, cotton, citrus, or other cash crops.

Children are growing up disconnected from nature because nature is not readily available to them. In addition, children are heavily influenced by mesmerizing sedentary activities—television, videos, computer games, smart phones, and social media sites such as Facebook. As a result, even if natural landscapes were accessible, we question whether children would be drawn to them as in the past. Gary Paul Nabhan and Steve Trimble provide evidence that rural kids in remote areas of Mexico, Alaska, and the American West learn more about nature from television than from firsthand experience.[11] A fourth-grader interviewed by Louv said, "I like to play indoors better 'cause that's where all the electrical outlets are."[12]

The Irony of Educational Nature TV

Television programming includes some excellent nature shows. Yet even well-respected programs send a wrong message in part. The problem is twofold. First, even the best programs instruct that nature is something that is learned about inside and "that it is passive, prepackaged, apart from human existence."[13]

Second, these programs create false expectations. Kids can watch the development of a baby cub into a full-grown grizzly bear in an hour. Anything they might observe firsthand in nature, by comparison, is going to be less spectacular and will require more effort and patience.

Barbara Kingsolver, in *High Tide in Tucson*, quotes Robert Michael Pyle's pointed question, "If we can watch rhinos mating in our living rooms, who's going to notice the wren in the backyard?" Kingsolver adds, "The real Wild Kingdom is as small and brown as a wren, as tedious as a squirrel turning back the scales of a pine cone, as quiet as a milkweed seed on the wind—the long, slow stillness between takes."[14]

One novel suggestion to motivate kids to get out into nature more is to fight television with television. Marshal Case said, "Getting kids back to nature through the visual media is probably the only way we're ever going to turn the tide. ...We have to take what's been doing the damage and turn it around. And I think we can do that if people get serious about producing some really good, solid materials that are aimed at getting kids back out to nature. I haven't seen anyone concentrate on this."[15]

As appealing as this solution appears to be—and we fully endorse it—it is perhaps unlikely. The television industry is aware that any widespread success in getting kids outdoors would, in the long run, compromise their business. At least in past actions, the TV industry has been reluctant to embrace this level of altruism out of concern for the public good.

The solution to the problem is more likely to arise through proactive measures in the home that get kids outside and in comprehensive environmental education offerings in the schools. Furthermore, the interpretive field contributes by offering programs that introduce babies to nature so that they don't fear it later and by providing stimulating children's programs as the kids grow.

"Nature is Frightening and Disgusting and Uncomfortable"

Not only are there no electrical outlets, but nature for many children is a fearful, dreaded, and alien place. Some children are familiar with natural landscapes through family excursions, summer camp, or similar experiences. Others, however, without such previous opportunities, may hold negative preconceptions about natural areas. They may be overwhelmed by their lack of familiarity with the sights, smells, and sounds of natural settings. Even when no immediate dangers exist, children may fear the unknown and may exhibit various phobias. These fears often stem from misimpressions of natural environments portrayed via movies, videos, television, newscasts, and ill-informed word-of-mouth.

Robert Bixler and his colleagues surveyed interpreters at nature and environmental education centers to determine the anxiety reactions of children. Interpreters were asked to recall and list fears by children on field trips to wildland areas. Major categories of fears and discomforts were ranked and those results follow.[16]

As may well be predicted, the fear of snakes was the most common response (87%). The second ranked response was fear of insects, primarily bees (79%). The third ranked response, fascinatingly, was fear of nonindigenous animals (73%). We may speculate that television and zoos contributed to the frequent references to these latter fears. For example, many children, having no concept of what to expect, expressed fears of being attacked by such predators as lions, tigers, and alligators. In addition to a litany of other fears (including, but not limited to, poisonous plants, spiders, bats, and getting lost), Bixler and his colleagues found that children reacted with disgust (as opposed to fear) to various organisms such as slugs and the odor of decaying plants.

> Interpreters may have to provide special assistance to apprehensive children who carry negative and unpleasant perceptions of nature.

Also of concern to some children in these field settings was their lack of comfort. That is, children were anxious about getting dirty or wet, or becoming too hot or too cold. This may be explained in part by the fact that many urban children have a narrow comfort range due to their dependence on more sterile settings and modern heating and air conditioning.

One of the challenges for those who interpret to children is that programs may have to include corrective as well as formative measures. Interpreters may have to provide special assistance to apprehensive children who carry negative and unpleasant perceptions of nature. This should be accomplished early by explaining any misconceptions, generating a sense of security, and establishing the child's confidence in the interpreter's knowledge and competencies.

In *Beyond Ecophobia*, David Sobel suggests that the early years of childhood, ages 4-7, should offer an emphasis on empathy with the natural environment, including sensitivity toward the animals that live in the wild. He notes that stories, songs, imitating animals, celebrating seasons, and promoting a "sense of wonder" should be primary activities during this stage.[17] At 7-11 years of age, children should be encouraged to explore the landscape firsthand. Typical activities for this stage would include following streams, taking care of animals, and searching for natural treasures.

Environmental educator Michael Weilbacher notes, "Eight-year-olds should not be asked to become warriors or worriers. Children have much more important work to do: Watch ants. Grow flowers. Dance between the raindrops. This is sacred work, and childhood needs to be preserved just as much as rain forests and wetlands."[18]

Only later should concerns associated with social action be introduced. A focus on social action may occur as children reach the age of 12 and beyond. Sobel observes, "As children start to discover the 'self' of adolescence and feel their connectedness to society, they naturally incline toward wanting to save the world."[19] Appropriate activities at this stage include managing school recycling programs, having speakers come to the school to address critical local issues, planning trips to learn about and observe environmental problems, and becoming involved with the political process. Sobel concludes that the interplay of empathy, exploration, and social action will remain complex as youth grow older, and these areas will work together as a source of joy and strength for the demands of social commitment in later life.[20]

Inoculating Babies with Doses of Nature

Perhaps the best action to ensure that children's interpretive programs are successful is to start early. Through exposure to nature (early inoculation), children can learn to enjoy natural settings before it becomes too late and they come to fear them. They can learn firsthand that there is very little to fear, that the disgusting can alternately be perceived as the fascinating, and that getting dirty and exploring with all the senses is fun.

At the Austin Nature Center in Texas, interpretive programs were designed and offered specifically for one-and-a-half to two-and-a-half-year-olds.[21] This "Babies and Beasties" program included basic "instruction" and self-awareness activities. In three different classes, the babies learned about themselves in comparison to other animals. In the mammals class, they were exposed to similarities among all mammals. In the birds class, they made comparisons between characteristics such as beaks and mouths, arms and wings, and feathers and hair. The reptiles class was the "climax" of the program: "Many people have an aversion to reptiles, but by demonstrating an accepting attitude to these 'slimy' and 'horrible' creatures, perhaps some of this accepting attitude will rub off on the participants, both babies and parents."[22] This observation sums up the importance of such programs. Children who are provided an accurate perception of nature from early firsthand experiences are more likely to be "inoculated" against accepting the inaccurate depictions of nature, which are so prevalent in the media or through word-of-mouth myths and misnomers.[23]

> **Through exposure to nature (early inoculation), children can learn to enjoy natural settings before it becomes too late and they come to fear them.**

Similarly, the Missouri Department of Conservation has developed a nature walk for those up to two years of age (and their parents) titled, "Babes in the Woods."[24] This is a 45-minute guided walk with parents pushing children in strollers. For obvious reasons, these programs are offered at times that avoid weather extremes, as well as early morning, mealtimes, and early afternoon nap times. A short trail with a smooth, level surface is best for this type of walk. The intent of the program is to expose babies to nature in a positive way.

Just as adults can never be too old, children can never be too young to enjoy nature. During the walk, babies are encouraged to imitate their parents in using their senses to explore natural objects. The program literature explains, "Even though babies may not converse with their caregivers, they gain just from hearing words, the tone of a voice, and the enthusiasm."[25] The overall goal of the program is to allow the child and adult to become familiar with, and feel comfortable in, their surroundings. As just one example, participants learn experientially about trees. Parents and their babies explore the textures of bark, compare shapes of leaves, smell bark or foliage, and listen to the rustling of leaves in the wind.

Adults learn what to do with their children by modeling the interpreter and get to experience firsthand that shared nature outings are a rewarding way to spend time with their babies. The babies, in turn, develop a connection to nature.

Providing Quality Interpretation for Children

From a general and practical perspective, Tilden and Mills agreed that children are capable of rapid learning, delight in the superlative, are generally lacking in inhibitions, desire personal examination of items through all of the senses, relish companionship, and thrive on a sense of adventure.[26] With these broad insights in mind, the interpreter attempts to answer the question, "How can interpretive programs be designed to be exciting and effective for children?" Interpreters should keep in mind, and plan for the fact, that attention span is limited and proportional to age (younger children have shorter attention spans). Children will want to move and be vocal. With thoughtful planning and program management it is possible to direct movement and vocalizations into something positive and related to the program.

Gary Machlis and Donald Field explored the concept of "connecting" interpretive programs with children. Connecting children with interpretation requires consideration of children's social groups.[27]

> Just as adults can never be too old, children can never be too young to enjoy nature.

The intent of the group will have a bearing on the message. The role of the interpreter may range from inspirational to educational to recreational. The group size also will have a bearing on the structure of the program. Small groups are more conducive to learning and inspirational experiences than larger groups.

The group's composition is another important consideration. Knowing the age range of the children, as well as social and educational backgrounds, is useful. What is of interest to the children? What have they been studying in school? To what degree do they have experiences in natural landscapes? What are their fears? What would they like, or what do they need, to know? Ideally, knowledge of the group's social context can be used as a motivational tool to "connect the group" to the interpretation. This knowledge can be useful in providing briefing materials for the group prior to the visit.

The interpretive approach for children, according to Machlis and Field, is derived from three basic modes of human expression: action, fantasy, and instruction.[28] Allowing children to become involved in the interpretation is critical. They learn best through action and appropriate participation. Demonstrations that involve children in an activity are especially effective.

Fantasy can be a "powerful and far-reaching mode of interpretation" for children.[29] For example, interpreters can effectively combine action with fantasy to engage children in play-acting to replicate past events and to provide a notion of how and why people responded as they did. Although children are often involved in imaginative pursuits, "this approach is seldom openly used by interpretation planners and programmers."[30]

> Children from Nature's Book and School stand highest in the examinations of life and carry life's richest treasures: health, individuality, sincerity, wholesome self-reliance, and efficiency.
>
> —ENOS MILLS

For children, as with adults, the success of instruction is related to its degree of meaning and usefulness. A combination of action, fantasy, and instruction approaches can be orchestrated to educate, motivate, and inspire any given children's group. This, as with all good interpretation, takes thought, research, planning, and care.

Tilden suggested, in terms of the cost and staffing of children's programs, "there is no preserve so small that it cannot employ some devices [for interpreting to children], if it desires to do interpretation at all."[31] Enos Mills considered the end result as follows, "Children from Nature's Book and School stand highest in the examinations of life and carry life's richest treasures: health, individuality, sincerity, wholesome self-reliance, and efficiency."[32]

Teenagers

When I was a boy of fourteen, my father was so ignorant
I could hardly stand to have the old man around.
But when I got to be twenty-one,
I was astonished at how much he had learned in seven years.

—**Mark Twain**

As Mark Twain observed, teenagers can be judgmental, harsh, self-centered, and incorrigible. They are sometimes stereotyped as living in a world consumed by themselves and their peers. Adolescence is a difficult time of transition between childhood and adulthood, a transition full of potential pitfalls associated with social relationships, and the temptations of drugs and alcohol. The good news is that teenagers can have enormous amounts of energy, zeal, and ambition. Most teenagers are good citizens who desire increased responsibility in their families and community. Through an understanding of teenagers, and with careful planning, interpretive programming can effectively reach this age group.

People working with teens must be genuinely interested in them. Teens will be able to tell if this is so or not. This does not mean interpreters should act like teenagers by adopting their vocabulary and mannerisms. Interpreters should treat teenagers as young adults, emphasizing mutual respect and responsibility. Working with teens requires special wisdom as teens look to peers for direction but also seek adult opinions in addition (often preferred) to those of their parents. With appropriate discretion, interpreters can play an important role in a teenager's life. Teens need time, and working with them requires much physical and emotional effort, but the life-changing rewards can be great.

> **Through an understanding of teenagers, and with careful planning, interpretive programming can effectively reach this age group.**

Teens typically prefer being with their peers, which is an important consideration in targeting them. They want independence from parents and traditional family groups. Teens are action-oriented and enjoy physical challenges. They want to do something. Allow for fun times. For example, visit other nature centers, go canoeing or hiking, or eat pizza together. Get them working on a task together and they can be seemingly unstoppable. However, in allowing them to work together, interpreters must be careful not to allow cliques to form. As they work, give teens as much responsibility as you can within their comfort levels and competency. Teens are confident, at least on the outside; but like all of us, they need positive support. Let the teens know that what they are doing is important.

Teenagers tend to focus on their future rather than their short history. Therefore, designing historical messages to relate past events to current or future consequences would be worthwhile.

Burr Oak Woods Conservation Nature Center in the Kansas City area offers programs for teenagers under the umbrella title "Wild Ones." Specific programs include: Sketching Wildflowers (the basics of sketching wildflowers and other natural objects), Fly Tying (tying three or four fishing flies), Geocaching Adventure (GPS units provided), Creek Crawl (looking for wildlife signs and picking up trash), Surviving the Wild (finding food, shelter, fire, and reading the landscape), and three- to five-mile hikes off the beaten path, sometimes bushwhacking cross-country where teens can test their orienteering techniques.[33]

Another approach to attracting teens at Burr Oak is through the volunteer program. Teens go through the same volunteer training as the adults, but are asked to commit to only six hours of service per month. Teens love to help with outdoor skills-type programming, especially activities like canoeing, fishing, and geocaching—anything adventurous! Interpreters use this program to introduce teens to the field of interpretation and to expose them to all of the Divisions within the Missouri Department of Conservation so they might explore related career choices. Burr Oak staff has found teens to be enthusiastic and highly motivated.[34] This motivation comes from a desire to gain job experience, to be with friends, to be part of a group (such as scouts or a church youth group), to give back to their community, or to get out of the house and enjoy the outdoors.[35]

At Runge Conservation Nature Center in Jefferson City, Missouri, teen volunteers are even given responsibility for giving presentations and leading walks. When asked to lead a hike or give a program, "teens are not afraid and will give the presentation with zeal and gusto."[36] In an interview with a local newspaper about the importance of teaching others about conservation, one teenage volunteer noted with maturity and insight, "Earth's natural ecosystem is being altered, and in some cases, destroyed by man. I think that we should learn to conserve earth's resources and encourage others to do so before it is too late."[37] Teens are a tremendous resource and an excellent and worthy audience for interpretive efforts.

Seniors

Age is not all decay; it is the ripening, the swelling,
of the fresh life within,
that withers and bursts the husk.

—George MacDonald

One view of aging suggests that the older years are a period of steady decline. This perspective focuses on the older years as a time of social uselessness, loneliness, and personal hopelessness. The other view is of the older years as a time of personal growth and accomplishment.

We will advocate the view that each year of life provides occasions for renewal as well as vitality. Although aging does result in losses, primarily physiological, aging also has positive aspects.

We are experiencing the graying of America. More people age 65 and over live in this country than ever before. Furthermore, older individuals are generally more healthy, financially secure, adventuresome, knowledgeable, independent, and vocal than previous generations of seniors. Serving older persons through quality interpretation will be increasingly important in interpretive programming.

Seniors have a strong intrinsic interest in subjects dealing with the past. At historical sites, older persons may have lived through the events or heard tales of those times. They like to reflect on the past. Sometimes interpretation will trigger important memories.

> We will advocate the view that each year of life provides occasions for renewal as well as vitality.

Seniors appreciate depth in interpretive programs. Their knowledge and experience allows them to make connections between concepts. They have a sophisticated grasp of time, so they may relate better to interpretation of complex life cycles and long-term processes such as succession or eutrophication. Sixty-year timber rotations and 100-year-old buildings mean more to them than to children or teenagers.

Older persons tend to visit interpretive sites more frequently in the off-seasons when they are less crowded. They often stay longer than other visitors and therefore are more likely to understand the resources on a deeper level and to ask more questions. This interest and attentiveness can make for rewarding interpretation.

Interpreters can involve and reach older persons through rewarding volunteer opportunities. Retired people, having worked all of their adult lives, often seek out meaningful ways to use their retirement time in a disciplined, productive manner.

Certain physical limitations may limit participation by older persons. These limitations, associated with the aging process, include lack of stamina, vision, hearing, and mobility. However, all of the common ailments of the elderly can be mitigated (by taking shorter hikes to accommodate those with less stamina, using larger print for visual impairment or assisted listening devices for hearing impairment, and paving surfaces with gentle slopes for those with restricted mobility). In an age when older persons run marathons, those who are physically fit should be encouraged to participate in more demanding interpretive activities.

Researchers studied elderly visitors to national parks and concluded that interpreters should consider age-specific programs for seniors.[38] They found that older persons appreciate social interaction with peers. Special programs for seniors allow for a common ground of sharing between participants. These programs also negate the possibility of disruptions by unruly children. (Older persons are not especially tolerant of unruly children, unless they are the grandparents of those children.) Typically, seniors prefer day rather than evening programs.

Overall, eliminating distractions, mitigating age-related impairments, scheduling activities at favorable times, and creating a synergistic and enthusiastic atmosphere between peers enhances and promotes interest by older adults. Moreover, when we use larger print, gentler slopes, and other accommodations for seniors, we help everybody receive interpretive messages more clearly and efficiently.

Interpreters can meet the needs of people throughout the lifespan.

Interpreters can meet the needs of people throughout the lifespan—from the tender stem of young growth, to the budding flower, to the green formative fruit, to the ripe fruit bursting with new life.

Segmenting and serving children has grown tremendously in the past few decades in interpretive-related ventures. We expect to see similar growth in serving teenagers and seniors in the future. This is the gift of targeted programs as we interpret through the lifespan.

S.P. 595
Same step
mat

© Tsuyoshi Matsumoto

C H A P T E R

7

The Gift of Personalizing the Past

Every place has a history. Interpreters can bring the past alive to make the present more enjoyable and the future more meaningful.

There is no peculiar merit in ancient things, but there is merit in integrity, and integrity entails the keeping together of the parts of any whole, and if those parts are scattered throughout time, then the maintenance of integrity entails a knowledge, a memory, of ancient things. ... To think, feel or act as though the past is done with, is equivalent to believing that a railway station through which our train has just passed, only existed for as long as our train was in it.

—Edward Hyams

Interpreting history, like all good interpretation, relies on relating to the audience, revealing deeper meaning and truth, and inspiring individuals. To be effective, interpreters of history must personalize the past and relate it to the present with an eye toward the future. In this chapter, our focus will be on living history, a distinct and particularly effective approach in making the past come alive and relevant to today's audiences.

In many respects, interpreting historical objects and events is not significantly different from interpreting natural resource themes. The fundamental principles and techniques of effective interpretation do not change with the subject. Heritage interpretation and natural resource interpretation take place in similar settings. Both occur in museums and visitor centers, along trails and roadsides, and at public parks and private tourist attractions. Every natural area has a history to interpret and every historic site is linked to a natural resource base that can be fruitfully interpreted.

Living History

History interpreters give talks and lead walks, sometimes in costume, sometimes in uniform. Living history has been defined as "the recreation of specific periods of the past or specific events utilizing living interpreters usually clothed and equipped with the correct tools and accouterments of a depicted era."[1]

When the interpreter is playing the role of a specific person from the past, it is considered "first-person" living history interpretation. When the living history interpreters are in costume but are speaking about the historic characters or events rather than presenting themselves to be an actual person from that time period, then it is considered "third-person" style. Third-person living history is also referred to as "costumed" interpretation. Some contemporary historical interpreters consider third-person costumed interpretation to be outdated and less effective than first-person interpretation.[2]

> **Every natural area has a history to interpret and every historic site is linked to a natural resource base that can be fruitfully interpreted.**

Some first-person living history interpreters portray common people carrying out typical activities associated with life in a particular period. Others portray famous individuals or reenact important events. For example, for many years, Lee Stetson has entertained and educated audiences at Yosemite National Park with his portrayal of John Muir. Similarly, professional actor Earll Kingston gave a captivating portrayal of John Wesley Powell to evening crowds at Grand Canyon National Park.

In conducting first-person interpretation, the interpreter becomes totally immersed in the identity of the historic person portrayed. This involves more than merely wearing authentic clothes, exhibiting authentic objects, or demonstrating certain skills. The best living history interpreters know the subtle mannerisms, perceptions, and attitudes of the individual they are portraying. They delve into the mind of the character to fully understand and "become" that person.

Such "visitors from the past" feign total ignorance of events that have occurred since "their time" and act oblivious to modern conveniences and lifestyles. First-person interpreters must think quickly and respond in character
when visitors challenge the time period context (by calling attention to a plane
flying overhead, for example) or ask unsolicited questions that would draw the
interpreter out of character. Experienced interpreters anticipate such interrup-
tions and respond with good humor without compro-
mising their character or the program. For example,
at a state historic site, a question about a low flying
plane by an audience member who wanted to draw
the interpreter out of character was met with the light-
hearted retort, "You're seeing things flying through
the sky? Oh, you must be the boy I heard about who
got kicked in the head by a horse."

> **Living history has
> many advantages as an
> interpretive approach.
> It provides tremendous
> opportunities for
> visitor involvement and
> enjoyment.**

Living history has many advantages as an interpretive approach. It provides tremendous opportuni-
ties for visitor involvement and enjoyment. Participants can see, hear, touch, and
even, at times, smell the past. Visitors can easily slip back in time and become
emotionally immersed in the presentation. Most of all, living history programs
can be fun.

Living history provides opportunities for serious amateurs to demonstrate
skills and share their interest in history. Results can be impressive when individuals from specific ethnic groups perform authentic interpretation of their
heritage and culture. In short, for both participants and observers, living history
presents the "closest tactile conception we have of our past."[3]

Jay Anderson, in *Time Machines: The World of Living History*, identified the
following three characteristics, which insure its significance as an effective way
to interpret history.[4]

- Living history strives for what T. S. Eliot called "felt truth." It challenges us
  to think and feel. To living historians, empathy is as important as understanding.
- Living history lies outside the boundary of established academic and public
  history. It thrives on independence. Each museum, each project, and each
  unit makes its own covenant with historical truth and determines the way it
  will carry on its dialogue with the past.
- Finally, living history rejects a linear view of the past. It argues that, before
  you can study a forest, you must become totally familiar with the trees. Living historians point out that the history establishment has often failed to
  study, interpret, and experience the everyday reality of ordinary people in
  the past.

The Process

The rewards associated with any interpretive activity will be commensurate with the amount of effort that went into planning and preparation. Living history is a labor-intensive but powerful interpretive strategy that connects people to the past. The following is a typical sequence of events that must take place to develop an effective living history program.

First, select a character (historical or fictional) who will best communicate the desired interpretive theme. This will require research and considerable thought. Then, you must develop this character. The interpreter needs to identify the character's place and date of birth, family information, social class, education, trades or skills, hobbies or talents, biographical highlights, national and world events that occurred during the character's life, and myriad other details.

> The rewards associated with any interpretive activity will be commensurate with the amount of effort that went into planning and preparation.

Next, the program itself must be considered. Interpreters must establish reasons for the audience's presence and the character's presence in the context of an interpretive story. Interpreters must establish the setting and construct or acquire props and costumes. Additional content to support the theme must be included and then, like any interpretive program, delivery must be practiced and polished, and audience reactions anticipated. Because living history interpreters interact directly and extensively with the audience, it is especially important for interpreters to anticipate and prepare for their varied responses.

John Luzader cautions that living history interpretation is more than just putting on a costume and working from a script. In fact, he believes the costume is the least important tool for living history. Instead, the interpreter's preparation and performance are the keys to success.[5]

Dilemmas in Delivery

Although living history programs are especially good at immersing the audience in the past, these approaches have some limitations. As we have seen, living history programs are labor-intensive, requiring considerable advance preparation. Besides the normal planning and research that would go into any interpretive endeavor, living history requires collecting—or creation—of accurate artifacts, props, sets, and costumes.

Staffing living history programs also can be challenging. Conducting living history, particularly in the first-person style requires special people. The ability to think quickly, some acting talent, and a high level of commitment are necessary to make the performance believable. Due to the high level of audience involvement, living history interpreters must be able to ad lib while also staying on topic. Living history interpretation also requires an ability to gauge the audiences' comfort level and willingness to participate.

Costumed interpreters pretending to be living in the past may confuse or intimidate visitors. Interpreters need to prepare visitors in advance for being receptive to unconventional deliveries by using signs, brochures, or announcements to allow them to make informed decisions about whether to get involved. During this visitor preparation process, we can encourage involvement by revealing the enriching fun and learning that results from participation.

As will be discussed below, living history has limited application in interpreting historical events associated with human suffering and death. When the topic is war or the exploitation and mistreatment of humanity applying living history approaches becomes challenging.

Heroes or Villains?

A difficulty with interpreting history (using living history or any other interpretive approach) is that the values that form our interpretations of historical events change. Society judges historical characters by a continually shifting framework, so our assessments of their actions shift. For example, in recent decades, General George Custer and Spanish Conquistadors have undergone a metamorphosis from heroes to villains in the eyes of many people. With other historical figures, the metamorphosis is incomplete. Although Christopher Columbus is still celebrated with a holiday complete with Columbus Day parades, festivals, and even closed schools in some cities, public demonstrations vilifying him are held simultaneously in other cities.

> Ultimately, the role of history is to provide the opportunity to examine ourselves and how we have become what we are today.
>
> —JOHN GOLDA

Similarly, when the Smithsonian's National Air and Space Museum announced an exhibit marking the 50th anniversary of the end of World War II featuring the refurbished B-29 Enola Gay, a heated battle was fought over how history should represent dropping an atomic bomb on Japan. Many veterans, veterans' organizations, and other Americans who were alive at the time and deeply affected by the war took issue with museum administrators and a group of historians over how the Enola Gay story would be told and what would be considered an "authentic" message. Congress got involved, as did the pilot of the Enola Gay, Paul Tibbets, who many considered a war hero. Protests continued (including an act of vandalism) even after the Enola Gay was relocated to the National Air and Space Museum at Dulles Airport.

John Golda, in considering how to interpret controversial historical figures, concluded, "In their actions, one can see the best and worst of human nature. In examining the interpretations of their history, one is given a mirror on the ideals and concerns of generations of Americans. Ultimately, the role of history is to provide the opportunity to examine ourselves and how we have become what we are today."[6]

Moreover, our culturally diverse audiences present interpreters with the challenge of offering an objective program. Native Americans at the Little Bighorn Battlefield, Japanese visitors to Pearl Harbor, and southern visitors to Civil War battlefields require sensitive treatment. Interpreters must be thoroughly informed to correct misconceptions, they must be prepared to bring different perspectives together in a balanced manner, and they must stress universal concepts such as courage and patriotism. Interpreters should reinforce that both sides were dying for what they thought was right and both sides fought bravely for their beliefs.[7]

As heritage interpreters develop themes, their choices should acknowledge changing perspectives over time. They also should be aware of, and sensitive to, audience members holding diverse values through which they interpret historical events.

History Interpretation as Entertainment

David Saxe observed, "The threshold between academic values and entertainment poses a dilemma for museum and historical site managers. When traditionalists hold sway, clutching to the high standards of decorum and dignity, this is a nonissue; entertainment has no place in the world of serious museum exhibition and historical interpretation. However, when the public enters the equation the thing itself on display in a room full of other objects is often not enough to keep the public engaged (and visiting)."[8] He goes on to point out that the entertainment issue is not so much about traditionalists and institutional dignity as it is about the bottom line, or "keeping the institution healthy and financially viable." He added, "From the best endowed institutions to the least, operators cannot avoid visitor demands (and expectations) for entertainment."[9]

Examples of historical sites that have learned the value of adding entertainment are Mount Vernon, where attendance has increased fivefold since the opening of a new high-tech visitor center that includes artificial snow falling in the theatre and other entertainment, and Colonial Williamsburg, where attendance has increased since a live-action outdoor drama called "Revolutionary City" was added.[10]

> The threshold between academic values and entertainment poses a dilemma for museum and historical site managers.
>
> — DAVID SAXE

The popularity of living history presentations makes them particularly vulnerable to becoming merely entertainment. The lure of potential profits may corrupt heritage interpretation by determining which themes will be presented and in what ways. Sites that generate revenue from fees may want to "jazz up" a historical presentation to make it more entertaining even if it means drifting from the facts. Moreover, making any theme pertaining to war entertaining is difficult without offending the visitors' sensibilities.

The challenge of being accurate and entertaining surfaced nationally when the Disney Corporation proposed building a historic theme park in Virginia. Disney Chairman Michael Eisner said the theme park would "include reminders of the painful, disturbing, and agonizing chapters in our history, from the introduction of slaves to the struggle in Vietnam."[11] However, the park's general manager said, "The idea is to walk out of 'Disney's America' with a smile on your face. We don't want people to come out with a sour face. It is going to be fun with a capital F."[12] Can "agonizing chapters in our history" be made fun—with a capital F? Columnist David Broder noted, "... the more Disney rewrites history into myth and converts America into Fantasyland, the more popular the park may be."[13] When trying to make painful chapters of our history entertaining, interpreters risk either glorifying or trivializing them.

Battle Reenactments

One genre of living history interpretation is military reenactment. Often hobbyists come by the hundreds from all over the country to reenact wartime events, usually a battle. Realism is something to strive for in interpretation, but reenactors fall short of total commitment to this concept on the battlefield for obvious reasons. Moreover, certain events are not appropriate for human reenactment.[14]

Volunteer reenactments should be consistent with the mission and interpretive objectives for the site. If this is the case, working with these groups ahead of time ensures that they present an accurate reenactment. Ideally, reenactors should receive training regarding the site's interpretive objectives, appropriate themes, visitor background, and principles of interpretation. In this way, the reenactment can supplement other interpretive efforts at the site.

To responsibly interpret war, including its tragic impact on humans is necessary. However, a gruesome, sensationalistic manner will detract from interpretive objectives, and simulations of suffering and death often offend audience members. For that reason, the NPS uses oral history accounts, slide shows, exhibits, film footage, books, and brochures to interpret warfare, rather than reenactments.[15]

Even exhibits about war may risk offending visitors. During the Vietnam War, Chicago's Museum of Science and Industry opened a popular exhibit—a replica of an Army helicopter complete with gunner's chair. While sitting behind a mounted machine gun, visitors could shoot and score "hits" on villages and people passing below as the helicopter gunship flew over the forests and rice paddies of Vietnam. Families stood in long lines to experience this high-tech, hands-on exhibit. To the child's mind, it was a novel shooting gallery. Others in the community protested the exhibit. They believed an exhibit in which killing becomes the object of participation trivialized war.

Because of these thorny issues, interpreters may be tempted to selectively interpret relatively safe aspects of war such as the technology used or strategies employed, while ignoring the grim realities of the human impact of war—the pain and sorrow associated with death, devastation, and destruction. In doing so they fail to present the complete and accurate picture of war and its related events and impacts. Finding a proper balance is the dilemma of interpreting war.

Interpretation of Evil Acts

An excellent treatment of wartime atrocities that is both appropriately heart-wrenching as well as uplifting can be found at the Holocaust Memorial Museum in Washington, D.C. This museum offers a powerful interpretation of the persecution and murder of six million Jews and millions of other victims of Nazi tyranny from 1933 to 1945 using a variety of emotionally moving exhibits. The museum's mission is to inform Americans about this unprecedented tragedy, to remember those who suffered, and to inspire visitors to contemplate the moral implications of their choices and responsibilities as citizens in an interdependent world.[16] The museum does a masterful job of interjecting hope and spiritual uplift amidst the horror of the holocaust. On the final floor after completing the stunningly sad tour through the permanent exhibition, visitors are presented with exhibits about the liberation of the Nazi camps, the Allied victory over Nazi Germany, and heroic rescue and resistance efforts. Visitors, most now emotionally drained and dazed by the powerful experience, can view the film *Testimony*, which introduces visitors to survivors, rescuers, and liberators sharing their inspiring experiences. Guests leave enriched with a sense of hope as they hear and see strong survivors, courageous non-Jewish neighbors who risked death or imprisonment to help people escape the Nazis, the Danish rescue of 7,000 Jews, and Raoul Wallenberg's activities to save Jews in occupied Europe.

> Interpreters of painful historic events can promote healing.

Interpreters of painful historic events can promote healing. An excellent example of interpreters performing this healing function is found at the Oklahoma City National Memorial and Museum that interprets the bombing of the Murrow Federal Building. The Memorial's mission, as expressed prominently on the focal point of the monument itself, states: "We come here to remember those who were killed, those who survived and those changed forever. May all who leave here know the impact of violence. May this memorial offer comfort, strength, peace, hope and serenity." Interpreters here personalize the past in a most dignified manner.

Lessons on Tolerance

Several units of the national park system focus on themes such as tolerance and inclusiveness. At Manzanar National Historic Site, interpretive exhibits and presentations remind visitors of the internment of Japanese Americans during World War II. Japanese Americans were removed from their communities and relocated to "camps" throughout the western United States. They lost their homes, their businesses, their pets, and almost all of their belongings. In all, more than 120,000 Japanese Americans were incarcerated in ten camps, one of which was Manzanar, located 200 miles northeast of Los Angeles, California. The inclusion of Manzanar in our system of national parks was initially controversial. So many of the early parks represent the extraordinary beauty of the American landscape and a cultural legacy in which we take pride. Should the parks also include places that represent shameful episodes in our national experience?

According to Yale historian Robin Winks, "Education is best done with examples. These examples must include that which we regret, that which is to be avoided, as well as that for which we strive."[17]

> Education is best done with examples. These examples must include that which we regret, that which is to be avoided, as well as that for which we strive.
>
> —ROBIN WINKS

A former superintendent at Manzanar National Historic Site noted, "How the Government treats its citizens—that's our story."[18] The lesson at Manzanar is about protecting citizens' rights, particularly in times of national crisis. This is a lesson that continues to be pertinent to our lives.

At the Brown v. Board of Education National Historic Site interpretive themes also deal with tolerance and equality—in this case desegregation of schools. Brown v. Board of Education is one of several national park sites devoted to interpreting civil rights history. From the park brochure: "We hope that you will leave this site with a personal commitment to tolerance, inclusiveness, and equality in your daily life."[19] And as an excellent example of personalizing the past the brochure concludes, "Brown teaches us that the struggle is not over. Freedoms are fragile and must be safeguarded by each generation. ...Brown succeeded because people like you demanded equality. It leaves us with a legacy and a responsibility to 'Pass it on.'"[20]

Despite the challenges associated with changing societal values and deal-ing with themes of war and exploitation, living history has proven a valuable interpretive medium. It is popular with the public, and this popularity contin-ues to grow. Living history speaks powerfully to people today. Clay Jenkinson, a Jeffersonian scholar, conducts living history presentations as Thomas Jeffer-son. Dressed as President Jefferson, he answers questions about contemporary issues using Jefferson's words.[21] Jenkinson has spoken to oenophiles about Jef-ferson's wine cellar and to Mayo Clinic staff about Jefferson's medical theories. He has made presentations from elementary schools to the White House. People have an interest in what Jefferson has to say to them today. They seek his wisdom and, according to Jenkinson, they want Jefferson's approval. Modern Americans don't want Jefferson to be disappointed in what has become of the United States.[22]

For reasons of both celebration and introspection, we must not forget our past.

Interpreting history serves an important societal function. David Mc-Cullough stated, "We need the past for our sense of who we are. We need the past for a sense of our civic responsibility, how all these benefits and freedoms came to us, and what it is our duty to protect. But we also need the past because it is an extension of the experience of being alive."[23] Historical interpreters can enrich and enthrall us with stories about heroic deeds. They can cause us to empathize with and be inspired by common people who lived their lives in a different time and place. History interpreters re-create the past in such a way as to make the past relevant to our modern lives.

As the opening quote states, keeping together the parts of any whole has merit as does maintaining a memory of ancient things. Historical interpretation allows humanity to celebrate our astounding achievements as well as remember our errant ways. For reasons of both celebration and introspection, we must not forget our past. A healthy society has a vivid and accurate memory. Interpreters play an essential role in keeping that memory alive and in making those memo-ries speak to the issues of today, which is the gift of personalizing the past.

Over the West Walls of the Palace
near the North Gate   mt '68
S.P. 136

© Tsuyoshi Matsumoto

CHAPTER 8

The Gift of Illumination
Through Technology

Technology can reveal the world in exciting new ways. However, incorporating this technology into the interpretive program must be done with foresight and thoughtful care.

*The central struggle of men has ever been to understand one another, to join together for the common weal.
And it is this very thing that the machine helps them to do!
It begins by annihilating time and space.*

—Antoine de Saint-Exupéry

Enos Mills and Freeman Tilden are unlikely to have imagined the possibilities associated with using current technologies in interpretation. New tools are constantly being made available to interpreters as technology races ahead, opening doors to new worlds, both virtual and real. Computers allow people to travel to interpretive sites with a click of the mouse or touch of a screen. Through technology, local nature centers and the smallest museums have expanded their sphere of influence both on-site and to the world beyond. They have created a presence in cyberspace so people from the community and all over the world can learn about their programs and resources. In innumerable ways, technology has made the interpreter's work more efficient and effective.

Through technology, local nature centers and the smallest museums have expanded their sphere of influence both on-site and to the world beyond.

However, throughout their writings, Mills and Tilden honor and revere humanness. Machines cannot express exhilaration or wonder. They cannot respond emotionally to members of the audience. Looking toward the future, Sydney Harris said, "The real danger is not that computers will begin to think like men, but that men will begin to think like computers."[1]

Obsessed with Technology

We live in a time in which technology permeates and transcends everything we do.[2] Recent studies indicate that we spend more and more time on our computers, smart phones, and social networking sites.[3] One observer notes that technology is becoming our worst addiction.[4] Scientists are investigating how incoming texts, emails, tweets, and other stimuli undermine our ability to focus and suggest that technology is rewiring our brains.[5] On a practical level, overuse of technology is resulting in more traffic accidents, less time for deep thought and creative pursuits, and less time for friends, family, and firsthand experiences in nature. Furthermore, the effectiveness of multitasking has proven to be a myth; researchers have discovered that people are less focused, less accurate, and less productive, in the long run, when trying to do two or more things at once.[6] According to scientists at the University of Utah, less than 3% of the population can effectively juggle multiple information streams.[7] Finally, a lack of downtime has been associated with anxiety, fatigue, learning difficulties, and memory problems.[8]

Brain scientists explain that trying to manage many streams of incoming information plays to a primitive impulse we have to respond to immediate opportunities and threats.[9] Reacting to immediate stimulation provokes a moment of excitement that has a physiological explanation—dopamine injected into the system—and many people cannot resist the possibility that something new and interesting might be occurring. Researchers are particularly concerned about children and digital stimulation because their brains are still developing and they already struggle to set priorities and resist impulses.[10]

One promising area of research suggests that experiences in nature have a positive influence on reining us in from the deluge of digital information.[11] Esther Sternberg, a physician who has studied "healing places," wrote: "Implicit in an understanding of the mind-body connection is an assumption that physical places that set the mind at ease can contribute to well-being, and those that trouble the emotions might foster illness."[12]

With the advent of more time spent with technology is an increasing divide between people and nature. Furthermore, an "urban lifestyle" separates people from the outdoors. Americans spend 95% of their time indoors, leaving little time for outdoor pursuits.[13] Sedentary lifestyles that entail so much time inside and behind a computer screen result in increased stress, obesity, high blood pressure, heart disease, and mental health problems.[14] The park and recreation profession, including interpretive professionals, promotes the physical and mental health of individuals by providing sites for outdoor recreation, and interpretation of those sites for more rewarding and enriching experiences (see Chapter 14).

> One promising area of research suggests that experiences in nature have a positive influence on reining us in from the deluge of digital information.

Technology in the Parks

The history of our parks includes countless examples of people getting into trouble because they weren't aware of the dangers of the site they were experiencing. Misguided visitors feed bears and get too close to other wildlife as they attempt "great" photographs. Now cell and satellite technology figures into such mishaps. Search and rescue missions have increased for the past five years due to people attempting challenges beyond their experience levels, knowing that help is only a phone call away.[15]

Visitors are less attuned to their surroundings as they send texts, photos, or emails—or play games or talk—on their cell phones. The National Park Service has now added a new category of "contributing factors" to park accidents: "inattention to surroundings."[16]

Although cell phones have been helpful in saving people who have truly found themselves in trouble, they also have caused problems for park rangers who find that some lost visitors want to be catered to. Rangers have received calls for refreshments (including hot chocolate) from those who have reached a summit at Grand Teton National Park, and at the Grand Canyon a group of hikers pressed the emergency button on their satellite location device because, as they explained to rangers arriving for the second time, their water supply "tasted salty."[17]

In other ways, technology has been helpful to rangers in protecting cultural and natural sites. As just one example, several men thought they had managed to urinate undetected into the Old Faithful Geyser in Yellowstone National Park. They were surprised to be confronted by rangers right after their stunt. The park had installed a camera so that people all over the world could experience Old Faithful online 24 hours a day. Viewers notified rangers immediately.[18]

Interpretive Technologies

On the one hand, technology-based interpretation can be expensive, impersonal, complex, and therefore counterproductive. High-tech exhibits that threaten audiences with their complexity or sophistication result in technological arrogance. Without friendly interpreters to personally encourage, assist, and guide visitors, machines can drive away those not accustomed to the most recent technology. Furthermore, some interpreters believe that the availability of wireless Internet connections, satellite dishes, and smart phones in parks has resulted in lower attendance at interpretive programs. Others fear that the virtual visit or virtual program will be more convenient and therefore more attractive than the real visit or program.

> Technological approaches allow visitors to view objects that previously could not be seen, experience environments that could not be experienced, and manipulate and respond to stimuli that previously could not be perceived.

On the other hand, interpreters can use modern technologies to reach people who otherwise would not be reached with their messages. Technological approaches allow visitors to view objects that previously could not be seen, experience environments that could not be experienced, and manipulate and respond to stimuli that previously could not be perceived. These advances expand, rather than stifle, interpretive opportunities.

Fresh and exciting visual and audio information resulting from new technology can bridge diverse learning styles. We can open new worlds to our visitors. This is the gift of illumination through technology, although it must be conducted thoughtfully and in concert with traditional firsthand approaches.

Three important attributes characterize proper application of technology. First, the technology should be engaging. Interactive activities must be perceived as fun and rewarding. They must be challenging enough to be interesting without being so difficult that they frustrate participants. However, gadgets that are strictly fun, but not educational, have no place in an interpretive setting. Such technology distracts people from more meaningful experiences.

Second, the technology must be dependable. High-tech exhibits must consistently perform well and be quickly serviced when they do not work. Technology can be expensive and requires regular maintenance, which is costly. Before a commitment is made to use certain technology, we must consider the costs in terms of what must be given up to acquire and maintain it. Frustrated interpreters in facilities with undependable technology have echoed Thoreau's lament, "Lo! Men have become tools of their tools."[19]

Third, the best use of technology is to reveal something. The power of many new technologies, whether in the fields of medicine, astrophysics, or interpretation, lies in their ability to allow people to go beyond their unaided senses to see things as we have never seen them before.

Technology can be engaging, and dependable, and may reveal startling new perceptions about our world, as noted in the following example.

The Owl Box

A nature-loving couple in San Marcos, California, put an owl box with a night-vision camera in their backyard.[20] It sat empty for two years before a female barn owl took up residence. The couple named the owl Molly. Before long, Molly was joined by a male owl.

To share live video of the owls on the Internet with family and friends, they asked their grandson, who was better versed in technology, to help them. He installed the necessary special equipment (when the owls were absent), including 150 feet of computer cable to the house, a new night-vision camera, a color camera for daytime viewing, and a microphone. Now, every aspect of the owls' lives in the owl box could be viewed on a computer. The computer link given to a handful of family and friends was passed on to other friends, who sent it to their family and friends.

When Molly laid her first egg, hundreds of people were watching on their computers. By the time she had laid six eggs in 12 days, thousands of people were watching online and talking in computer chat rooms, speculating on how many of the eggs would hatch and of those that did, how many would survive to adulthood. A month later, Molly pushed an egg aside and ate it. Perhaps there was no sign of life or perhaps she just had too many eggs. Whatever the case, viewers were witnessing the cycle of life.[21]

Shortly after this, the first egg hatched, to the joy and wonder of those viewing. By the time the other eggs hatched, several million people had watched the owls live on their computers. The family of owls were featured on television news shows and made front-page news in local papers. Many schools began following the activities of the owls on the Internet for educational purposes.

At one point, Molly uncharacteristically left the owl box for a night. The chat rooms were in a panic, worried about her and what might happen to the owlets, before she eventually returned. Ultimately, Molly and her family captivated tens of millions of viewers in countries all over the world.

Through technology, people were able to observe owl behaviors, including the owlets finally spreading their wings and leaving the nest. Also through technology, the viewers were able to learn more about owl behavior from educational resources posted online.[22]

Looking to the Future

When Enos Mills wrote *Adventures of a Nature Guide*, he worked directly with guiding people firsthand in the Rocky Mountains without any technology at all. When Freeman Tilden wrote *Interpreting Our Heritage* he acknowledged that many "gadgets" were coming into use. He suggested that technology would be used in interpretation to a much greater extent in the future. Tilden predicted, "This means, explicitly, more automatic projection equipment, more sound installations, more recorders and tapes, more gadgets to be self-operated by visitors, more motion pictures of fidelity and professional skill, and so on."[23] Of course, these technologies seem quaint to us now.

> Technology will continue to evolve in ways that we can't imagine.

In previous editions of *Interpretation for the 21st Century*, we wrote about technology advances that Mills and Tilden never could have imagined including animatronics, holograms, videos, DVDs, distance education, digital photography, and remote sensing.[24] At this writing these former frontiers are commonplace.

Now the emphasis is on podcasts, eHikes, smart phone apps, and avatars; yet these, too, will be advanced upon. Technology will continue to evolve in ways that we can't imagine. Nonetheless, we next provide a brief summary of some of the technologies that are proving effective in the interpretive field, noting that a human element, and encouragement to experience our cultural and natural history firsthand, is integral to the mix.

Interpreting Via the Internet

Interpreters reach the world with information about their sites over the Internet. People travel to parks and museums without leaving home. At each site they might play an interactive learning game, download a teacher's manual, or watch an educational video. From home computers, people can print interpretive brochures, articles, technical documents, program schedules, photographs, and maps that may better inform an actual visit to the site. Via the Internet, people can get up-to-the-minute weather or campground information or make reservations for special events. To gain additional perspectives and insights about a place, potential visitors can link to websites or social networking pages of individuals who have recently visited and who have posted photographs and/ or trip journals.

Web-based interpretation has advantages of being on duty all day, every day of the year, and it is relatively inexpensive. It reduces consumption of printed brochures and information sheets. Messages can be "posted" back and forth on the website between users and naturalists or curators. People can ask questions about specific topics such as birds, astronomy, wildlife, or current environmental issues. Park agencies and museums use the Internet to disseminate information to increasing numbers of people each year, many of whom would not normally visit a park or museum. Interpretive sites often offer Web-based curricula linked to curricula in schools or special learning opportunities for concerned citizens.

However, this technology cannot substitute for firsthand adventure. Ideally, technology motivates on-site experience.

The Internet can help interpreters, too, in serving as a valuable research tool to find facts about an organism or event or current information about a controversial issue. Interpreters can ask questions or share ideas and information with other interpreters in special interest chat groups. Information provided on government websites, sites of professional organizations, or academic websites are subject to peer-review or editorial processes that result in a high rate of factual accuracy. Unofficial sites are less reliable sources.

The possibilities for human enrichment through Internet travel are endless. The Internet can be both a source of information for interpreters and a means for interpreters to interpret their site to the world. However, this technology cannot substitute for firsthand adventure. Ideally, technology motivates on-site experience.

WebRangers

The National Park Service promotes a WebRangers program for children. The vision for this program in the next 10 years is to offer "a multimedia-based, multisensory experience that supports adventure learning."[25] WebRangers will support interactive opportunities and encourage park visitation. Connections to the parks through these experiences will lead to a sense of understanding and appreciation, and ultimately stewardship.

As discussed in Chapter 6, a movement is afoot to encourage children to spend more time outdoors. The intent of WebRangers is indeed to encourage youth to get outdoors, by meeting kids where they live on the Internet, and encouraging them to explore, care about, and care for the natural world around them. The program includes incentives and rewards, and provides a forum for community service.

Satellite Imagery and GIS

Geologic and archaeological features are often best identified from the air. These views also can be used to interpret land use changes, habitat types, or scores of other environmental and cultural themes. At Grand Teton National Park, interpreters used satellite imagery to make computer-generated panoramic photographs for interpretive wayside exhibits. This technology allowed interpreters to change the angle of view to show important features not always visible from the specific wayside exhibit. For example, visitors could see not only the mountains before them, but also lakes hidden at the base of the mountains.[26]

Geographic Information Systems (GIS) uses images and data points collected on the ground to create maps that reveal information. At Black Canyon of the Gunnison National Monument and other sites, students from local schools are using GIS and hand-held Global Positioning System (GPS) instruments to create full-color digitized maps on which they precisely locate their schools, homes, roads, habitat types, recreation areas, and other physical and social features.[27] Interpreters can use such activities to teach environmental science concepts and a variety of technical skills. This approach includes firsthand field experience. Molly O'Meara pointed out, "Although remote sensing, GIS, and other technologies can help us understand how we are changing the planet, they cannot substitute for firsthand knowledge of the environment."[28]

Interactive Computer Exhibits

Interactive computer exhibits can be used as reference devices, as personal tour guides, or they can offer simulations and educational games.

As a reference device, interactive computer exhibits allow visitors to retrieve written or graphic information about a topic of their choosing. For example, the "Since You Were Born" exhibit at "The Living World" exhibition center of the Saint Louis Zoo allows visitors to travel across time. Upon entering your date of birth, you receive a printout of environmental changes since then (such as acres of rainforest destroyed or population growth). Interactive computers also can direct visitors to a particular trail, program, or exhibit to meet their needs, interests, and abilities.

Interactive computers may serve as personal tour guides. Art museums have successfully used on-site computer exhibits to interpret works of art by directing visitors to make comparisons and contrasts, and by interpreting the meaning and significance of each piece of art just as a museum guide might do. At parks, visitors can get a guided tour of the park's features by using handheld interactive computer technology or a podcast sent to their smart phones. Along trails, auto tours, and scenic byways, portable devices or smart phone apps trigger interpretive videos at specific locations along the route using their built-in GPS capabilities.

Simulation exhibits encourage visitors to manipulate variables, observe effects, and respond to them to make discoveries, often in a problem-solving context. Computer games are immensely popular and can be educational. Computer games often require players to make choices, and wise choices are rewarded with points. For example, players can become a certain animal in the food chain of an ecosystem and score points by successfully consuming a sufficient number of calories or by eating the correct prey while avoiding being eaten themselves by other creatures.

At Mount St. Helen's, visitors can play the role of "pioneer species" using a touchscreen computer exhibit to make decisions about survival strategies in the post-eruption landscape. Participants learn about plant succession and how mammals, insects, and other organisms have reestablished themselves since the eruption. Such games teach ecological principles while the player is having fun.

> **Research suggests that interactive exhibits of any sort are more effective at attracting and holding attention and enhancing learning than passive exhibits.**

At Brown v. Board of Education National Historic Site, visitors use a touchscreen to choose specific people to be their allies in the fight against segregation. They soon learn if their choices were good choices.

Research has suggested that interactive exhibits of any sort are more effective at attracting and holding attention and enhancing learning than passive exhibits.[29] Interactive computer exhibits are no exception. They have been shown to strongly attract and hold attention and promote learning. A study at "The Living World" showed that computer interactives are second only to live animals in popularity, have the longest holding power of any exhibit, and are effective in teaching visitors.[30] Those who played a "Bat Game" that allowed them to use audio cues to hunt like a bat were far more likely to know that bats use echolocation and eat moths than those who did not play the game.[31]

Interactive computer exhibits have other advantages. They can store and make available to the public enormous amounts of information. Most important, by incorporating personal background information and allowing the participant to choose subjects and levels of difficulty, computers can "individualize" the material. For example, if an unknown technical word is used, a click of a button might provide both a written definition and an animated explanation.

Interactive computer exhibits promote non-sequential learning. Unlike an interpretive talk, brochure, slide show, or video where every person in the audience receives the same introduction, body, and conclusion, interactive computer exhibits allow learners to select the kinds of information they receive, the order in which they receive it, and the level of detail. Some of these are called "deep exhibits" because visitors can go as deep into the subject as they would like. For example, an interactive exhibit about prairie dogs could first offer opportunities to see what different species of prairie dogs look like and to see range maps and habitat descriptions. Learners could seek additional information in many directions. They could hear a prairie dog "bark" or they could go underground to experience subterranean life in the colony. Games and simulations involving these fascinating social creatures could offer fun learning experiences aimed at children. Detailed information about prairie dog population dynamics, research data, or complex and controversial policy issues involving prairie dog poisoning by ranchers or prairie dog sport hunting could be found for advanced and interested learners. People could then branch out to learn about black-footed ferrets and endangered species linked to prairie dog towns.

Interactive computer exhibits allow learners to choose the path, pace, and depth of information gathering based on their needs, interests, and abilities. This flexibility circumvents one of the most difficult challenges in interpretation—how to meet the needs of diverse individuals in a single exhibit.

Designing Interpretive Websites

Designers at Educational Web Adventures, an educational multimedia development firm, reviewed the Web-based learning literature and recommended using goal-based approaches. Goal-based Web education is characterized by developing skills and understanding—and providing extrinsic motivation and a sense of accomplishment—rather than merely learning facts. Specifically, these designers recommend goal-based strategies that use narrative, simulations, games, and guided creative activities.

These four goal-based approaches are consistent with principles presented in this book. Narrative in interactive computer media not only tells a story (Principle 3), but also can place the learner in the story and assign a task or mission to complete. Simulations and games can spark interest by relating to the learner (Principle 1), and they can reveal meanings without overloading the learner with too much information (Principle 2). Simulations and games provoke action (Principle 4), explore themes (Principle 5), and can be targeted for specific groups such as children (Principle 6). Guided creative activities make application of arts in interpretation (Principle 3). Users at some goal-based sites create their own works of art, write their own stories, or assume the role of an explorer or scientist and create art or literature from that context.

Web-based interpretation aimed at children is particularly effective. Many interpretive sites (such as the Children's Museum of Indianapolis, the Brookfield Zoo, and the Colonial Williamsburg Foundation) have Web pages specifically devoted to interpreting to children.

Besides being goal oriented, websites can encourage repeat visits. This requires designing a dynamic, regularly updated site with new information and new experiences. Like a visitor center that never changes its displays or programs, static websites offer little incentive for repeat visits.

Web-based interpretation can be efficient if Web pages are well-designed and accessible to all Internet users. The principles of traditional interpretation are just as relevant when interpreting in cyberspace as they are when interpreting on-site. Indeed, the 15 principles offered in this book should be adapted and applied when designing websites, interactive computer exhibits, podcasts, smart phone apps, and other interpretive technology.

Modern devices now allow us to see and experience our world differently. Although personal contact and on-site experience should always have a place, computers and other technology can be powerful tools to effectively interpret to multitudes of people and extend the interpreter's sphere of influence beyond the physical boundaries of the site.

When Diaghilev commissioned Stravinsky to write the ballet score for *The Rite of Spring*, Stravinsky asked what sort of music he should compose. Diaghilev answered, *"Étonnez-moi!"* (Astonish me!). We have heard the wonderful result. Today, visitors come to historic sites, museums, and parks with the same request, *"Étonnez-moi!"* Technology can be used effectively by interpreters to do exactly that—astonish people—and inspire them to seek further learning and firsthand experiences that will astonish them even more; the gift of illumination through technology.

S.P. 370
San Diego 6/13/73
mat

© Tsuyoshi Matsumoto

CHAPTER

9

The Gift of Precision

Interpreters must concern themselves with the quantity and quality (selection and accuracy) of information presented. Focused, well-researched interpretation will be more powerful than a longer discourse.

To gild refined gold, to paint the lily,
To throw a perfume on the violet,
To smooth the ice, or add another hue
Unto the rainbow, or with taper-light
To seek the beauteous eye of heaven to garnish,
Is wasteful and ridiculous excess?

—Shakespeare, King John, IV, 2

This chapter addresses the quantity and quality of information presented to the public. The quantity issue speaks to the tendency of interpreters to offer too much information or display too many objects. An excessive amount of information or number of artifacts overwhelms the audience's ability or motivation to process the information. The quality issue refers to the accuracy of information that is presented. In the case of misinformation or overstatement, Freeman

Tilden likens some interpretive efforts to the "florid exponent of chamber of commerce literature."[1] Discerning people dismiss overstatements and interpreters lose credibility.

Excess

Good interpreters become excited about the resources they are interpreting. Many museum and nature center storage areas burst with slide collections, rocks, pressed plants, assorted skins, skulls, fossils, invertebrate collections, and other good "stuff." The combination of abundant enthusiasm and available treasures tempt many interpreters to use everything at their disposal. Examples of excess abound in museums, nature centers, and parks. Talks exceed time limits and crowded artifacts push the limits of space and attention spans.

An expert carpenter once advised that to avoid splitting wooden shingles, do not give the nail the last tap. Tilden observed, "There are so many instances where, injuriously and to the detriment of an otherwise fine presentation, the nail has been given 'the last tap.'"[2]

Talks

We have all witnessed talks that have gone on too long. Our charge as interpreters is to keep our talks focused and interesting. Once talks go beyond what an audience can endure, they have progressively less value. Listeners who were previously inspired may leave, instead, tired. Successful provocation of audiences depends on not going overboard.

> Our charge as interpreters is to keep our talks focused and interesting.

Although flattering audience feedback can tempt interpreters to do more, interpreters must be vigilant against giving the public too much of a good thing. An old showbiz adage says to "leave the audience wanting to come back for more." This is sage advice for interpreters.

A good (and often well-intended) example of excess is the seemingly obligatory question-and-answer session at the end of programs. Interpreters should welcome the opportunity to answer individual questions, but not at the expense of the entire audience. As bold individuals begin to ask questions, others in the audience may wonder, "Can we leave now?" Interpreters should build up to a powerful conclusion and end the formal presentation on a high note.

Interpreters can make clear that they are happy to answer questions on a personal basis after the program. Those who have a true interest will stay. Those who were too shy or intimidated to ask a question in front of the group now have nothing to fear. This one-on-one interaction after the audience has been dismissed provides us with some of the richest and most productive interpretive opportunities we will experience.

Exhibits

Museums have their roots in building collections. Often, it is the curator's job to build a "type" or reference collection, requiring collection of many examples of the same "class" (category) of artifacts for future research or preservation. Whether china plates or canons, the collection curator's goal is to accumulate as many variations as possible, with storage space being the primary limiting factor at most sites. Dedication to this important museum function has manifested itself in a tendency for zealous curators to carry this "more is better" philosophy into the exhibit halls.

> The interpreter's responsibility is to display only those objects that are consistent with a well-thought-out interpretive theme, and then only in numbers that do not exceed the visitor's attention span.

Military museums are notorious for cases filled with scores of rifles, swords, or medals, all looking superficially identical to the untrained eye. Musket balls and arrowheads are among the most over-displayed artifacts. A significant battle could be waged with all that is on display at some museums. Tilden noted that seeing too many of one class of object leads to a diffusion of interest that, in turn, leads to a numbness: "You have seen nothing because you have seen everything."[3]

Both the collections curator and interpreter need to be sensitive to their respective goals and needs. The mission of the curator is to collect, catalog, and store large numbers of objects. The interpreter's responsibility is to display only those objects that are consistent with a well-thought-out interpretive theme, and then only in numbers that do not exceed the visitor's attention span.

Our obligation is to determine how many examples are necessary to accomplish the interpretive objectives. Then we must discipline ourselves to display only that number. When several examples of the same thing—whether rifles, rocking chairs, bowls, or bullets—are displayed together, the interpretive challenge is to show the differences and explain the significance of those differences. If we do not do this, our exhibits will be excessive for most visitors.

Research generally supports the notion that excess leads to a loss of attention.[4] The classic study by George Miller (see Chapter 5) described our limited short-term memory as being able to handle only seven pieces of information (plus or minus two) at one time.[5] Researchers have since documented satiation (also called museum fatigue) at sites ranging from zoo reptile houses to prestigious art galleries.[6] Regardless of the setting, the most attention is given to the first exhibits encountered, and visitors spend decreasing amounts of time viewing exhibits or paintings as the number encountered increases.

"Information overload" is another problem related to excessive material.[7] Overload occurs when the audience members fail to process information because they receive too many simultaneous stimuli. Like children tearing through a pile of gifts that compete for their attention on Christmas morning, eager visitors may flit from exhibit to exhibit, always distracted by the next one.

Other variables such as audience characteristics, comfort, the topic's intrinsic interest, the exhibit's physical characteristics, time constraints, competing stimuli, and a host of other factors influence how much is too much. Further-

Research generally supports the notion that excess leads to a loss of attention.

more, time standing in front of a display does not necessarily mean individuals are processing information. While conducting an evaluation of exhibits at the Birmingham Zoo Predator House, researchers noted that visitors spent more time viewing an empty exhibit than they did viewing a small mammal exhibit with animals present. Undoubtedly, the visitors were searching in vain for animals in an empty enclosure.[8]

A study at Chicago's Field Museum of Natural History found that about three-quarters of the visitors stopped at less than 40% of the exhibit cases in the animal halls, and visitors spent an average of less than 12 seconds at each case. Nevertheless, the researchers state (in their provocatively titled paper "Stuffed Birds on Sticks"—from one visitor's description of the museum's animal halls), that exhibit planners should not concern themselves with trying to answer the questions, "What percent of the cases should a visitor look at?" or "How much time should a visitor spend looking at an exhibit case?" Instead, they suggest "it doesn't matter, because we assume that visitors can and will and should look at whatever appeals to them in the manner they wish. We are not attempting to control their patterns of looking, which are highly influenced by such difficult to quantify factors as fatigue, number and mood of children, personal experience, prior knowledge, weather, parking meters, and time since last meal, etc."[9]

These researchers shift the focus from exhibit quantity to quality. They direct planners to create ways to entice visitors to stay longer, to get them to say: "Yes, this exhibit was designed with me and my interests in mind, and I want to come back again and look at more of these cases." The researchers concluded, "We do not expect or predict that many visitors will want to or be able to see it all. Rather, the quality of their experiences, however and wherever they choose to spend their time, will be improved."[10]

Clearly, the perception of what is excessive is related to the quality of the display. A common approach to thinking about displays uses a cost-benefit model. The expected benefits from interacting with an exhibit must exceed the perceived cost in time or effort, or the consumer will not purchase the experience by expending time and energy. Excessive text lowers the expected reward by appearing boring and difficult, and it requires greater effort to read. Because many people are reluctant to read, graphics or photographs should be used to illustrate the points being made. Moreover, whatever text is absolutely necessary should be presented in short paragraphs and in short sentences or bullet points.

Facilities

Facilities themselves can be excessive, although tight budgets seldom allow extravagant interpretive facilities. Yet, occasionally an agency or a private organization experiences a political windfall that is devoted to "bricks and mortar." Structures are excessive when they detract from the interpretive messages. Just as people engrossed in a cathedral's beauty or interesting architecture may miss the more important spiritual message, visitors to a museum or visitor center may be so taken with the architecture or technology that they ignore interpretive messages.

Humor

The use of humor in interpretation must be handled very carefully. Humor usually depends on creating mental incongruities or contradictions that produce a surprise. However, what is humorous to some doesn't work for others. In deciding whether humor is excessive in a given interpretive venue, follow the rule of "if in doubt, leave it out."

The key to using humor effectively and appropriately is to recognize that all humor is not the same. Awareness of the different types of humor and their utility can make the difference between driving home a message or driving people away. In general, puns are the safest form of humor. Carefully selected jokes, riddles, and witticisms also can be safe and effective. Obviously, jokes directed at any one individual, gender, or ethnic group will be offensive and have no place in interpretation.

> The key to using humor effectively and appropriately is to recognize that all humor is not the same.

As with all aspects of interpretation, we must know the audience to use humor effectively. Jokes that are too sophisticated or require a higher level of knowledge or reasoning than people possess will "go over the heads" of audience members. On the other hand, if jokes are too simple or silly, the interpreter looks foolish. If interpreters perform for an audience of both children and adults, indicating when humor is directed to the children is important.

In addition to knowing how to use humor, considering how much humor to use is essential. Humor cannot be used continually or you place an impossible burden on yourself and the members of your audience. People need a chance to process your interpretation.

When using humor, whether written or spoken, the audience must know the intent is playful. And, like all interpretive efforts, the important points being communicated must come through. If done well, humor can enhance the effectiveness of interpretation by holding the attention of people, making the interpretation more enjoyable, and helping people to retain the information.

Painting the Lily, Adorning the Rose

"A mouse is miracle enough to stagger sextillion of infidels," wrote Walt Whitman.[11] Everything in nature is a miracle, and no living thing needs embellishment.

The tendency for interpreters to exaggerate is not born of deceit. Sometimes it is a matter of ignorance—interpreters parroting erroneous information they have heard or read. Often, misinformation is a manifestation of the love interpreters have for the resource. This affinity may feed a propensity to accept and disseminate interesting and favorable information about a subject without questioning it. Like proud parents touting their offspring, good interpreters love to sing the praises of their site.

> Everything in nature is a miracle, and no living thing needs embellishment.

Occasionally overzealous interpreters misinform audiences concerning natural history information. A widespread example of this is the myth that purple martins eat mosquitoes. Tens of thousands of people, as well as nature centers and municipalities, have purchased martin houses to help eradicate mosquitoes. Yet research has shown the martins generally do not eat mosquitoes; in fact, they eat dragonflies, which do eat mosquitoes.[12] Purple martins are certainly worthy of appreciation and protection, but by assigning martins attributes they do not possess, interpreters are "adorning the rose."

Historical Myths

Many historical figures deserve appreciation, honor, and reverence, but some interpreters assign false characteristics and actions to them. Some historical sites and individuals have bodies of myth that seem to exceed bodies of knowledge. George Washington, Betsy Ross, Abraham Lincoln, and Davy Crockett are among the most fictionalized characters. Historic sites such as The Little Bighorn Battlefield National Monument and The Alamo have been misinterpreted for decades.

The National Park Service has made a special effort to eliminate myths surrounding Custer and events at Little Bighorn Battlefield. They have adjusted interpretive content to put both the person and the battle in historically proper perspective. In light of competing misinformation, however, this is not easy.[13]

For example, films and popular paintings may launch and perpetuate misinterpretations. Since the first Custer film in 1908, many Hollywood movies have been made, each giving a different version of history. *They Died With Their Boots On*, made in 1941 and starring Errol Flynn, portrayed Custer as a heroic martyr while fueling the sale of war bonds. In 1970, at the height of the Vietnam War, an anti-war film, *Little Big Man*, portrayed Custer and the 7th Cavalry as villains. Some equated the Plains Indians with the North Vietnamese.

Paintings also perpetuate myths. "Custer's Last Fight," painted by Otto Becker in the 1890s, is the most popular and famous painting of the battle. The initial printing was 150,000 copies and the total number hanging in saloons and family dens now numbers in the millions. What's wrong with the painting? Just about everything but the landscape! The painting shows Custer with long hair (he had short hair at the time), carrying a decorative saber (sabers were not taken into battle), and wearing buckskin (he took it off before the battle). It shows the Indians mounted on horseback (this was a dismounted battle by both sides), carrying shields not used by Plains Indians, and wearing Iroquoian headdresses worn by woodland tribes from the eastern United States.

Challenging the folklore surrounding cultural icons requires courage because the truth is sometimes difficult for the public to accept. Historians sometimes become the targets of ridicule and charges of false motives. One noted spokesperson who seeks to correct misconceptions is James Loewen, who has written books on the subject and gave a keynote address at a National Association for Interpretation conference.[14]

The Myth of Chief Seattle

A commentary titled, "Are We Ministers of Misinformation?" identified common fallacies propagated by some interpreters, including the debunked "Web of Life" speech by Chief Seattle.[15] This "speech" is well-known to an enormous number of interpreters. It includes the following:

> Every part of the earth is sacred. … All things are interconnected. What happens to the earth happens to the sons and daughters of the earth. … Man did not weave the web of life, he is merely a strand in it. Whatever he does to the web, he does to himself. … Where is the thicket? Gone. Where is the eagle? Gone. What is it to say goodbye to the swift pony and the hunt? The end of living and beginning of survival.

As it turns out, the speech was written by Ted Perry, a screenwriter for the 1972 film documentary *Home*, which was produced by the Southern Baptist Convention. Perry did not intend to be deceptive; the producers of the film simply neglected to credit him for his script. This oversight has fueled the dissemination of a fallacy that has been referred to as "The Gospel of Chief Seattle." Indeed, it continues to be evoked around campfires and other interpretive venues across the country and around the world despite several exposés including the front page of the *New York Times*.[16]

What To Do?

The following recommendations are offered: 1) We must work even more diligently to ensure personal competency, and 2) The interpretive profession must evolve as an institution that provides an environment for responsible, considerate, professional criticism.[17]

Costa Dillon encourages interpreters to take a proactive approach when confronted with myths. He presented several principles summarized here.[18]

Know the Myths

Interpreters should make a point of reading novels and seeing television shows and movies about the subjects they interpret. Then we are in a position to reveal deeper meaning and truth. We can maintain a list of misconceptions and myths for reference and training of new interpreters.

Don't Have a Superior Attitude

Those who believe myths are not necessarily unteachable. Knowing a myth in itself is often an indication that a person has an interest in the subject. We should take advantage of that interest.

Use the Myth as an Entry Point

We can acknowledge the popular misconception and then use it to reveal facts and show how the myth relates to the truth. For example, many believe the Gettysburg Address was written on the back of an envelope. Lincoln, in fact, wrote many drafts knowing that it was a tremendously important speech. The myth can be a springboard into the discussion of why it was such an important speech and the care Lincoln took in preparing it.

Address the Reasons and Origins of the Misconception

The reasons behind the Parson Weems fables about George Washington (such as chopping down a cherry tree) tell us something about the formation of American culture. Likewise, the Betsy Ross myth (that she sewed the first U.S. flag) tells us something about the flag as a symbol and the feelings of Americans during the country's Centennial when the story first circulated.

Know Credible Sources

We must critically evaluate sources and be prepared to give references when challenged.

Make the Interpretation as Good as the Myth

People remember myths because they are good stories. Interpreters must research, formulate, and tell memorable stories.

The interpreter's job is not to bust myths or deflate legends. Our charge is to "make the reality available, accurate and believable."[19] An overt attempt to knock a hero off a pedestal or deflate an image of patriotism will lead to bad feelings and conflict. As Dillon noted, "If someone leaves your site secure in their long-held misconception, then so be it."[20]

Myths are important in all cultures. They help us define and understand our world and ourselves. Interpreters should eagerly take myths and use them as tools to bring people to the truth.[21]

Application: From the Visitor's Perspective

Thomas Hoving, a former director of the Metropolitan Museum of Art, offers several recommendations for museum visitors.[22] To begin, he suggests acknowledging that you can't see it all and focusing on just a few personally meaningful displays. Better to fully enjoy and revel in a few great works of art, than to attempt to see it all. To determine what those few displays will be, Hoving suggests visiting the bookstore first where images of the best artwork appears on postcards. Then show the postcards to an employee who can direct you to the displays that will provide the most pleasure. Hoving also suggests you trust your own instincts and not strive to understand something that doesn't make sense.

> We are reminded that the word museum comes from muse, the mythological source of inspiration.

In order to focus directly on what the museum best has to offer—the original displays—Hoving recommends skipping the audio guides that will only detract from a richer firsthand experience. Finally, he suggests setting a time limit so you don't become weary. Rather than trying to see it all in an exhausting day, plan on returning to the museum for another relaxing, high quality experience. How much more rewarding it is to revel in a few great objects. We are reminded that the word museum comes from muse, the mythological source of inspiration.[23]

In Chapter 1, we quoted Anatole France, who cautioned against, "satisfying our vanity by teaching a great many things. ..." To avoid excess, interpreters must teach a few great things well.

Reining ourselves in a bit and making sure we speak the truth need not put a damper on our interpretive efforts and certainly will not limit our effectiveness. As we gain and maintain credibility, we will be more effective because our audiences will sense our authority and take our messages more seriously. Teaching a few great things well is the gift of precision.

Our job is to integrate these various truths into the whole truth, which should be our only loyalty.

—Abraham Maslow

© Tsuyoshi Matsumoto

C H A P T E R

10

The Gift of Professionalism

Before applying the arts in interpretation, the interpreter must be familiar with basic communication techniques. Quality interpretation depends on the interpreter's knowledge and skills, which must be continually developed over time.

Interpretation is a voyage of discovery in the field of human emotions and intellectual growth, and it is hard to foresee that time when the interpreter can confidently say, "Now we are wholly adequate to our task."

—Freeman Tilden

Becoming a good interpreter takes practice. We must learn methods that contribute to quality interpretation and we must practice them. Some of this learning may seem tedious or extraneous. Many of us have struggled through difficult or seemingly irrelevant courses. Furthermore, we all must go through the gut-wrenching process of our first talks in front of an audience. The learning and practice is not much different than that required in other artistic endeavors.

For example, consider the techniques musicians must learn before they create personal styles. First they must master notes and scales. This is repetitious and laborious, but it must be done. Only after a musician has command over notes and scales can we expect a virtuoso performance.

To a certain degree, the interpreter goes through a similar process of learning the basics of communication. After the basics are mastered, we become artisans of the craft—in a sense "painting" a program by interjecting our own personal styles. We can inspire the confidence of our listeners by paying attention to basic communication strategies and then moving on to hone personal nuances.

Effective Presentations

An intimate knowledge of the breadth and depth of the subject matter is essential. So, too, is an ability to convey the material. People often assume that they can give a talk on a subject they know about, regardless of whether they have been trained in effective speaking techniques. Yet, plenty of evidence exists to the contrary. Indeed, a disorganized, rambling, monotone speech can do more harm than good. The following discussion offers basic direction on how to present effectively.[1]

The Fear Factor

According to WebMD, fear of public speaking is the number-one fear in humans. Even the most experienced speakers will feel apprehension. This is normal. To avoid being overcome by fear, several useful strategies may be employed.

Most important, for the sake of the audience and the interpreter's degree of confidence, is that the presentation is impeccably prepared. The wise interpreter uses apprehension as a motivating force for researching and organizing an excellent presentation. Some of us choose to write out the entire story, whereas others choose to make an outline. However the presentation is constructed, remember to speak, not read.

After assembling the structure of an inspiring talk, the conscientious interpreter will want to rehearse it. You may isolate yourself and practice, try your story on someone you know (and trust), or record the presentation and listen carefully for areas of improvement. As a check on attention to detail, you might also answer the following question: "What are the indicators that my story was adequately and carefully prepared?"

> **The wise interpreter uses apprehension as a motivating force for researching and organizing an excellent presentation.**

Interpreters should not anticipate being afraid of the audience. Rather, they should use any nervous energy to project excitement. Rehearse with confidence that the presentation will be well-received. Arriving early and talking with visitors builds rapport and can have a settling effect.

Under no circumstances should the interpreter apologize for apprehension. A little quavering in the voice or other signs of nervousness may not be noticeable and will soon disappear. However, if you announce your apprehension, the audience will be more attuned to it.

In most instances, sticking with the game plan—what has been prepared—is best, even if supposedly better ideas occur just before the presentation. Of course, there can be extemporaneous elements of the talk, although sticking with prepared opening and closing lines is well advised. When a speaker panics and attempts to reconstruct a presentation on the spot, it inevitably shows.

While speaking, make eye contact with members of the audience. Seek out those who have "friendly eyes" and are obviously interested in what you are saying. This positive reinforcement will build confidence. Try not to focus on those who are not paying attention; they may have distractions in their personal lives that have no bearing on the quality of your talk.

Speaking Ability

Developing the ability to speak in public situations comes with practice. Especially early on, getting constructive feedback is important. A supervisor or colleague can offer insights that you, as the speaker, may not be aware of. The following speaking skills are essential so the message is received with clarity, because voice is the key link between the interpreter and the audience.

A good speaking voice is one that is conversational and natural. Seek to speak in a friendly tone and be certain that you clearly articulate your words and avoid verbal crutches (such as "uh"). Speaking at a slower pace may correct poor articulation or verbal crutches.

An effective voice should be balanced between extremes of volume, pitch, and rate. Speak at a volume that is pleasant and can be heard by everyone. Vary the loudness or softness of your voice to add emphasis or provide an element of drama. Likewise, speak with a different pitch to your voice to convey emotion and conviction. Change voice inflections so that you are not speaking in a monotone.

> Because you are speaking on a topic that you truly believe in, express your sincerity by putting your entire self into the talk.

Finally, speak at a rate that is neither too fast nor too slow. Speakers who move along too quickly will lose their listeners and those who speak too slowly will put them to sleep. However, varying your speaking pace to emphasize points or to indicate mood changes is beneficial. Silence is also a powerful tool. A confident speaker is aware of the potency of a silent pause.

Overall, strive to speak with vitality, providing the impression of confidence and conviction. This keeps the audience alert to your message.

Body Language

Body language is also a critical component of effective speaking. Hand gestures and facial expressions work in tandem with the interpreter's vocal skills to bring sight and sound into harmony.

As you launch the presentation, be certain that you are standing upright, but not rigid. Your hands, when you are not gesturing, should be at your sides. Be careful not to cross your arms in front of your chest, for this signals self-consciousness, a symbolic barrier between you and the audience.

Because you are speaking on a topic that you truly believe in, express your sincerity by putting your entire self into the talk. Facial expressions that reflect the various moods of your presentation should come naturally, although these may not be visible to the whole audience if you are speaking in front of a large group. The most visually expressive part of body language, therefore, is the use of hands and arms to illustrate your words and show what you mean. For example, gestures may reflect size, shape, direction, or importance. However, be careful not to allow gestures to take over the presentation; you don't want flailing arms to detract from your message.

As in many aspects of learning about effective speaking, observing how polished speakers use gestures that appear smooth, natural, and spontaneous is worthwhile. The interpreter may also rehearse body language in front of a mirror or videotape the presentation to evaluate progress.

Organize The Presentation

To ensure that the presentation is effective and makes sense to the audience, the material must be sequenced properly—in the form of a story. Accomplished speakers know exactly where they are going to begin and end. Even a well-intended and sincere speech that uses the best material will be ineffective if it is not organized carefully.

> **Accomplished speakers know exactly where they are going to begin and end.**

If the presentation is to make sense and generate results, the story must flow in a logical way. We should strive to arrange our presentations so they satisfy the audience. Do not ask, "What do I want to say?" but rather, "What does the audience seek to hear?" That is, "What will be useful and meaningful to the listeners?"

The best speakers spend a considerable amount of time planning how to maintain the attention of the audience. These experienced speakers know that the telltale way to determine whether a talk is making an impact is to watch the audience throughout the presentation. If listeners are focused on the interpreter's words and watching the interpreter with interest, then the talk is working.

The basic structure of most formal talks includes the introduction, the body, and the conclusion. A discussion of each of these components follows.

In the introduction, the interpreter arouses interest for the topic. The opening lines should capture the attention of the audience and express the theme or thesis. The introduction may include an overview of the presentation, a challenging statement, a quotation, or appropriate personal story. It may also include humor; however, a speaker should stay away from anything that is not central to the theme.

> Your audience members will be able to sense whether you are prepared, and they will be thankful for every hour you put into researching, organizing, and rehearsing the program.

The body of the talk is where we elaborate on the subject. Any number of illustrative devices can be used throughout: facts, examples, analogies, anecdotes, or references to related news events (see Chapter 3). Again, be sure to include only pertinent information. In the body, you continue a step-by-step progression toward the conclusion. This logical sequence will help to hold listeners' interest, just as a rambling discourse will surely scatter their attention.

The conclusion is the destination of the talk. At this point, the interpreter may tie comments back to the introduction, provide a summary of the points that have been made in the body, convey an illustrative message or quotation, or make a clear appeal for action. The end of the presentation should be forceful and conclusive, with no need to confirm "that's all there is." That point should be obvious.

Your audience members will be able to sense whether you are prepared, and they will be thankful for every hour you put into researching, organizing, and rehearsing the program. However, the audience does not care to learn about the time and effort you spent. That will be evident. To paraphrase a comment Annie Dillard made about writers, is it pertinent, is it courteous, for us to hear what it cost the speaker personally?[2]

Know Your Site and Be Available to the Audience

The interpreter should strive to know intimately the location and physical layout of where the presentation takes place. This familiarity will generate increased comfort and confidence.

Early arrival allows the interpreter to check the lighting, sound, and equipment. After everything is set up, you may interact with those who have arrived early. Mingling with the audience has several benefits, summarized by William Lewis as follows:

- It establishes a friendly, more intimate atmosphere.
- It helps weld the audience into a responsive whole.
- You may assess the general mood of the audience.
- It provides you with information you can use in your presentation.
- You may visualize the audience as a collection of individuals rather than a mass of humanity.
- It removes nervous tension as you make the transition from talking with smaller groups of people to the entire audience.[3]

Likewise, making yourself available after the presentation is important. Your availability should be announced in your introduction to avoid distracting from a powerful conclusion. Afterward, you may talk casually with those who were inspired by your presentation or perhaps provide further information for those seeking additional knowledge or experiences.

The Storyteller's Responsibility

Barry Lopez explains that the storyteller's responsibility is not to be wise; "a storyteller is the person who creates an atmosphere in which wisdom can reveal itself."[4] When Lopez writes a piece of nonfiction, he makes a bow of respect to the material and a bow of respect to the reader. The interpreter, similarly, pays tribute to the subject matter and to the visitor.

> ...a storyteller is the person who creates an atmosphere in which wisdom can reveal itself.
>
> —BARRY LOPEZ

Lopez sums up his respect toward the material in the following way: "Listen. Pay attention. Do your research. Try to learn. Don't presume. And always imagine that there's more there than you could possibly understand or sense."[5] The interpreter owes this same level of deference to the subject matter, be it a natural landscape or historical event.

In paying respects to the reader, Lopez says, "I have assembled this material. I have tried to bring order to these disparate elements. I have tried to use the language elegantly. I have sought, everywhere I could, illumination, clarity. I have tried to organize things with a proper sense of the drama of human life, I have tried to think hard about all these things. I have tried to get rid of all that is unnecessary for you to understand the story."[6] Again, the interpreter owes this same degree of attention to the recipient of interpretation. This standard requires substantial effort.

Building on the Basics

Only after we master the basics of communication—using nervousness to advantage, learning speaking skills and expressive body language, orchestrating the flow of information—can we effectively move on to incorporating the various arts. To attempt the art of storytelling or interpretive drama without knowing about voice projection, the importance of eye contact, or basic organizing and attention-holding principles would certainly be worse than a bad speech, although neither are desirable.

As basic techniques are mastered—and this progresses over time—we continue to grow in our knowledge and expertise. Many channels promote our growth.

Interpreters must continue to read widely. This helps us to be well versed in our subject matters and assists in our program preparation as we consider how written material is organized for optimal effectiveness.

We must also keep abreast of news events. Awareness of what is going on in the rest of the world—regionally, nationally, and internationally—helps us avoid becoming shortsighted and narrowly focused. As wondrous as our interpretive site is, a whole world is out there, and both our site and visitors are connected to it.

> Continued professional growth is essential to the quality of the interpreter's work.

Continued professional growth is essential to the quality of the interpreter's work. We should be members of professional organizations, and, better yet, active participants. In the United States, the National Association for Interpretation (NAI) has been the foremost national organization devoted to "inspire leadership and excellence to advance heritage interpretation as a profession."[7] The diversity of this organization is represented by its many sections.[8] Other national and international organizations include Interpretation Canada, InterpEurope, InterpChina, Interpretation Australia, and the Association of Heritage Interpretation in Great Britain.

Attendance at regional, national, and international conferences promotes our growth through listening to experts in the field, networking and meeting new friends who may face similar challenges, being exposed to new resources and program ideas, and coming away inspired to serve our clientele even better.[9] Furthermore, this association with other professionals enhances our commitment to our life work; provides a sense of belonging to a larger group with similar interests, goals, and aspirations; and affirms the validity and mission of the profession.

In addition to active reading, seeking knowledge, and participating in professional organizations, we grow professionally by attending seminars and pursuing additional coursework. For many of us, learning other languages or new technologies that may be applied to better serve our visitors is useful.

Competencies and Certification

Some agencies have developed competencies that correspond to increasing skill development for interpretive staff. For example, the National Park Service created three categories that make up an increasing range of knowledge, skill, and ability. The interpreter must demonstrate competency at each level before moving to the next level. The three basic categories and competencies are:

- *Entry level*: interpretive talks and informal visitor interactions.
- *Developmental level*: interpretive writing, conducted activities, curriculum-based education programs, and demonstrations and other illustrated programs.
- *Full performance level*: developing interpretive media, planning park interpretation, interpretive training and coaching, and interpretive research and resource liaison.

The National Association for Interpretation (NAI) now offers (since the first edition of this book) a professional certification program. Certification allows interpreters to document important knowledge and skills that help them perform effectively in the profession. Minimum qualifications consisting of education and/or experience must be met prior to requesting a certification package. Upon successful completion of the requirements, the interpreter is certified in one of four professional categories: Certified Heritage Interpreter, Certified Interpretive Planner, Certified Interpretive Manager, and/or Certified Interpretive Trainer. In addition to the four professional categories, NAI also offers a certification program for those who do not meet minimum qualifications of education and/or experience. The Certified Interpretive Guide (CIG) option was created as a training program for those who interpret cultural or natural history, but do not have academic credentials or field experience. This program was designed to increase basic knowledge and skills in interpretation for seasonal employees, volunteers, docents, and others who lead tours or conduct interpretive programs. Finally, the Certified Interpretive Host training program integrates customer service principles with communication strategies for those who don't give formal programs, but otherwise come in contact with the public such as maintenance workers, law enforcement rangers, receptionists, and sales clerks.

Tim Merriman, Executive Director of NAI, estimates that more than 300,000 potential CIGs are serving in interpretive roles in the United States alone. Merriman further estimates that the total number of public contact people who may offer interpretation in the overall tourism sector is in the range of two to five million. Extraordinary advancement of the profession may occur in this arena.

*I'll interpret the rocks, learn the language of flood,
storm, and avalanche. I'll acquaint myself with the
glaciers and wild gardens, and get as near the
heart of the world as I can.*

—John Muir

Many avenues contribute to our professional growth. As we continue to work at a particular site we grow in our knowledge of the place, we grow in our experiences there, and we grow to love the place. Our enthusiasm inspires our visitors. We fine-tune existing programs and try new ones.

How does one pursue enhanced interpretation? Ultimately, the process is a personal endeavor—like a journey. Each of us is unique and our interpretation is unlike the interpretive efforts of any other person past, present, or future. Interpreters perform through the lens of their own experiences and with their own creative approaches and passions.

As students we determine how best to prepare ourselves for entering the profession by selecting appropriate coursework, relevant fieldwork and internship experiences, and meaningful volunteer opportunities. We build a foundation.

As practitioners we deliberate on how to structure our time to meet our own expectations for excellence. We learn from our colleagues, supervisors, and visitors. We continue to seek information and to read widely. We collaborate, take on progressively more challenging tasks, contribute our expertise to professional organizations, write for various publications, and share our experience with entry-level interpreters. This constant learning, and the assistance we provide to others, keeps us fresh.

As managers of interpretive programs, we keep current in all aspects of interpretation as well as create supportive environments for our interpretive employees and volunteers to excel. Our work ethic, our passion for the resource, our concern for the welfare of visitors, and our investment in continual growth serves as a model for our employees.

We are on a journey and our success—our contribution—will depend on the foundation we establish and what we make of opportunities to grow along the way. Among other possibilities, we now have the opportunity to seek certification in a number of professional categories, both to advance our knowledge and skills, as well as advance the profession. Our investment in professionalism is a gift to ourselves, our workplace, our profession, and our audiences.

There is a life force, a quickening that is translated through you into action,
and because there is only one of you in all time, its expression is unique. And if
you block it, it will never exist through any other medium and be lost.
The world will not have it.

—**Martha Graham**

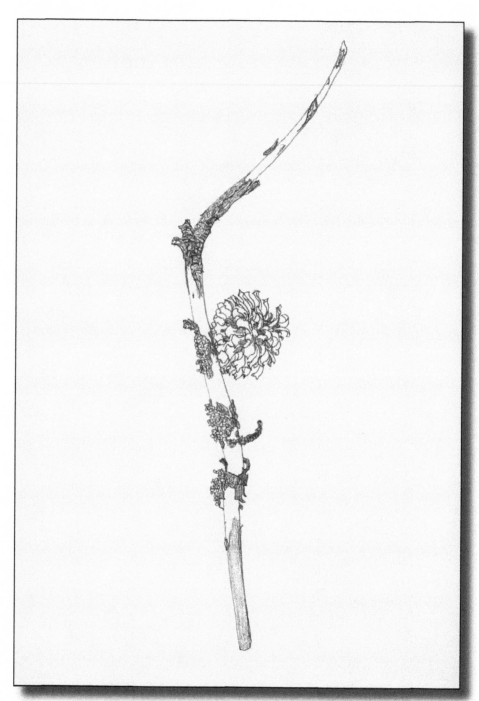

© Tsuyoshi Matsumoto

CHAPTER

11

The Gift of Interpretive Writing

Interpretive writing should address what readers would like to know, with the
authority of wisdom and its accompanying humility and care.

Write as if you were dying. At the same time, assume you write
for an audience consisting solely of terminal patients.
That is, after all, the case.

—Annie Dillard

Our purpose in this chapter is not to teach the reader specific writing techniques, but to present general principles that contribute to good writing. When
Tilden wrote about the mission and complexities of interpretive writing, his focus was on writing "inscriptions"—meaning the text of signs and labels. He
claimed that adequate inscription is the result of 90% thinking and 10% composition and noted that perfect composition without sound thought will be fatally
flawed, whereas a well-considered piece that contains composition flaws may
still communicate something meaningful.[1] But, composition flaws may lead to
confusion; therefore, both thinking and composition are necessary to create a
well-written piece. These two processes—thinking and composition—provide
the organizational framework for this chapter.

Thinking

Thinking About the Content

The two most engaging powers of an author are to make new things familiar, and familiar things new.

—Samuel Johnson

Interpreters first must think about choosing a subject to be addressed in their writing. What new things should be made familiar? Which familiar things should be made new? In answering this question of what to write about, Tilden said that writers often make the mistake of asking only "What is it I wish to say?"[2] The more important consideration is what the prospective reader wishes to read. All writing, and indeed all interpretation, should begin with the audience. The needs and interests of readers will direct your decisions.

> Interpretive writing should communicate the essence of the place and the reason for its existence.

Tilden also suggested that writers ask themselves if they can write something in "brief, inspiring, and luring terms" about the potential topic.[3] The goals of interpretive composition are to interpret information in such a way that it relates to the lives of the reader (Chapter 1) and reveals insights, meanings, and deeper truth (Chapter 2). To be able to write in inspirational and luring terms, and to meet the goals of interpretation, the interpreter must have a thorough understanding of the subject.

Communicating a sense of place is also important in choosing content. Interpretive writing should communicate the essence of the place and the reason for its existence. Identifying, and then interpreting, the site's genius locus is the hallmark of good interpretation. We cheat visitors when we distract them with writing having nothing to do with the site. Although this may seem like common sense, the authors have seen polar bears interpreted at a prairie park and antique automobiles interpreted at a Civil War battlefield.

Sometimes content is determined by others when interpreters are assigned messages to convey. For example, an important function of modern interpretation is as a management tool. Because interpretation is the communication link between the interpretive site and the visitor, and because interpreters should be expert communicators, administrators call on them to effectively communicate management messages. In these instances, interpreters might be asked to write messages presenting an agency policy or to explain organizational mandates and priorities.

When given the choice of what to write about, interpreters would do well to consider the advice of author Barbara Kingsolver that, ". . . it's emotion, not event, that creates a dynamic response in the mind of the reader. The artist's job is to sink a taproot in the reader's brain that will grow downward and find a path into the reader's soul and experience, so that some new emotional inflorescence will grow out of it."[4] Most importantly, in selecting content, writers should be enthusiastic about the subject and excited about the prospect of finding that path into the reader's soul and experience. Tilden wrote, "Whatever is written without enthusiasm, will be read without interest."[5]

> The artist's job is to sink a taproot in the reader's brain that will grow downward and find a path into the reader's soul and experience, so that some new emotional inflorescence will grow out of it.
>
> —BARBARA KINGSOLVER

Thinking About the Process

Many aspiring writers are stymied as they wait for some magical moment of inspiration. Some interpreters passively wait their entire careers for the muse to appear. Inspiration is difficult to predict and control, but writers can encourage it by carefully observing their surroundings and listening to other voices—the voices of nature as well as human voices.

Perhaps the best source of inspiration is reading. Reading provides ideas, information, and illustrations, all of which make inspiration more likely. Samuel Johnson said, "The greatest part of a writer's time is spent in reading, in order to write; a man will turn over half a library to make one book."[6] Moreover, he sharply criticized another writer by saying, "He wrote more than he read."[7] Reading well-written pieces has the bonus of serving as models of good writing.

Most professional writers consider time spent reading part of their writing time. Annie Dillard observed, "The writer studies literature, not the world. He lives in the world; he cannot miss it. …He is careful of what he reads, for that is what he will write. He is careful of what he learns, because that is what he will know."[8]

Author Barry Lopez was once asked for advice about becoming a writer. He offered three suggestions: to read (particularly the classics), to travel, and to become someone.[9] In encouraging reading, he noted, "No one can fathom what happens between a human being and written language. She [the reader] may be paying attention to things in the words beyond anyone else's comprehension, things that feed her curiosity, her singular heart and mind." Lopez then suggested not just geographical travel, but travel into unfamiliar territories by learning a new language, living among different people, listening to new voices, trying new things. Such "traveling" can also be done close to home and provides the writer with a fresh understanding of the familiar. Finally, Lopez said to write well, writers must become someone. They must find out what they strongly believe and write from those beliefs. In this way writers develop their own voice. If writing does not speak to readers from deep personal beliefs and meaning, it is merely "passing along information, of which we are in no great need."[10] Writers must write courageously. They must not fear putting their thoughts, emotions, and beliefs on paper for the world to see. This is a gift to the reader.

> **Writers must write courageously. They must not fear putting their thoughts, emotions, and beliefs on paper for the world to see. This is a gift to the reader.**

Inspired writing is a difficult, often demanding process. Interpreters attain inspiration only through effort—observing, listening, reading, traveling, and being somebody. Then comes the discipline of putting the words down. "Genius is 1% inspiration and 99% perspiration," said Thomas Edison.[11] Tilden also noted that, "inspiration is usually the mirrored reflection of hard work."[12]

Another key to strengthening one's writing is to write frequently. While waiting for inspiration to strike, write. The more one writes, the easier it becomes. Furthermore, when writers write about important subjects with heartfelt convictions, the writing can be rewarding and enjoyable.

Composition: Putting Thoughts into Words

Wordsmithing

> *Words should be an intense pleasure to a writer just as leather should be to a shoemaker.*
>
> **—Evelyn Waugh**

Writers build manuscripts with words. Composition involves choosing the best words and using them concisely and correctly. One writer said, "For the born writer, nothing is so healing as the realization that he has come upon the right word."[13] Good writers first consider their audience's characteristics when choosing the best words. Identifying the best word is difficult and changes with the characteristics of the readers, and thus is an audience-driven choice. At the same time, the word must precisely convey the meaning and emotions of the writer. Reading levels, vocabularies, and connotations change with age, education, and culture. Interpreters must write with sensitivity to all readers.

Selecting precise words is the starting point. Organizing the words together in a correct and logical way is the next step. Correct grammar not only enhances clarity, but also the writer's credibility. If grammar is notably poor, readers may assume the information is suspect. Moreover, if the writing appears careless, readers may think the agency is careless in carrying out its mission.

Brevity is a critical component of good composition because it enhances clarity and readability.[14] Avoiding tedious detail and saying only what is necessary enhances the reader's interest. Readers often choose what to read based on the perceived level of difficulty. Thus, short paragraphs and more white space tend to promote reading of the text. The paradox of brevity is that concise writing takes more effort and time. Mark Twain noted this paradox when he reportedly wrote to a friend that he would have written a shorter letter, but didn't have time.

As with most everything, moderation is called for in regard to brevity. Messages may be so brief they are incomplete. In striving for brevity, writers may omit important contents, leaving the reader confused. No specific rule or word count formula exists to determine if something is too brief or too long. Writers must use discernment so they do not say less than the occasion demands, nor more than is needed.

> **Brevity is a critical component of good composition because it enhances clarity and readability.**

In some cases, there should be no written interpretation at all. Tilden noted that some signs "accost" visitors.[15] Like Mozart, who suggested his rests were more important than his notes, interpreters should be sensitive to circumstances in which a sign or label would detract from the desired experience.

Concise writing enhances readability. Well-chosen nontechnical language arranged in short sentences and short paragraphs encourages the reader to keep reading. Likewise, writers maintain interest and make sentences succinct and lively by using active, rather than passive verbs. Many other such considerations regarding style, tone, and technique go into making a well-written piece. Grammar texts and writing manuals, both popular and academic, abound to help writers with the basics of good writing. Among many possibilities is the classic slender volume by William Strunk Jr. and E.B. White, *The Elements of Style*, one of the best of this genre.

Quotes

Writers have conflicting views about quotes. Emerson said, "Don't recite other people's opinions. I hate quotations. Tell me what you know."[16] Others disagree. Clifton Fadimn said, "I think we must quote whenever we feel that the allusion is interesting or helpful or amusing."[17] Montaigne said, "I quote others only the better to express myself."[18] Tilden acknowledged that "sometimes a quotation will be found more effective than anything we can currently invent, to project the right mood into the mind of the reader."[19] We encourage interpreters to use quotes to create a mood, stimulate reflection on the origin of the words, or stop readers in their tracks with a profound idea that came from someone else.

Revision

"You watch, you set it down. Then you try again." That is how Barry Lopez described the writer's life.[20] The "trying again" is what separates great writers from the ordinary. Serious writers are not easily satisfied with their efforts.

In some cases, there should be no written interpretation at all.

They sense an urgent need to work until their prose is precise and perfect. For example, when writing a book, Ernest Hemingway would start each working day by re-reading and editing everything he had written to that point. This meant that he worked through each book manuscript several hundred times. He claimed to have revised the ending of *A Farewell to Arms* 39 times before he felt satisfied, thereby illustrating the writing axiom that there are no great writers, only great re-writers. A person knows he or she has arrived at becoming a writer when he or she learns to appreciate the tedious, detail-oriented task of revision as much as the creative act of writing the first draft.

Revising is "more than just changing a few commas and running a spell-checker," wrote noted writing instructor Philip Gerard.[21] "It is re-envisioning your work. Stepping back from it in light of what you know now, what you have written, and determining if you have done what you set out to do."[22] For this reason, experienced authors recommend setting aside a manuscript for a period of time between revisions to allow scrutiny with a fresh eye for detail and possibly even a new perspective.

The act of revising stems from a serious concern and commitment to composition—using the best words in the most powerful way. As William Zinsser declared, "the essence of writing is rewriting."[23]

Interpretive Writing

In his book titled *Interpretive Writing*, Alan Leftridge promotes this style of writing as a genre. He notes that interpretive writing is distinguished by making intellectual and emotional connections between the reader and the interpretive subject and must be goal-oriented. Leftridge concludes that "interpretive writing is enjoyable, personable, relevant, creative, purposeful, humorous, organized, thematic, and informative."[24]

The written word can be a powerful means of communication. John Steinbeck noted, "Great writing has been a staff to lean on, a mother to consult, a wisdom to pick up stumbling folly, a strength in weakness and a courage to support sick cowardice."[25]

> The essence of writing is rewriting.
>
> —WILLIAM ZINSSER

The gift of written interpretation has certain advantages over other interpretive media. Written materials can be read at the reader's own pace. They can be read off-site. They can be read repeatedly. They can last for generations. All of these factors make the well-written word a powerful interpretive medium.

Tilden said to be an effective writer, you "must be in love with your material and in tune with your fellow man."[26] When these conditions exist, writers write enthusiastically with dedicated thinking and inspired, careful composition—a wonderful gift to readers.

When love and skill work together expect a masterpiece.

—John Ruskin

SUNDAY, June 25, 1978
T.P.S.R.
from the driveway to
the museum
mat

© Tsuyoshi Matsumoto

CHAPTER 12

The Gift of Relationship

The overall interpretive program must be capable of attracting support—financial, volunteer, political, administrative—whatever support is needed for the program to flourish.

He who has a thousand friends has not a friend to spare,
And he who has one enemy shall meet him everywhere.

—Ralph Waldo Emerson
(who attributed it to Omar Kahyyám)

For much of the 20th century, interpreters operated under the premise that interpretation was free of economic concerns, politics, and public opinion. In many respects, interpreters approached their profession almost like a religion, with dedication and a devout altruism. However, we have come to understand clearly that financial, political, and public support matter. In times of limited and shrinking budgets, interpreters face the challenge of convincing the public and their administrators that interpretation is not a luxury, but an essential service providing multiple benefits to society and sponsoring organizations. Interpreters can succeed in this important task by forming friendly, supportive relationships.

Financial Support

Interpretation in the commercial sector has always had to make a profit to survive. In response to taxpayer revolts and a general trend of government budget reductions, many public sector interpretive programs must generate financial support or face elimination. Entrance fees, program fees, or a variety of fundraising strategies can raise revenue for interpretation.

High-quality interpretation in a park sometimes will more than pay for itself. Jay Miller, Chief of Park Interpretation, has seen first-hand the financial benefits of having interpretation in Arkansas State Parks. Old Davidsonville State Park is a small historic site in northern Arkansas. Davidsonville was home to Arkansas' first post office, first two-story courthouse, and first land office. Located along the famed Southwest Trail, the town welcomed travelers from St. Louis and points east who were on their way to Mexico. The town was abandoned by 1830. The State Park was almost as abandoned and forgotten as Old Davidsonville itself until Wes Field, a dedicated and talented interpreter, became the first full-time interpreter at the park. Through special events, consistent programming, living history, working with local schools, and courting the media, Wes made Old Davidsonville a popular place. Specifically, one year after his arrival, programs increased from 22 to 109, visitor contacts increased from 1,524 to 10,410, park attendance increased from 28,342 to 79,119, and revenue increased from $7,407 to $23,522. "Why doesn't every park across the country have an interpretive staff? Beats me," Miller said. "I find it hard to believe that any park system, which wants to be successful, doesn't put interpreters in every park as soon as they open the doors to the public."[1]

> High-quality interpretation in a park sometimes will more than pay for itself.

Fee or Free

As tax dollars have dwindled and costs of providing services have increased, some organizations have adapted by changing to fee-based programming. For example, the Park Board of Johnson County (Kansas) Parks and Recreation Department mandated that interpretation programs be fee-supported. Visitors do not pay park entrance fees, but they pay fees for interpretive programs. Although tax dollars subsidize utilities, maintenance, and parts of some salaries, fees support 100% of the direct programming costs. In fact, fees collected at programs cover more than 80% of the entire interpretation budget.[2]

Johnson County interpreters develop a budget before offering any interpretive program. The cost of brochures, advertising, supplies, staff salaries, equipment, and administrative costs are calculated, and a pricing scheme is set based on estimates of minimum and maximum attendance. Administrators recognize that some programs, such as wildflower walks or bird walks, cannot be sold at fair market value and break even, so revenues generated from highly profitable interpretive hayrides and summer camps subsidize the interpretation of wild-flowers and songbirds.

Decisions about which programs to provide are market-based. In Johnson County, every program is evaluated to get customer feedback on the program's quality and to assess future demand. Staff regularly conducts surveys of visitors and non-visitors to determine their needs and desires. For stability and planning purposes, interpreters must have "base programs" upon which they can rely to generate revenue each year (such as contractual arrangements with local schools to provide a set number of programs). Once such a base is established, programs are added based on market research.

Interpreters must think of interpretation programs as a business that manufactures and sells interpretive experiences. We need to recognize that competitors produce substitute experiences. Like any manufacturing process, interpreters must consider the quality and quantity of the experiences they produce.

Charging fees has advantages and disadvantages. The disadvantages are that some will resist new fees, saying, "You've never charged before." Others will claim that they have already paid with their tax dollars and that, philosophically, public programs should be available to everyone. In some cases, fees might represent an economic barrier to participation. However, interpreters can offer a voucher system or scholarships to disadvantaged individuals or groups. Moreover, if interpreters use other revenue-generating strategies along with fees, then fees can be kept low to minimize economic barriers.

Collecting fees offers some advantages. Fees reduce "no-shows" because fee payers who register for a program have made a commitment to participate and are unlikely to forfeit their fees. Interpreters have a great incentive to provide a high-quality program, because the expectations of a paying audience will be greater and because the interpreter knows that a better product will generate even more financial resources. These resources, in turn, can subsidize other worthwhile programs that would otherwise not be financially viable. At Johnson County Parks and Recreation and many other park departments, zoos, and museums, relationships have been nurtured within the community whereby people have become willing to pay for quality programs.

Donations

As indicated by the title of this chapter, fundraising is a matter of fostering relationships with people outside the organization's normal sphere of influence. Fundraising is friend-raising.[3] Turn acquaintances into friends before approaching them about opportunities to give. The key is to understand why the individual would want to give and then help them achieve their goals. The giver also must benefit from the gift transaction.

People give for one or more of the following reasons: tax benefits, gratitude for service rendered to them or their community, belief in a program's mission, for personal recognition today, or to achieve immortality (or at least remembrance) in the future. If interpreters know which of these motivates donors, they can strategically target the donors' interests to particular projects. If the donors' interest is in increasing their recognition, they may want to sponsor a weekend festival. If their interest is immortality, they may want to help with a building project involving naming rights. Regardless of the potential giver's motivation, personal solicitation of gifts is the most effective way of raising donations. Seeking donations is not about badgering people, but making friends and giving them an opportunity to become part of an important and successful venture. As noted in Chapter 4, studies by Sam Ham have shown that targeted interpretation can significantly increase philanthropic giving.

> Seeking donations is not about badgering people, but making friends and giving them an opportunity to become part of an important and successful venture.

Special Events

Special events raise money through entrance fees and sales. Most importantly, they attract people from the community who otherwise would not visit the site. New audiences are introduced to the interpretive site and its programs and are given an opportunity to sample them. Tim Merriman is legendary for his creative special events that pulled The Greenway and Nature Center of Pueblo (Colorado) from the brink of bankruptcy. These included casino nights, art fairs, rummage sales, dances, raft races, and field trips. Existing trails were adapted seasonally to become Halloween Spook Trails and Easter Egg Trails. Merriman also established a restaurant, a plant store, and gift shop. Through hard work and ingenuity, he generated the financial support necessary to allow this private interpretive site to thrive.[4] As mentioned in the Johnson County example above, special events can be profitable and can support less profitable but important interpretive programs.

Partnerships and Sponsorships

One way to stretch dollars is to develop relationships with other agencies or organizations. Many nature centers, museums, and zoos are forming partnerships with local school districts. Schools are looking for ways to teach science and history. Because many states have specific learning goals for each grade, interpreters can help schools meet them. Joining with schools brings strong support from parents, local business, civic and service groups, and the public.

Some interpretive sites are partnering with other nearby sites. For example, in the Kansas City area, an Interpretative Site Coalition (ISC) was formed by bringing together personnel from 13 sites to form a unified cooperative effort. ISC has pooled and shared resources to produce workshops, share volunteers and staff, generate free publicity by cross-marketing their programs, and conduct an annual city-wide interpretation event called "The Passport to Adventure Hunt." This activity promotes all the member organizations by enhancing awareness and visitation as participants get their passports stamped at each cooperating site. ISC gains sponsors, donations, and publicity

> One way to stretch dollars is to develop relationships with other agencies or organizations.

that would not have been possible if the sites were acting independently. Such mutually beneficial relationships are possible anywhere interpretive sites exist in close proximity.

Interpreters also can form relationships with the business community. Branded sponsors raise funds for interpretive sites in exchange for exclusive rights to sell their products at specified events. In exchange for these rights, sponsors pay cash, give discounts on products, or assist in advertising and marketing. Free advertising is sometimes the most valuable compensation interpreters can receive. Firms provide advertising space on their websites, vehicles, or packaging to encourage attendance at interpretive programs.

Likewise, in return for advertising on park materials and venues, companies will sponsor specific interpretive programs, trails, or websites. Maintaining these resources would be beyond the budgets of the park, zoo, or museum. Partnerships with the private sector have always been important for the National Park Service since the first years when railroads partnered to promote and develop the parks. Today some park sites and programs operate almost exclusively through partnerships and many have a clear mandate to form partnerships. For example, Ford Motor Company, in conjunction with the National Park Foundation and Student Conservation Service, sponsors Transportation Interpreters who work on buses, trolleys, trains, and ferries in national parks to share information about alternative forms of transportation as well as other themes appropriate to the site.[5]

> Much ingenuity with a little money is vastly more profitable and amusing than much money without ingenuity.
>
> —ARNOLD BENNETT

However, in building relationships with the private sector, interpreters must 1) work only with companies that are respected members of the business community, and 2) maintain control of the interpretive messages, so as to not be accused of "selling out" to a particular firm.

Relationships with private sector partnerships can be profitable to all parties. The keys are to maintain open communications, build trust, and strive for diplomacy and consensus while still being able to confide in one another.

Volunteers: Putting Friends to Work

Interpreters produce the gift of relationships in the form of volunteers as they encourage and motivate people to care about, and for, the site or facility. Volunteers have become an important force in providing interpretive services. For example, the National Park Service benefits from the Volunteers-In-Parks (VIP) program. These volunteers are indeed VIPs (in the Very Important People sense) because 172,000 volunteers donated 5.7 million hours to our National Parks at a value of over $100 million in a recent year.[6]

Some large interpretive sites use hundreds of volunteers to do the work of dozens of full-time employees. Interestingly, many nature centers have found that teenagers are among the best and least tapped populations for recruitment of volunteers (see Chapter 6). They have the ability, interest, and energy to make outstanding contributions to interpretive programs and facilities.

> Interpreters produce the gift of relationships in the form of volunteers as they encourage and motivate people to care about, and for, the site or facility.

Sometimes volunteers coalesce to form "Friends" groups that benefit all facets of the operation, not merely interpretation. These groups enter into formal partnerships with the agency. They assist by conducting fundraising that would not be allowed within the agency. Friends groups can organize to receive tax-deductible donations, resulting in a much more competitive position when seeking financial gifts. Friends groups also may operate bookstores and gifts shops and assist with maintenance, cleanups, and publicity and advocacy campaigns. For example, at Homestead National Monument the Superintendent may spend up to 20 hours per week with the Friends group. In return, besides providing a reliable cadre of volunteers, the Friends group raised over $500,000 for a new Heritage Center, generated enough funds to exceed by 100% a match necessary for a land purchase, provided testimony in Congress to support the NPS and the Homestead National Monument, and manages a 140-acre tract that eventually will be donated to the park.

Keeping Your Volunteers

In many ways, volunteers should be treated like paid staff. This begins even before they become volunteers. Just as prospective employees are interviewed, potential volunteers should be interviewed to determine their interests, motives, and needs. Job descriptions, policies, and time commitments should be presented and discussed before the volunteer is accepted. Like employees, volunteers should be evaluated to provide feedback on their performance.

After they are selected, volunteers need training. For example, volunteer naturalists with the Missouri Department of Conservation are required to attend formal training of 24-32 hours. During the training, volunteers learn about the agency's history, the specific interpretive facility, interpretive methods, communications skills, and a variety of natural history topics.

Volunteers should be provided with their own work space, uniforms, or identification badges, as appropriate. They should be made to feel like an important part of the interpretation team. This means keeping them informed of all relevant agency communications and listening closely to what they have to say about policies and practices.

Volunteers must feel needed and respected. They should be regularly thanked, privately and publicly, and formally shown appreciation for their contributions. Volunteers do not "work for nothing." Volunteers benefit richly from the experience. In fact, if the experience is not rewarding, volunteers will look for opportunities to serve elsewhere.

> Many volunteers find profound pleasure and personal fulfillment in sharing their energy and interests with others.

A study of volunteer interpreters' motivations for serving found that of nine potential motivations measured, the three most important were "enjoyment of nature," "learning," and "benefiting nature and society."[7] Although the motives of some volunteers, particularly younger ones, may be pragmatic, such as gaining experience to adorn a resumé, or trying out a potential employer or career path, many volunteers just want to feel useful, taking to heart Dickens's observation that, "No one is useless in this world who lightens the burdens of another."

Many volunteers find profound pleasure and personal fulfillment in sharing their energy and interests with others. Interpreting cultural and natural resources can be tremendously rewarding personally (see Chapter 14).

In return, the organization receives a dedicated and enthusiastic labor pool to help it carry out its mission. Because volunteers are often on the front line interacting with visitors, the volunteer's enthusiasm is contagious and may positively affect not only visitor's mood, but also staff morale.

The strongest professional friendships must be mutually beneficial. Interpreters must find ways to meet the needs not only of visitors, but of volunteers, donors, and other partners as well.

Friends in High Places

Political Support

To a large extent, political support is a function of public support. Most politicians and policymakers will support a consensus of their constituents, particularly if they are well organized and vocal. Expanding the interpretation program's sphere of influence through publications, mass media interpretation, and off-site programs broadens the base of public support. Another way of expanding the base of support is through family ties. Children's programs have powerful political impacts. As a Danish saying goes, "If you take the child by the hand, you take the mother by the heart." In other words, if you captivate the children, you've captured the support of parents. Similarly, programs at nursing homes and assisted living centers enhance the quality of life of seniors, thereby garnering the additional support of their families and the staff. Having the privilege of presenting programs to the aged enriches interpreters' lives, too.

Politically, having advocates and allies in the form of other organizations or agencies is critical. Linkages to schools and health care facilities are especially valuable because health and education lend themselves to strong community support.

> Most politicians and policymakers will support a consensus of their constituents, particularly if they are well organized and vocal.

The best insurance against unfavorable political decisions is providing a high-quality product—one that the customers would hate to lose and would fight to keep. Interpretation programs must become as customer-oriented as any business. Many interpretation organizations use business concepts to meet the needs and exceed the expectations of their visitors. Satisfied customers who are willing to influence policymakers are a strong defense against political setbacks.

Agency Support

Sometimes the lack of support for interpretation is not from the outside, but from within the organization. Although interpretation has been used as a resource management tool since the early days of the National Park Service, some administrators do not recognize the benefits of interpretation. To thrive, interpreters must win their administrators' support and become respected members of the overall team.

Examples abound of interpretation being used as a management tool to reduce vandalism, littering, leaving designated trails, and other depreciative behaviors, as well as to increase desirable behaviors such as increasing participation in conservation-related activities, compliance with rules, and public support of agency policies among visitors. A bibliography of interpretation literature listed 154 entries under the heading "Management and Administration," and almost 100 more publications were listed under the topic "Resource Management."[8] Most of these citations speak to the important role interpretation can play in assisting administrators to meet their management goals.

Possibly the most powerful of these examples are those illustrating how interpretation can enhance safety and even save lives. Interpretation has been used to reduce bear, bison, and alligator attacks, but perhaps the most well documented success stories are those where interpretation has prevented drowning.

J. Patrick Barry relates the following stories of interpretation's ultimate value—saving lives.[9]

- At Bonneville Lock and Dam, anglers drowned annually from improper anchoring in the swift water. When the anchor rope is too short in the deep, fast-moving water, the short anchor line tightens and pulls the bow under the water. Barry, an interpreter with the Corps of Engineers, recalled, "One of the most frustrating feelings I've ever experienced was the sense of defeat I felt while searching in vain for survivors from a capsized boat." Rangers implemented an interpretive strategy using flyers, posters, video, and bumper stickers. This strategy has resulted in nobody drowning due to improper anchoring in the past 15 years.
- A Park Ranger at Lake Kaweah in California gave an evening interpretive program that depicted what people look like when they are drowning. The next day a woman from that audience saw two girls drowning and, along with another person, saved the two girls. She said she knew they were drowning only because she attended the program the night before.
- A ten-year-old girl saved her eight-year-old cousin after he fell off a fishing dock into Lake Leon in Texas. She remembered what she learned from a park ranger who came to her fourth grade class. He taught the children to "reach or throw, but don't go." She reached for the boy and pulled him from the lake.

Grant Sharpe stated that interpreters need to ask how they can be part of the management team. He noted, "Too many interpreters still think of themselves as interpreters only, often making little or no attempt to work with management in solving or reducing management problems .... Interpreters should make themselves so valuable in problem solving that they become indispensable."[10] That sage advice holds as true today as it did when he spoke those words decades ago.

> To thrive, interpreters must win their administrators' support and become respected members of the overall team.

Arkansas State Parks have taken the use of interpretation as a management tool to an entirely new level at Parkin Archeological State Park. This park went through an interpretive planning process to define park mission, to develop an overall guiding interpretive theme (based upon the park's mission statement and the special resources found in the park), and to outline visitor experience goals. The interpretive prospectus became the guiding force for park management.

Staff work plans are now developed to meet visitor experience goals that are in turn linked to the interpretive themes. Supervisors link work plans to performance reviews. Through this process, managers measure how much effort is being invested toward various aspects of the visitor's experience. If the manager sees one portion of the operations being neglected, improvements can be made.

Interpretation is intertwined with every facet of park operations and interpreters work closely, and in a mutually beneficial way, with park superintendents.

The data can be combined with other statistics (visitation, revenue, and facility reports) that paint a complete picture of the park operation. Then those data can be transformed into requests for equipment, personnel, policy changes, facilities, fee changes, and other management-level decisions all based around an interpretive mission and theme.

In this way, interpretation is intertwined with every facet of park operations and interpreters work closely, and in a mutually beneficial way, with park superintendents to achieve the mission of the park as well as to communicate the park's interpretive themes to the visitor.[11]

Interpreters need to seek and build support in financial, volunteer, political, and administrative arenas. Our goal should be to build relationships: to touch acquaintances in a way that makes them want to be our friends and supporters. This gift of building relationships is part of the overall gift of interpretation.

Granger, a character in Ray Bradbury's classic *Fahrenheit 451* said it well regarding the touch of his grandfather: "Grandfather's been dead for all these years, but if you lifted my skull, by God, in the convolutions of my brain you'd find the big ridges of his thumbprint. He touched me."

Our mission should be to leave our gentle enriching thumbprint on our visitors, donors, volunteers, policy-makers, and administrators. If we do this, we will garner the support we need and leave a legacy worthy of future support.

© Tsuyoshi Matsumoto

C H A P T E R
13

The Gift of Beauty

Interpretation should instill in people the ability, and the desire, to sense the beauty in their surroundings—to provide spiritual uplift and to encourage resource preservation.

Dostoyevsky once wrote, "Beauty will save the world."
But who will save beauty?

—Yevgeny Yevtushenko

Beauty defies definition. For centuries, the subject has attracted the attention of the world's greatest writers and artists. Yet the most articulate among them have struggled to capture the full character and meaning of beauty. Beauty is too personal, and therefore too subjective, to lend itself to a universal definition. One person experiencing something as beautiful does not necessarily make it so for everyone. Interpreters must heed this warning. Freeman Tilden believed that a broad generalization about the beauty of an area contributes to establishing an appropriate mood while leaving individuals free to make their own judgments about the beauty of any particular objects.[1] He said that among the roles of the interpreter is to prepare visitors to be receptive to beauty and "do all that discreetly may be done to establish a mood, or sympathetic atmosphere."[2] Enos Mills noted, "One of the best lessons gained from the wholesome atmosphere of the Parks is the duty of preserving natural beauties."[3]

Classifying Nature's Beauty

The notion of beauty is difficult to articulate because much of what is beautiful is revealed beyond the senses to the soul; an uplift of one's spirits, a rejoicing in the presence of symmetry, elegance, harmony, grace. Yet wild nature and beautiful human artifacts have powerful appeals, some of which may be captured.

Robert Marshall compared nature's beauty to that of great works of human art. When asked how many wilderness areas this country needed, he replied, "How many Brahms symphonies do we need?"[4] Marshall insisted that beauty in any form should not be destroyed, that we could never have too much. According to Marshall, although natural beauty is comparable in its magnetism and appeal to human art, it is distinctive for several reasons.

First, nature's beauty possesses timelessness that is not found in the art of the painter, the poet, the sculptor, the musician, or the architect. Even the paintings of the Renaissance are anchored in time. John Muir understood this when he extolled Nature's beauty: "This grand show is eternal ... Eternal sunrise, eternal sunset, eternal dawn and gloaming, on sea and continents and islands, each in its turn, as the round earth rolls."[5]

Robert Marshall compared nature's beauty to that of great works of human art.

Second, the immensity of natural landscapes has a special aesthetic power. We are humbled by the sheer size of nature as we gaze from the lip of the Grand Canyon or from a lofty mountain summit. We feel like a speck in the universe and are exalted at the same time. Barry Lopez wrote, "To the explorer the land becomes large, alive like an animal; it humbles him in a way he cannot pronounce. It is not that the land is simply beautiful, but that it is powerful. Its power derives from the tension between its obvious beauty and its capacity to take life."[6]

Third, in natural settings we are immersed by nature's artwork. As Marshall suggested, "One looks from outside at works of art and architecture, listens from outside to music or poetry. But when one looks at and listens to the wilderness he is encompassed by his experiences of beauty."[7]

Fourth, natural beauty is dynamic; it changes through the seasons and the years showing autumn leaves, the snow of winter, spring wildflowers, and verdant summer meadows. According to Marshall, a Beethoven symphony, a Shakespearean drama, a landscape by Corot, or a Gothic cathedral, when they are finished, become virtually static.[8] In contrast, the landscape is in constant flux. Sigurd Olson wrote, "I never watch a sunset without feeling the scene before me is more beautiful than any painting could possibly be, for it has the additional advantage of constant change, is never the same from one instant to the next."[9]

A fifth distinctive quality of nature's beauty is that it encompasses all of our senses: The smell of the forest after rain. The breath of a cool alpine breeze. The song of a meadowlark or trembling aspen leaves. The sweet taste of a mountain stream. The colorful flash of a monarch or tiger swallowtail on the wing. Or the unfurling leaves of a black oak in spring—the ineffable colors of a ripe peach. Diane Ackerman observed, "Much of our experience . . . is an effort to get away from those textures [of the senses], to fade into a stark, simple, solemn, puritanical, all-business routine that doesn't have anything so unseemly as sensuous zest."[10] Nature stimulates and quickens all of our senses.

Finally, Marshall noted that nature offers the best opportunity for "pure esthetic enjoyment." He wrote, "This requires that beauty be observed as a unity, and that for the brief duration of any pure esthetic experience the cognition of the observed object must completely fill the spectator's cosmos."[11] This deep and powerful response to beauty is consistent with Abraham Maslow's concept of peak experiences that he explained simply and profoundly as moments of highest happiness.

All of Nature is Beautiful

People are drawn to the deepest canyons, the highest mountains, the spectacular coastlines, and the tallest trees. Alfred Runte refers to this inclination toward nature's spectacles as monumentalism.[12] The "jewel" scenic parks inspire, uplift, and overwhelm us. But are they more meaningful than other natural areas? Are they really more beautiful?

Barry Lopez noted that "unheralded landscapes are still part of the face of God."[13] Walt Whitman wrote about the beauty of understated landscapes when writing about prairies. He noted, "As to the scenery (giving my own thought and feeling), while I know the standard claim is that Yosemite, Niagara Falls, the Upper Yellowstone, and the like afford the greatest natural shows, I am not so sure but the prairies and plains, while less stunning at first sight, last longer, fill the esthetic sense fuller, precede all the rest, and make North America's characteristic landscape."[14]

Likewise, Muir lamented, "Tourists make their way through the foot-hill landscapes as if blind to all their best beauty and like children seek the emphasized mountains—the big alpine capitals whitened with glaciers and adorned with conspicuous spires." He optimistically hoped that in the future "lowlands will be loved more than alps, and lakes and level rivers more than water-falls."[15]

Tilden wrote that nothing in nature can be ugly. "The seeming exceptions are simply facets of beauty we have not yet grasped," he said.[16] And Ralph Waldo Emerson stated the "inevitable mark of wisdom is to see the miraculous in the common."[17] Agreement can be found in the writings of Aldo Leopold, Edward Abbey, Sigurd Olson, and an anonymous writer who wrote, "Genius is recognizing the uniqueness in the unimpressive. It is looking at a homely caterpillar, an ordinary egg, and a selfish infant and seeing a butterfly, an eagle, and a saint."

> Interpreters help people ... see beauty in the ordinary, miracles in the mundane.

Interpreters help people understand that beauty is not merely a matter of size and ruggedness and help them see beauty in the ordinary, miracles in the mundane.

Interpreting Beauty in Practice

Establishing a mood conducive to perception and appreciation of a beautiful scene or object means freeing visitors from distractions so they can focus on the beauty. It also means having the audience in the proper frame of mind to maximize the impact of the beauty. A quiet, understated exposure to beauty will enhance the effect on the viewers.

Creating a sympathetic atmosphere is more than merely keeping the audience focused and minimizing distractions; it also entails cultivating peoples' ability to perceive beauty. As discussed above, some glorious scenes in nature are universally appreciated, such as the Grand Canyon. But what about dank cypress swamps? We are intrigued by eagles and grizzlies, wolves and deer. But how many visitors understand the wonders of a bat? How do we create a sympathetic atmosphere for things that, on the surface, are not as spectacular and may even be perceived as revolting or disgusting?

Aldo Leopold explained these differing levels of appreciation as follows: "Our ability to perceive quality in nature begins, as in art, with the pretty. It expands through successive stages of the beautiful to values as yet uncaptured by language."[18]

To further Leopold's analogy of art, ask the average person on the street to name a favorite painter and many may answer with artists such as Norman Rockwell or Remington, whose paintings are easy to understand and appreciate. Few mention acclaimed masters as Dali, Picasso, or Kandinsky. Their paintings are not as accessible in terms of being "pretty" and their meanings are not as obvious. Appreciation of nature's beauty is similar, and the same may hold true in historical settings. Beautiful craftsmanship of a chair, for example, or architecture of a building, is not always immediately discernible to the untrained eye.

The public may appreciate the beautiful stained glass of a cathedral, but may be oblivious to the handiwork in the pews.

Instead of looking upon people with reproach, our role is to assist them, to guide them without condescension, to point beyond finding beauty only in obvious grandeur. This returns us to the second principle in which we strive to reveal meaning—the beauty of subtle landscapes, unusual organisms, or complex objects.

Like a master teaching an art appreciation course, interpreters can help people see or feel the beauty that is not readily apparent. It takes time, effort, and exposure to develop one's capabilities. We have all started at the beginning, and we can make reference to and apply our own journey toward understanding more subtle beauty to assist others. We can sensitize and motivate visitors to exert the effort to appreciate successive stages of the beautiful. This is part of the gift of sharing beauty.

Helping People to Possess Beauty

John Ruskin, 19th century poet, artist, and philosopher, devoted much of his life's work to understanding beauty. He believed that people respond to beauty and have an innate desire to possess it.[19] People attempt to possess beauty through such acts as leaving their mark on it in the form of personalized graffiti, buying souvenirs or artifacts to take home with them, or by taking photographs to capture it. But Ruskin believed that people can fully possess beauty only by first noticing it, and then understanding it. Further, he believed the most effective way to achieve this understanding of a beautiful place or object is through drawing it and/or writing about it, regardless of the drawing or writing skills of the observer. To this end, he taught drawing classes. The goal had little to do with drawing well, but had everything to do with getting people to slow down and notice details. Drawing taught his students to see, not merely to look. Ruskin told a story about two men who went to the market. One man came out "no wiser." The other man noticed a bit of parsley hanging over a butter-woman's basket and "carries away with him images of beauty which in the course of his daily work he incorporates with it for many a day."[20] Ruskin wanted his students to notice details like that bit of parsley. He noted that even the prettiest tree seldom detains a passerby. But to draw the tree takes the time, attention, and concentration necessary to see the

> Interpreters help people possess beauty by getting them to slow down, by directing their attention to the details, and then by helping them understand the significance and meaning of the place or object.

details. Likewise, writing about the tree causes one to slow down and reflect about the characteristics and meanings of the tree.

How can interpreters respond to this universal need to possess beauty? Interpreters help people possess beauty by getting them to slow down, by directing their attention to the details, and then by helping them understand the significance and meaning of the place or object. This can be accomplished in many ways but, journaling, with both its sketching and writing components, perfectly mimics Ruskin's approach to helping people truly possess beauty.

Beauty and Stewardship

Perceiving something as beautiful will cause us to care. And if we care about something, we will care *for* it. Again we can turn to art for an example of how beauty causes us to care. In 1972, a 33-year-old Hungarian-born Australian geologist named Laszlo Toth climbed over the guardrail of the chapel of the Pieta in St. Peter's Basilica and attacked Michelangelo's Pieta with a hammer, breaking off the nose and the translucent shell of the left eyelid from Mary's face and breaking her right arm off at the elbow. Although artists were able to restore this nearly 500-year-old sculpture, this brazen act outraged people around the world. The most passionate called for the death penalty. The vandal served nine years in prison. When people perceive a work of art, a work of nature, or even the site of a historic event as beautiful, they will passionately nurture it and protect it.

The gift of beauty reconciles people with nature or with historic events. Upon return to Paris during the winter, Hemingway, in *A Moveable Feast*, noted that the bare trees against the sky became sculptures when he became "reconciled to them." Reconciliation—restoration of compatibility, friendship or harmony—allows people to appreciate and value objects or events that maybe have had neutral or negative meanings.

Interpreters put people on friendly terms with their environments and history. Beauty inspires stewardship as it restores harmony and causes us to care.

Landscapes of Nature and the Mind

Barry Lopez distinguished between the exterior and interior landscape. The exterior landscape is the one we see and experience. Eventually, with time and practice, we learn not only the identities of organisms in the environment, but also to perceive their relationships—"like that between the sparrow and the twig."[21] The interior landscape is within the self (our thoughts, our moods), but it is a projection of the exterior landscape. That is, the interior landscape responds to the attributes of the exterior landscape.

Yi-Fu Tuan advanced the idea that beauty is essential in our individual lives and is, collectively, the driving force and ultimate goal of culture. The pervasive role of the esthetic is reflected by its root meaning of "feeling" and is suggested even more by its opposite, anesthetic, "lack of feeling." Tuan reminded us, "The more attuned we are to the beauties of the world, the more we come to life and take joy in it."[22]

Mills observed that in places such as national parks "the geological wonders, the forests, the wild bloom, the folk in fur and feathers are protected for their higher values, for uses in education, for enjoyment, for giving relaxation and universal sympathy, for inspiring visions, and for enriching the imagination."[23] Likewise when Ruskin was helping his drawing students to "possess beauty," he noted, "My efforts are directed not at making a carpenter an artist, but to making him happier as a carpenter."[24] Should that not also be the motivation of interpreters? We should interpret beauty not to make visitors into historians or naturalists, but to make them happier—more alert, more observant, more appreciative—people.

> We should interpret beauty not to make visitors into historians or naturalists, but to make them happier—more alert, more observant, more appreciative—people.

The Spiritual Dimensions of Beauty

Tilden wrote that "the finest uses of national parks, or indeed any of the preserves that come within the range of interpretive work, lie ultimately in spiritual uplift."[25] Perhaps no other writer has so eloquently pursued the fleeting and ineffable nature of beauty as John Muir. He struggled, "Everything is so inseparably united. As soon as one begins to describe a flower or a tree or a storm . . . up jumps the whole heavens and earth and God Himself in one inseparable glory!"[26]

Muir's absorption with beauty was undoubtedly influenced by a time in his late twenties when an accident caused him to lose his sight. While working in a carriage factory, a sharp file slipped from Muir's hands and pierced his right eye; the aqueous humor dropped into his cupped hand. His other eye also became blind from sympathetic nervous shock. Muir was confined to a bed in a dark room for a month. Terrified by his loss of sight, he bemoaned his fate: "Closed forever on all God's beauty!" Seeing only glimpses of light at first, Muir slowly regained his vision. For the rest of his life Muir equated light with God. He bestowed upon his precious Yosemite and Sierra

> In beauty we reflect wonder and compassion.

the highest honor: "the range of light." Muir concluded, "No synonym for God is so perfect as Beauty."[27]

Muir believed that God's glory was written over all His works. Furthermore, exposure to nature's beauty transforms a person. Overwhelmed by beauty, Muir exulted, "You bathe in these spirit-beams, turning round and round, as if warming at a camp-fire. Presently you lose consciousness of your separate existence: you blend with the landscape, and become part and parcel of nature."[28] In this rapturous state, Muir believed that one might experience the fullest human integrity, the fundamental truths of existence, an understanding of the harmony of nature, the spiritual dimensions of beauty.

> No synonym for God is so perfect as Beauty.
>
> —JOHN MUIR

In the presence of beauty we feel oneness with the universe. We sense the order and perfection of nature. We rejoice in the moment amidst the harmony of the timeless whole. We feel peace and joy. The experience rings with truth. In beauty we reflect wonder and compassion.

Interpreters can carry out the profound act of interpreting beauty only if they first perceive it themselves and know strategies to bring it to the attention of others. Ultimately, the appreciation of beauty is deeply personal. It is not, as the cliché suggests, so much in the eye of the beholder, but in the heart of the beholder. Antoine de Saint-Exupéry, in his classic *The Little Prince*, wrote, "It is only with the heart that one can see rightly: what is essential is invisible to the eye."[29] This is the mystery of beauty. Interpreters celebrate this mystery by turning hearts toward beauty; and in bestowing this gift of beauty, interpreters can elicit inspiration and spiritual uplift.

> *Beauty is truth, truth beauty,—that is all*
> *Ye know on earth, and all ye need to know*
>
> **—John Keats**
> (Ode on a Grecian Urn)

C.P. 66
Mr. Celson's Pines
Evening of 3 June '68

© Tsuyoshi Matsumoto

CHAPTER
14

The Gift of Joy

Interpreters can promote optimal experiences through intentional and thoughtful program and facility design.

The conscious desire is to achieve a state, even momentarily, that, like light, is unbounded, nurturing, suffused with wisdom.

—Barry Lopez

Aristotle came to the conclusion, some 2,300 years ago, that more than anything else, people seek happiness. What defines happiness and what contributes to happiness? Mihalyi Csikszentmihalyi, a leading scholar on optimal experiences and best-selling author, has discovered that happiness is not contingent upon money or power or fame. It is not the result of random chance. It doesn't depend on outside events, but rather on how we interpret (perceive) them. Happiness comes as a consequence of being totally involved in our living.[1] Optimal experience, according to Csikszentmihalyi, is when we feel a sense of exhilaration, a deep sense of enjoyment, that comes when our bodies and minds are "stretched to [their] limits in a voluntary effort to accomplish something difficult and worthwhile."[2] Csikszentmihalyi called these moments of peak enjoyment "flow."

Settings that are effective in advancing learning and promoting optimal experiences are characterized by the absence of anything that might induce anxiety or stress. An attractive element of parks, museums, zoos, aquariums, historic sites, and other interpretive areas is that these are informal places generally free of stress and have inspirational qualities. Within these informal settings, we can promote situations in which joyous experiences are likely to occur.

Visitors in Flow

Interpretive professionals are in the business of creating and managing opportunities for enjoyment. They do not, however, produce that enjoyment. Only the visitor can do that.[3] Nonetheless, interpretive sites are conducive to the attainment of optimal experiences. Furthermore, interpreters can encourage optimal experiences through intentional and thoughtful program and facility design.

> Interpretive professionals are in the business of creating and managing opportunities for enjoyment. They do not, however, produce that enjoyment. Only the visitor can do that.

People come to places of cultural and natural significance during their leisure, although leisure means different things to different people and can range from relaxation to pushing oneself to the limits. At one end of the spectrum, many people simply need directions or basic information. Perhaps they will achieve an optimal experience when they reach their destination. Others are seeking a pleasurable and relaxing time, but nothing too demanding. Perhaps this moment of rest will serve as a foundation for subsequent growth. Some want to push themselves, even though they may not be consciously thinking in those terms. This concept of leisure is consistent with the Greek ideal of leisure (or "schole"), which was realized when individuals used their freedom to explore the limits of their potential. The value of leisure was not that it offered relaxation; on the contrary, it required effort to expand the range of one's physical, mental, or spiritual capacities.[4]

Although some dimensions of the flow experience are beyond the realm of interpreters' influence, other characteristics may be purposefully influenced. Csikszentmihalyi compiled eight characteristics that define optimal experiences. These have subsequently been reordered and renamed to form the acronym PACIFICS: purpose, attention, challenge, involvement, feedback, immersion, control, and sense of time.[5]

Purpose

The purpose of any given activity must be clear to promote optimal experiences. When we are unaware of why we are doing something, we are less able to achieve the goals. Therefore, purpose and expectations must be well-articulated before we can be fully goal-oriented.

Without purpose, we tend to lose focus and motivation, both of which are essential to achieving states of optimality. Interpreters should provide clear goals to their participants. Facilities should be designed so the purpose of exhibits, self-guiding trails, and other nonpersonal interpretation is evident. In personal interpretation, a stated purpose must capture the visitors' curiosity and attention and engage sustained interest so visitors can become fully involved in their experiences.

Attention

When we are in flow our attention is completely focused on the task at hand. This high level of concentration, when we are operating in the "here and now," is necessary to fulfill the conditions of a flow experience. Interpreters should strive to make their interpretation compelling enough to fully engage the attention of the audience members.

Challenge

If the challenge facing us is too demanding, we quickly lose interest or become anxious. This is why, for example, we don't ask third graders to read William Faulkner. But if the challenge is too simple, we tend to lose interest through boredom. Therefore, we don't ask university students to recite the letters of the alphabet. The challenge of the task must be equivalent to one's knowledge or level of skill to enable full involvement in the activity. Otherwise, we become anxious or bored, and our attention is not focused on the task.

Different visitors require different interpretive accommodations in which the challenges meet the skills of those participating. Enjoyment appears at the boundary between boredom and anxiety, when the challenges are just balanced with the person's knowledge or physical ability.[6] To meet the needs of a wide diversity of visitors, parks often offer a wide spectrum of trails that differ according to their length, type of terrain, and overall difficulty. Likewise, programs may be designed, as discussed in Chapter 6, specifically for children, teenagers, or seniors to meet the level of their interests and abilities.

> Enjoyment appears at the boundary between boredom and anxiety, when the challenges are just balanced with the person's knowledge or physical ability.

Application of this characteristic of flow could also be made at the level of visitor center or museum design. For example, information can be organized to reveal progressively more complex concepts. Perhaps the most simple information, presented via colorful illustrations and simple diagrams, would be at the height of children and more complex information and graphics would be presented at a higher level. Of course, this approach would have to be structured with sensitivity and with accessibility of the information to all visitors, including those in wheelchairs. Another possibility would be to design zones of information in increasing levels of complexity (such as having different areas of a museum or visitor center set aside for different levels of interest and knowledge). Finally, computer technology offers almost limitless possibilities for meeting varying degrees of complexity associated with the knowledge and skills visitors possess.

As a person's knowledge and skills increase, he or she tends to seek greater competence. An internal mechanism urges the individual to seek novel and increasingly complex challenges.[7] Interpreters must ask: "Are there provisions for developing skills at gradually increasing levels of competence?"[8]

Involvement

When people experience flow, they are not consumed with other less pleasant aspects of life. They are not worried about the past or concerned about the future. Csikszentmihalyi referred to this dimension of flow as the merging of action and awareness—people are completely absorbed in the experience.[9] What they are doing is inseparable from what they are thinking about.

Interpreters can promote high levels of visitor investment and involvement in the program to help accomplish a merging of action and awareness. Ideally, this will encompass the use of many different senses.

Feedback

Linked with the importance of clear goals is feedback, as appropriate, for those striving to reach the goals. Feedback allows those who are involved in an activity to track their progress. Feedback can also be a motivating factor that encourages people toward further learning or skill development.

Interactive computer-based exhibits can give immediate feedback acknowledging success. Quiz boards and many less sophisticated displays also can give immediate feedback. Sometimes goals may be far-reaching (over a long span of time), and feedback may be possible only in return visits to the site. In any case, providing feedback is important and may be accomplished by acknowledging progress and perhaps giving participants inexpensive but memorable items (such as certificates) for successful completion of the goal.[10]

Immersion

We noted above that when a mental or physical challenge is equivalent to one's aptitude or skill, one is immersed in the activity and does not regress into consideration of past or future concerns. According to Csikszentmihalyi, "One item that disappears from awareness deserves special mention, because in normal life we spend so much time thinking about it: our own self."[11] Being able to move, temporarily, beyond preoccupation with ourselves tends to be both healthy and enjoyable. It allows us, in the long run, to expand the concept of who we are.

Interpreters face the challenge of immersing participants in the interpretive event and assisting them to see beyond themselves temporarily. In flow, people are enriched by new attainments of knowledge and skill. Such achievements occur when we lose our self-consciousness, yet the self (as would be expected) emerges stronger after the experience, because we have grown.

Control

Optimal experiences are stimulated when people perceive that they have some sense of control. Allowing visitors control over their experiences can be promoted by interpreters who encourage a degree of choice or input in their programs. Although establishing a purpose is important, so is allowing individuals to express themselves within the context of the overall goals for a program. Settings that facilitate optimal experiences support personal autonomy and responsibility.

> **Being able to move, temporarily, beyond preoccupation with ourselves tends to be both healthy and enjoyable. It allows us, in the long run, to expand the concept of who we are.**

A sense of control also can be facilitated through nonpersonal interpretation. In active visitor center exhibits with multimedia technologies, visitors can have control by allowing them to select the nature, pace, and outcome of information presented.[12]

Sense of Time

The last defining quality of optimal experience is that when we are engaged in a challenging task, our perception of time is altered. This characteristic of flow may be expressed in two ways: 1) time seems to accelerate (hours seem to pass like minutes) or 2) the opposite occurs (minutes seem to pass like hours). Most often, in flow, time seems to pass quickly: time flies when we are having fun. Either way, our sense of time is quite different from the actual passage of time as measured by the clock. Although this is not necessarily a prerequisite for enjoyment, it is one of the most common descriptions associated with optimal experiences.[13] Interpretation that contributes to flow experiences may result in an altered sense of the passage of time—usually with visitors wondering how the time passed so quickly.

Interpreters in Flow

Yet another way to pursue the application of optimal experience theory, as it relates to interpretation, is to focus on flow experiences of the interpreter. Indeed, several professions involve work that is conducive to achieving a flow state. Csikszentmihalyi's research revealed that surgeons, music composers, basketball players, and modern dancers experience flow according to the eight dimensions set forth above.[14] Enos Mills commented, "Daily association with inspiring and ever-varying nature and the companionship of thoughtful people mean pleasure and steady development." The interpretive guide, Mills continued, "makes good by growing."[15]

Interpreters must understand the purpose and ramifications of what they are doing. Assisting interpreters in understanding both their privileges and obligations is the intent of this book. Without a sense of professional purpose we lose direction. We also lose motivation.

Clear goals must be set at several levels. First, the agency must have a clear purpose as stated in a mission statement. What is it that the agency wants to create, to offer, to contribute? Second, the interpretive supervisor must have a clear sense of direction. His or her sense of purpose will infiltrate the ranks of field interpreters. Third, interpreters themselves must have a clear sense of what they are striving to do. Interpreters are autonomous, self-sufficient, and generally self-directed. Therefore, we are responsible for developing and continually examining our own goals for meeting the needs of visitors.

As interpreters, ideally, we devote full attention to what we are doing in our work. We should be able to concentrate on the task at hand. This means that we should be able to have work spaces that are free of distractions. Furthermore, those areas where we perform our interpretation should be conducive to eliciting our best efforts. Site managers are responsible for seeing that work conditions are such that interpreters can concentrate without undue disruptions.

The competent interpreter is motivated to become even more so.

Just as visitors react to varying levels of challenges according to their skills, interpreters respond to various levels of work complexity. For example, it would be asking too much to require first-time seasonal interpreters to make a presentation in front of an audience of 250 people, or to interpret a controversial topic, in their first week of employment. Yet it is precisely this level of challenge that inspires the veteran interpreter. Without increasing levels of complexity, people become bored with what they are doing, but if the challenge is beyond their capabilities they become anxious.

The National Park Service developed a list of competencies that correspond to increasing skill development (see Chapter 10). In the National Park Service model, the competencies are made up of an increasing range of knowledge, skill, and ability. The interpreter must demonstrate competency at each level before moving to the next level. This framework is consistent with matching challenges to skills to promote optimal experiences. As Csikszentmihalyi noted, "One needs to grow, to develop new skills, to take on new challenges to maintain a self-concept as a fully functioning human being."[16] The competent interpreter is motivated to become even more so.

The most successful work output is that which fully involves us. We are most effective and most productive when we are totally engaged with the task at hand. Our work experiences should be structured so we may be completely invested in our interpretive efforts. Much of the success in this realm of optimal experience is dependent on the interpreter's ability to keep the mind from wandering, although this prospect is lessened if the activity is challenging and engaging.

To operate at the peak of our potential we must be attuned to the feedback we receive. One aspect of feedback comes from supervisors. Supervisors should be able to assist interpreters in meeting the needs of visitors, and in developing and presenting effective interpretation of the place. If the interpreter faces problems in the workplace, the supervisor should be able to help resolve them. Otherwise, the interpreter will be compromised in his or her pursuit of realizing full potential. Interpreters also receive audience feedback. Interpreters who are in a flow state when they perform in front of others are effective and enthusiastic communicators.

Interpreters may become fully immersed in their work. Moving temporarily beyond preoccupation with ourselves is mentally beneficial and enjoyable. We are fortunate to be in a profession in which the work is sufficiently stimulating that this full immersion occurs. Yet, as we shall see in the concluding chapter, it is what we have to offer that is most rewarding to us.

Total immersion in our work may proceed in several areas of our responsibility. For example, we may lose our self-consciousness through immersion in our research and study. We may become fully consumed in our creative organization of materials in the composition of the interpretation. We may become totally engaged in interpretive planning processes with our colleagues. Or we may be wholly invested in the presentation of an interpretive program. When we lose our self-consciousness is, undoubtedly, when we perform at our best.

As with others who achieve optimal experiences, interpreters must have some sense of control over their work environment. First, we must feel as if we are trusted; that we have flexibility to exercise independent judgment. Second, interpreters must be assured that responsible risk-taking is encouraged and rewarded in our efforts to achieve excellence. Failures should be considered acceptable learning experiences. Third, we must be allowed sufficient time to foster creativity and innovation. This reflective time should be incorporated into our schedules so we have time to think in imaginative ways. Fourth, supervisory roles should be structured to emphasize guiding, educating, advising, and encouraging, rather than regulating and controlling.[17] Interpreters should be given the fullest responsibility consistent with their capabilities. This empowerment, through controlling one's own contribution to the workplace, allows interpreters to continue growing to their fullest potential.

Interpreters fully engaged in their work will lose track of time. We often wish we had more time in a day. Time distortion may occur as we immerse ourselves in our study of the place or when we create a mix of our experience and knowledge that becomes our interpretation of a subject. It may occur when we are "on stage." Our sense of time becomes distorted when we are doing something for the love of the task.

With an understanding of optimal experience theory, interpreters are better equipped to serve visitors. When visitors are engaged in optimal experiences, in our places of cultural and natural wonder, they will be inclined to seek out further enjoyment, learning, and inspiration.

With an understanding of optimal experience theory, interpreters are better equipped to serve visitors.

With an understanding of optimal experience theory, interpreters can maximize enjoyment, productivity, and effectiveness in their own work. If we are joyous and enthusiastic, visitors will sense this positive energy, and it will be contagious, paving the way to powerful and enriching interpretive experiences. In all of its many nuances, this is the gift of joy.

Snatches of high insight, glimpses of beauty, stirrings of passion, excitement, or enthusiasm, communion with God may come when we are in harmony with the whole, at any time—in the eyes of a loved one, or the touch of a hand. One does not have to climb [a] peak; it can be felt when looking at a blossom, smelling fresh rain, leaves, and needles, or sensing gladness in a child. The important thing is to be aware—never a day without some event that springs of the spirit.

—**Sigurd Olson**

Sunday, June 4, 1978
Driveway to the Museum
mat SP 780

© Tsuyoshi Matsumoto

15

The Gift of Passion

Passion is the essential ingredient for powerful and effective interpretation—passion for the resource and for those people who come to be inspired by it.

*There is a single magic, a single power,
a single salvation, and a single happiness,
and that is called loving.*

—Hermann Hesse

Carl Sharsmith loved Yosemite National Park. He also loved interacting with visitors to the park over a career that spanned some 50 years. As a seasonal interpretive naturalist, his enthusiasm for Yosemite and for those to whom he interpreted its beauty was undiminished. He influenced thousands of visitors and the affinity he shared was reciprocal. As children who attended Sharsmith's interpretive programs grew up, they brought their own children to go on interpretive hikes with him. Sharsmith interacted with seemingly countless visitors who wished to experience and understand Yosemite's grandeur.

In the latter part of his career, Sharsmith was approached by a woman with a limited itinerary and an age-old question. She asked, "I've only got an hour to spend at Yosemite. What should I do? Where should I go?" In a slow, deliberate voice the elderly interpreter replied, "Ah lady. Only an hour. I suppose if I had only one hour to spend at Yosemite, I'd just walk over there by the river and sit down and cry."[1]

Carl Sharsmith, and interpreters like him, embody a noble passion for the resource they interpret and those who have come to be inspired by it. Tilden wrote that the "priceless ingredient" for effective interpretation is love.[2]

The Interpreter's Passion for the Resource

One does not generally speak about love, in modern culture, except in the most trivial sense of the word. Those who call upon others to practice brotherly and sisterly love are as likely to be ridiculed as to be taken seriously.[3] But as the priceless ingredient of interpretation it has a precise meaning. Interpreters can and do love the forests, the deserts, the canyons, the coasts, all the various landscapes, and the cultural sites at which they work. This passion for the resource, this intimacy, grows over time.

> In addition to being passionate for the interpretive site, the interpreter has a passion for sharing his or her knowledge and wisdom with others.

As with human love for one another, this expression takes meaning as we renew constantly our capacity for the complexity and wonder of the place we interpret. Eventually, a reciprocal relationship with the land becomes established in which we become aware that the landscape is aware of us. What can be achieved through this "erotic" bond is a spiritual connection with the place that brings peace, joy, astonishment, and fulfillment.[4]

In some countries interpreters demonstrate their love for the resource by making the ultimate sacrifice in protecting it. In the West African country of Cote d' Ivoire, two or three park rangers (functioning as guides and interpreters) are killed each year by poachers. At Comoe National Park, Lobi tribesmen hunt and kill both game and rangers with poison arrows. Empowered by the village fetishers, the poachers gain psychological if not spiritual advantage over the rangers. The ill-equipped rangers are often less familiar with the terrain than poachers and may lack proper shoes, functioning guns, binoculars, radios, or other equipment. They are no match for the local hunters. Those who do not die protecting the parks also pay a severe price. Park rangers are social outcasts and are subject to ridicule. They also may work for months without paychecks. These African rangers work because they love the landscape and want to protect their vanishing forests and wildlife.

In addition to being passionate for the interpretive site, the interpreter has a passion for sharing his or her knowledge and wisdom with others.

The Interpreter's Passion for People

Love is patient, love is kind.

—1 Corinthians 13:4

Interpreters enthusiastically share their passion for the resource with others. This does not mean that the interpreter loves audience members in a romantic sense, but rather has a passion for educating, enlightening, and inspiring them. We feel a sense of obligation, out of respect for the resource and those who have come to enjoy it, to craft a worthy interpretation of the place.

Many people do not have the luxury of enjoying their work or of having a career that becomes an intricate part of their lifestyle. Barry Lopez wrote, "Such a life speaks to a need many of us have but few can attend to—long-lived intimacy with a place, being able to speak of it knowledgeably to others."[5]

Throngs of the employed battle traffic and suffer long hours indoors, often doing mundane chores, in contrast to work enjoyed by interpreters in places of natural or cultural beauty. And that is precisely what Tilden suggested we remember when we are dealing with less than courteous visitors: "the pestiferous, the unmanageable, the ineducable, and some whose apparent reason for existence is to provide the hangman with work."[6] The interpreter's role is to understand these people, to be patient, and to enlist visitor's higher capacities to appreciate where they are at the moment. This is empathetic love.

> Such a life speaks to a need many of us have but few can attend to—long-lived intimacy with a place, being able to speak of it knowledgeably to others.
>
> —BARRY LOPEZ

Interpreters must treat their clientele with respect. Although we may know more about a certain segment of history, or the ecology of a place, we may not have the medical, mechanical, musical, or management expertise of those who are with us. So we may assume, for the essential sake of our own humility, that some members of the audience may be at least as accomplished as we are.

Our relationship to the visiting public has yet another dimension. In our quest to satisfy the visitor, we must not lose our integrity. The purpose of the interpreter is not to fill a void for the visitor who has come expecting to be entertained.[7] Furthermore, if a visitor becomes abusive—disturbs other people or harms the resource—then, and only then, but at that point decisively, the interpreter must notify the unwelcome guest that he or she has exceeded the bounds of reasonable decorum.

Of course, self-absorbed interpreters and self-indulgent visitors are the exceptions to the rule. If we treat others with respect and trust, we may expect the same in return.

Some interpreters have a passion for working in areas where both the human and natural resources may need restoration. An urban park or other setting may be used as a vehicle to help people.[8] Some interpreters' love for people is so great that they take personal risks to interpret to them. Interpreter Robin White, herself a former gang member, for years led Gary, Indiana, gang members into the Indiana Dunes National Lakeshore on day and overnight field trips. Debbie Chavez and her USDA Forest Service staff work with Los Angeles gang members by taking them to the nearby Angeles National Forest.

In addition to federal agencies, many private organizations introduce people to nature who would not otherwise experience it and who can benefit greatly from that exposure. The Student Conservation Association, Outward Bound, the Environmental Career Organization, and the North American Association for Environmental Education all have programs targeting inner-city youth.

Rather than taking people to distant natural areas, some programs interpret the resources that surround people in their neighborhoods. In Los Angeles, a program called WOW (Wonderful Outdoor World) uses city parks and playgrounds as camping and nature study sites. WOW is a partnership program with public agencies including the Bureau of Land Management, USDA Forest Service, National Park Service, California State Parks, California Fish and Game, Los Angeles City Parks, California State University-Long Beach, and private organizations such as the National Outdoor Leadership School and the Walt Disney Corporation. This program offers children the opportunity to camp in a Los Angeles city park. During the outing, environmental education activities teach ecological concepts to the children, and they learn map reading, fishing, and camping skills.

Interpreters with these programs care about people first, regardless of the quality of the surrounding natural resource base. When they cannot take people to natural areas, they love interpreting the magic of nature found in vacant lots, school yards, and city parks. They conserve lives, not just resources.

The Role of Passion in Inspiring Others

My message is my life.

—Ghandi

Passion plays a role in influencing visitors. It gives the interpreter a certain charm and credibility. Visitors are more likely to listen to someone who brims with enthusiasm, who is passionate about the place, and who is fired up about his or her work.

Why are some people passionate and others are not? We don't pretend to know the full answer, but we are compelled to delve deeper into this subject for no other reason than this world would be a better place if there were less deceit, less pessimism, less apathy—and more truth, optimism, and passion.

How can we, as interpreters, express the best in human nature? Although this question is ultimately reduced to the level of the individual, we offer some generic thoughts. Through our passion for the resources we interpret, we may bring out a similar passion in those to whom we interpret. To draw visitors into a full appreciation of the interpretive setting, the interpreter displays an affinity for the resource and a respect for humanity. We introduce to visitors something we love, not something we own.

> Passion plays a role in influencing visitors. It gives the interpreter a certain charm and credibility.

Interpreters may also convey their passion by hinting that what we do isn't a job or occupation, but rather a way of life. According to Barry Lopez, the calling is a high calling that many in our society don't recognize.[9]

We can promote our work by serving as role models to the public. We have the opportunity to reveal our quality of life as a result of staying close to, and continuing to learn from, the landscape and our heritage. This relationship with our world, marked by learning that turns to wisdom, and the sense of awe, appreciation, and joy it brings—this relationship is something that visitors will notice. And perhaps they will ask themselves what they might learn from an interpreter's connection to his or her place and consequent passion for life. For many interpreters this passion comes seemingly naturally. Others have to work harder at it. What can we suggest?

A Practical Guide to Passion

This is the day the LORD has made;
Let us rejoice and be glad in it.

—Psalm 118:24

Barry Lopez once told one of the authors that it is "terrifically difficult to be a decent human being." With full concurrence with Lopez's observation, we offer the following discussion.

Carpe diem: Sieze the day. With every sunrise come new opportunities to experience the world, to enjoy others, and to serve them through our work. Recognizing that we are responsible for choosing and defining our lives is essential. We must be open to growth and change—to pursue learning—from books, other people, introspection, our experiences. We should strive toward being proactive; to look at our options and choose wisely. As Leo Buscaglia insisted:

> We're afraid of living life, therefore we don't experience, we don't see. We don't feel. We don't risk. We don't care! And therefore we don't live—because life means being actively involved. Life means getting your hands dirty. Life means jumping in the middle of it all. Life means falling flat on your face. Life means going beyond yourself—into the stars.[10]

Nothing can change our lives more rapidly, or entail more real or imagined risk, than the consistent outflow of love and passion for life. Everything in our lives—career, family, friends, lifestyle, contributions to the community—can be transformed through love. Loving all aspects of life, regardless of challenges we may be facing, opens doors and brings forth energy and joy.[11] When we choose to live an inspiring life, we make a difference in the lives of everyone else with whom we interact.

We have the opportunity to reveal our quality of life as a result of staying close to, and continuing to learn from, the landscape and our heritage.

One of the greatest challenges facing the individual, and the world, finds its roots in a lack of love, a lack of a sense of interdependence. Regardless of the situations, or the people we may feel inclined to dislike, we must resist the temptation. Ernest Holmes wrote, "In some way we have to find something of value in them, no matter how big or little it may be. Find something to like."[12] This approach is not altogether selfless. Our health, both physical and emotional, is related to the amount of love or hate in our lives.

What I fear and desire most in this world is passion.
I fear it because it promises to be spontaneous,
out of my control, unnamed, beyond my reasonable self.
I desire it because passion has color, like the landscape
before me. It is not pale. It is not neutral.
It reveals the backside of the heart.

–Terry Tempest Williams

The Interpreter's Creed

As a Practicing Interpreter, I Shall:

- Seek to serve visitors; to be an ambassador for the place I work; to instill in visitors the ability and desire to sense beauty in their surroundings.

- Seek to respect all the visitors with whom I come in contact and welcome them as I would welcome guests in my home; and to share equally my knowledge and passion regardless of the visitor's age, gender, interests, physical abilities, or cultural differences.

- Seek to be agreeable, look good, have a polished presence, speak in a well-modulated voice, and be genuinely friendly.

- Seek to see the good, or the humor, in any situation and answer repetitious questions with enthusiasm, as if they were asked for the first time.

- Seek to convey only well-documented, accurate information.

- Seek to be an exemplary role model for environmentally responsible behavior by word and example.

- Seek to structure interpretive design and programming in such a way as to minimize the impact on cultural and environmental resources.

- Seek to improve my mind, continue learning about the resource, and expand my learning about the principles and processes of interpretation that will ultimately benefit visitors to the site.

- Seek to help other interpreters achieve their interpretive goals, particularly assisting new interpreters to develop confidence and abilities.

- Believe in myself; give my best to the world and expect that the world will give its best to me.

Sunday, June 18, 1978
Parry Grove Trail

© Tsuyoshi Matsumoto

CONCLUSION

The Gift of Hope

You give but little when you give of your possessions.
It is when you give of yourself that you truly give.

—Kahlil Gibran

We began this book with a celebration of the contributions of Enos Mills and Freeman Tilden to an ever-evolving philosophy of interpretation. Their work has permeated, in varying degrees, the principles set forth in the balance of the book. We now come full circle and return to them in our conclusion.

Mills (in *Adventures of a Nature Guide and Essays in Interpretation*) and Tilden (in *Interpreting Our Heritage*) agreed that the work of the interpreter is like that of an artist. Mills wrote, simply, "A nature guide is an artist."[1]

Quality interpretation demands background preparation and the learning of technique, just as in the traditional arts. And like in poetry, music, sculpture, theater, and painting, a certain creative element (personal, individualized) is associated with interpretation of cultural and natural history.

A nature guide is an artist.

—ENOS MILLS

Lewis Hyde, in *The Gift*, suggests that a work of art is a gift and not a commodity.[2] If interpretation is an art, and a work of art is a gift, then it follows that interpretation must be a gift. The interpreter, like the artist, bears a gift. In this book, we have presented 15 gifts that interpreters give to others.

The Interpreter's Plight

The gift-giving work of the interpreter, like that of the artist, is often misunderstood and unappreciated. W. B. Yeats, in the first stanza of a poem titled "Adam's Curse," seems to capture the plight of interpreters, who, like artists, labor out of love but are not always valued by the public. Their work is considered superfluous by some of the world, yet the commitment and perseverance to create inspiring art is far more difficult than the most demanding physical labor. Yeats wrote:

> We sat together at one summer's end,
> That beautiful mild woman, your close friend,
> And you and I, and talked of poetry.
> I said: 'A line will take us hours maybe;
> Yet if it does not seem a moment's thought,
> Our stitching and unstitching has been naught.
> Better go down upon your marrow-bones
> And scrub a kitchen pavement, or break stones
> Like an old pauper, in all kinds of weather;
> For to articulate sweet sounds together
> Is to work harder than all these, and yet
> Be thought an idler by the noisy set . . .'[3]

Interpreters interpret because they love their work and want to share the gifts of their profession. This includes the place itself—a place of cultural significance or natural wonder—and the interpreter's creative rendition of the place.

Creating the Gift

At one level, the interpreter has a gift. That gift is the interpreter's talent and "although a talent can be perfected through an effort of the will, no effort in the world can cause its initial appearance."[4]

In addition, the inspiration an artist receives is a gift. As an artist (interpreter) works, an idea pops into his or her mind—some aspect of one's artistic creation (interpretation) is bestowed upon the creator. D. H. Lawrence observed, "Not I, not I, but the wind that blows through me."[5]

Robert Finch, a nature writer, stays attuned to the creative impulse that often reveals itself in a sudden change: "right in the middle of things—from what you expected to find to what you do find."[6]

> Interpreters interpret because they love their work and want to share the gifts of their profession.

Gary Snyder, writer and poet, concurs: "You get a good poem, and you don't know where it came from. 'Did I say that?' And so all you feel is: you feel humility and you feel gratitude. And you'd feel a little uncomfortable, I think, if you capitalized too much on that without admitting at some point that you got it from the Muse, or whoever, wherever, or however."[7]

Note that these two elements of gift—talent and inspiration—are associated with the creation of the work. These elements are the gift at the level of the artist or the "inner life of art."[8]

Giving the Gift

Most interpreters, like many artists, are in their profession for reasons other than financial gain. The challenge and joy of the work is rewarding, along with the knowledge that one is giving a gift that cannot be measured monetarily.

The notion of gift, addressed above in terms of its "inner life," can be extended to its "outer life" as well. This "outer life" is when the gift is given and received. Even when a fee is involved, when we are truly touched by a work of art, something is bestowed upon us that has nothing to do with the price.[9]

Our response to the art may illumine our world, foster our recognition of beauty, generate an energetic optimism, stimulate our sense of truth, revive the soul, set us on a courageous course of action, or simply overwhelm the senses. In the presence of meaningful art, we feel as if we have been touched by a resonating chord. At its absolute best, this describes all art, including interpretation. Art communicates what cannot be said in mere words; it brings us to a point beyond the complacent and the mundane where our minds and spirits soar.

Keeping the Gifts in Motion

According to Hyde, "the spirit of a gift is kept alive by its constant donation."[10] This means that the gift must not be removed from circulation. Protecting a place of cultural or natural significance ensures that the gift will be available for all people and to future generations. Unless the site is exploited or compromised, its gift properties are constantly available. The first and most important lesson is: Do not destroy the gift.

> The challenge and joy of the work is rewarding, along with the knowledge that one is giving a gift that cannot be measured monetarily.

Another way to look at circulating the gift is in how people who introduced us to our passion, our life's work, have inspired us. We have all had mentors who shared the gift of nature or culture in the broadest sense. These mentors may have been grade school teachers or university professors. They may have been colleagues or supervisors. They may have been parents or writers. Our mentors taught us about nature or history, and they taught us how, by their example, to inspire others just as they had inspired us. By perpetuating the example of our mentors, we keep the gift in motion. Those who are now motivated by our words and actions continue to keep the gift alive as they share it with others. What is given is supposed to be given away again, not to the originator of the gift, but to someone else.

In tribal societies, such as the Kula of the South Sea islands near the eastern tip of New Guinea, this mode of circular giving involves tangible gifts—necklaces or armshells. Hyde notes, "When I give to someone from whom I do not receive (and yet I do receive elsewhere), it is as if the gift goes around a corner before it comes back. I have to give blindly. And I will feel a sort of blind gratitude as well."[11] Interpreters, although giving less tangible gifts, also give and receive blindly with a faith that a good gift has been given and a good gift will be received in turn.

A gift may also come from Nature or the Creator: watching the behavior of a wolverine or seeing the alpenglow of a mountain at sunset as a full moon rises above it, reflected on a lake. If we open ourselves up to receive them, we receive gifts that entertain, inspire, enrich, and restore us. We may pass these gifts along; that is, communicate them to an audience in such a way that they comprehend the wonder of what was observed and seek out similar experiences.

The Maori, natives of New Zealand, enlarge the circle beyond the body of the tribe to include nature and the gods. In the traditional hunting ritual, the forest provides food for the hunters, the hunters give to the priests, and the priests give back to the forest and the deities—giving thanks in return for the sustenance the forest provides. Here we find a spiritual dimension of gifts beyond the scope of this book. Yet we note that this passage into the unknown and mystical is invigorating.

> Art communicates what cannot be said in mere words; it brings us to a point beyond the complacent and the mundane where our minds and spirits soar.

We are exhilarated when gifts "arise from pools we cannot fathom."[12] Without a knowledge of boundaries we find that gifts are inexhaustible.

The Gift of Hope

And now these three remain: faith, hope and love.

—1 Corinthians 13:13

Although we have presented 15 gifts given by interpreters, as we look toward the future, we believe interpreters can offer one more gift—possibly the most important gift: hope. The world is a place of incredible beauty and great joy, while at the same time being a place of environmental degradation and tremendous human suffering. When we become blind to the beauty in the world and focus on the squalor, we are immobilized. If we lose hope that we can improve our personal lives, our communities, and our world, then we fall into despair and apathy.[13]

In March 1968, just before his death, Martin Luther King, Jr. gave a sermon titled "The Meaning of Hope." In his sermon, he noted that faith undergirds hope and love fuels it. Hope is in the center. He added, "Hope grows out of the faith that life has an ultimate meaning."[14] Hope for something better drives the possibility of it happening. Hope raises our awareness and motivates us in the right direction.

Hope allows us to be happy and productive in spite of circumstances. Vaclav Havel, while imprisoned, wrote these words, "Hope is an orientation of the spirit, an orientation of the heart; it transcends the world that is immediately experienced, and is anchored somewhere beyond its horizons."[15]

Martin Luther King, Jr. in the aforementioned sermon called unbound, unjustified optimism, "magic hope" and noted that, "Before Easter you have to get by Good Friday."[16] Interpreters can offer hopeful messages while acknowledging and confronting the many problems that shape our world.

> **Hope for something better drives the possibility of it happening. Hope raises our awareness and motivates us in the right direction.**

Admiral Jim Stockdale, a POW during the Vietnam War, sheds more light on the importance of a deeper faith in a brighter future. Admiral Stockdale, the highest-ranking officer in the Hanoi Hilton, was tortured more than 20 times over eight years and even beat himself with a stool and cut himself with a razor so that he could not be used in propaganda films as a "well-treated prisoner." In his book, *Good to Great*, author Jim Collins relates a conversation with Admiral Stockdale in which the Admiral explains how he survived and why others didn't.

When asked how he survived he replied, "I never lost faith in the end of the story. I never doubted that not only I would get out, but also that I would prevail in the end and turn the experience into the defining event of my life, which, in retrospect, I would not trade."[17]

> Interpreters can offer hopeful messages while acknowledging and confronting the many problems that shape our world.

The fact that Admiral Stockdale had hope in how the story would end is both amazing and encouraging. However, when he speaks about who did not make it, we can learn an important lesson. These prisoners thought they'd be out by Christmas. And when Christmas passed they thought they'd be out by Easter. And when Easter passed they thought they would be out by Thanksgiving. And then they were back at Christmas again. Stockdale said these prisoners "died of a broken heart."[18]

The lesson that Stockdale shared with Jim Collins is, "to never confuse faith that you will prevail in the end—which you can never afford to lose—with the discipline to confront the most brutal facts of your current reality, whatever they might be."[19]

Interpreters are uniquely positioned to offer hope in any situation and at any point in history. The beauty of human integrity commemorated in events of the past and the beauty of the intricacies of nature give rise to hope, and these are the tools of the interpreter.

Moreover, our role in giving the gift of hope increases during troubled times. G.K. Chesterton noted that hope is only a strength when things are most hopeless. "As long as matters are really hopeful, hope is a mere flattery or platitude; it is only when everything is hopeless that hope begins to be a strength. Like all Christian virtues, it is as unreasonable as it is indispensable."[20]

> The beauty of human integrity commemorated in events of the past and the beauty of the intricacies of nature give rise to hope, and these are the tools of the interpreter.

To offer hope, interpreters must possess that "orientation of the spirit" and a sense of something "beyond the horizon" about the potential of the human condition. This heartfelt conviction that we can make change for the better feeds our dedication. Without hope, there would be no purpose; without purpose, there would be no passion; and without passion, interpretation is hollow.

A Profession of Giving

We have the privilege of receiving gifts and the obligation of passing them along. The joy of the gifts, for the interpreter, is in the giving. The profession is a noble one in that we are serving others by providing life-enriching gifts. We do so with very little expected in return—mostly joy from giving the gifts.

We continue to learn and be inspired (receive), and we continue to interpret (give) from our wealth of knowledge and experience. Our gift is in helping others to see and in so doing we gain resolution in our own vision. As Mills wrote, "The essence of [interpretation] is to travel gracefully rather than to arrive."[21]

As interpreters, we are blessed with many gifts, and may it always be our obligation and blessing to share the gifts of interpretation with others.

H Kagan '11

EPILOGUE

Part I: About the Artwork and the Artists

When the raven delivered a pine cone to us as we walked along the shore at Torrey Pines State Reserve (TPSR), as detailed in the Prologue, we felt an impetus to change the title of this book. As we completed this edition, we decided to use an illustration of a Torrey Pine cone for the section breaks throughout the book. A quick Internet search brought up the Torrey Pines Association, a nonprofit that supports TPSR; its newsletter masthead features a Torrey Pine cone. This was going to be easy, it seemed. We just needed to find out who drew the pine cone and get permission to use it.

In the meantime, I recalled a simple publication that I had bought at the TPSR museum many years ago. The pages in the little booklet are hand-numbered and held together with two staples. The booklet contains hauntingly beautiful drawings of Torrey Pine trees by a Japanese artist. I appreciated that each detailed sketch conveyed the personality of the trees and that many were given names: "The Song of Faith," "The 1585 Tree of Joy," "Where You Touch Heaven," and "Happiness—The Sunset Tree."

The booklet is titled *The Story of Mat*, and as I read the brief content I learned that Tsuyoshi Matsumoto (Mat) was born in Hokkaido, Japan. Although his father, a medical doctor, was Buddhist, his mother converted to Christianity. Mat went on to study at a missionary college in Tokyo and seminaries in San Francisco and New York. Mat enjoyed painting in oils and drawing pine trees from around the world. He and his wife eventually settled in New York, where he managed his own gallery. In his retirement years, he was encouraged to travel to La Jolla to see the unique Torrey Pine. He was so enamored with these trees that he and his wife moved to La Jolla, where Mat spent his days at TPSR sketching trees. In the following years, he filled boxes of sketchbooks and sold some of the final prints to private collectors. At the end of the booklet's synopsis of Mat's life was a footnote thanking his family for their kind permission to use his drawings.

No one knew who drew the Torrey Pine cone for the newsletter masthead. Perhaps it was Mat. At this point, Ted and I were also interested in the possibility of using some of Mat's artwork in this volume. I eventually reached the president of the Torrey Pines Association, which led to contact with Helen Kagan, Mat's surviving daughter.

Helen and her husband live in a beautiful home that overlooks a nature preserve with a magnificent view of the Pacific Ocean. Three mature Torrey Pines adorn their yard. Upon entering the home you see a series of large framed panels: a panorama of Torrey Pines by Helen's father.

I explained the project and my belief that *The Gifts of Interpretation* was consistent with the spirit of Mat's art and his advocacy for conservation. I told Helen about the raven and the pine cone, and how that led me to her. I explained my academic discipline and the meaning of interpretation. Then Helen brought out several sketchbooks filled with Mat's drawings of pines. She told me more about her father and her family.

Mat was an artist of many talents: he painted, sketched, played the organ, and wrote poetry. Helen shared with me some of the poems her father wrote when he was suffering from a terminal illness; they were deeply spiritual verses about life's meaning, gratitude, and the wonders of the natural world. Helen conveyed that Mat loved to listen to Bach while sketching and would flick his wrist to the music as he drew the myriad pine needles. Helen's husband, Ron, indicated that he once mentioned to his father-in-law that he wished he had the patience to draw every pine needle in detail. Mat's response was to note that it wasn't about patience: It was all about passion.

Why was Mat so obsessed with pine trees? As I came to learn, Matsumoto (Mat's last name) means "root of the pine." Part of the answer also lies in his culture. The pine is a symbol of good luck and longevity in Japan. In winter, pines symbolize hope—longer days, new life, the advent of spring. The illustrations in this book feature pines Mat sketched from around the world, including those at the Imperial Palace in Japan, ancient bristlecone pines found in the highest mountains of western America, and Torrey Pines. Yet another aspect of Mat's passion for pines is that he saw in them a glimpse of the divine. He found solace among the pines, a sanctuary that offered inspiration and rapture; like John Muir, he found a place where he communed with God.

In the next several weeks, Helen and I held a series of long afternoon meetings. One visit, when we made the first round of selections that would be thematic for each of the book chapters, lasted more than five hours. Still, in going through all the sketchbooks, Helen could not find the illustration of the Torrey Pine cone we were seeking (and that artist, to this day, remains unknown). She found a beautiful drawing of a pine cone from another species, but not a Torrey Pine.

At one of our meetings, Helen shared her own paintings with me. Later that evening, it struck me that perhaps Helen would be willing to draw the pine cone that we hoped to have represent each gift. When asked, she said it might not be as good as her father's work, but she was willing to try. When I next came to visit, she had completed the drawing that is featured throughout this book.

Everything Helen provided—permission to include her father's artwork, her drawing of the pine cone, personal meetings with printers about scanning the images for publication, wonderful hospitality at her home—was a gift. As authors, we are deeply grateful for Helen's generosity and for how the artwork adorns the book and complements the written content for readers. And we recall that none of this would have come about if not for a raven dropping a pine cone, from high above, that landed at our feet; we are grateful for that gift as well.

Part II: The Torrey Pine

Visited Torrey Pines State Reserve the other day
Where everything, fauna and flora, is let naturally growing
God's own garden, incredibly beautiful, serene, peaceful, unified
All in perfect harmony.

—Mat

The Torrey Pine is among the rarest of pines, and is found naturally in only two geographically isolated locations. It grows on a narrow strip of land, four miles long and within a mile of the coast, just south of Del Mar, California. Remarkably, and somewhat mysteriously, a second and smaller population is found on Santa Rosa Island, part of Channel Islands National Park, 200 miles to the north. The *Pinus torreyana* was described as a new species in 1850, the same year California became a state. The species was named after Dr. John Torrey, one of the foremost American botanists of the time.

The Torrey Pine inspired conservation efforts beginning in the late 1800s. By the early 1900s, philanthropist Ellen Browning Scripps acquired several groves of the pines. Even so, the trees were being steadily destroyed for firewood. By 1959, land was conveyed to the State of California as a reserve, and an extension was added in 1974 as a result of citizen advocacy.

Although the population of Torrey Pines may have dwindled to as few as 50 trees during a dry period some 3,000 years ago (a theory supported by sediment records of relative pollen deposits), the population is estimated to be 6,000 today. The TPSR provides a case study of species conservation because the first step is to identify critical habitat encompassing the endangered species and set it aside for protection. Nonetheless, a number of threats remain, including climate change, exotic competitors, insect pests such as pine beetles, and heavy recreational use.

The physical characteristics of the Torrey Pine vary. Trees on eroding cliffs that face the Pacific Ocean are shorter and more scraggly than those that grow farther inland, which are erect and much taller. The coastal trees tend to have distinct growth patterns because they have been shaped by constant winds. Torrey Pine cones are large, thick-scaled, and require three years to mature. The seeds are hard and sweet, and were gathered by the native Kumeyaay. The seedlings grow in loose sandstone soils and seedling survival is low. Because obtaining water and nutrients is difficult, a small seedling's roots can go down three feet and an adult tree can have roots that extend 200 feet.

The Torrey Pine teaches us valuable lessons. If we are lucky to live long enough, we are certain to encounter hardship. Torrey Pines are survivors, stubbornly clinging to life in harsh conditions where other trees are unable to grow. Root systems develop slowly to build a firm foundation. Like people who have triumphed over adversity, each tree displays a character, a ruggedness—a beauty uniquely its own—that would not exist if it had an easier life.

Part III: One Last Word

Love.

We have already touched on love as the force behind passion in Chapter 15. We return to it here to complete the book. Freeman Tilden wrote, "If you love the thing you interpret, and love the people who come to enjoy it, you need commit nothing to memory." Love is a certain measure for success in our careers and in our lives. It is essential, now more than ever, in this complicated world we inhabit.

The atrocities that abound—crimes against nature, creatures, humanity— are a mirror of the lack of love. We need to stand up for what is right, while at the same time not perpetuating the violence, for hatred kills off life, beauty, relationships, and joy. Regardless of differences, we share this tiny speck of dust in the universe with a family of humans and other living things: a community of life. Operating from the wisdom of our hearts, we want to protect each of those sacred things, each a miracle, that comprises the community, but in ways that promote peace and harmony.

Many people are faced with a conundrum. On one hand, knowing what to do with our time is difficult because the world is so seductive and so much beauty is here to behold. Yet, on the other hand, so much work needs to be done to protect that beauty and so many causes require our engagement to make the world a better place. Therefore, planning one's day can be difficult. But interpreters are able to do both of these things simultaneously by balancing enjoyment of beauty with advocacy for beauty, thus inhabiting a place between the extremes where we can live without regret.[1]

We have something unique, something honest, something beautiful, something profound, something hopeful, something inspiring, something grand to share with others. This is the interpreter's covenant with the profession, to share the gifts of interpretation, which is indeed a labor of love.

It's time to marvel and rejoice amidst the wonders of our cultural and natural diversity. Concurrently, it's time to share those wonders with others in such a way that we ignite a spark in each of them, a spark that may one day save the world.

> *Nature is universal. She hoists no flag of hatred.*
> *The supreme triumph of parks is humanity. …Sometime it may be that an*
> *immortal pine will be the flag of a*
> *united and peaceful world.*

> **—Enos Mills**

© Tsuyoshi Matsumoto

NOTES

Preface

1. Mills, E., 1920, *Adventures of a Nature Guide and Essays in Interpretation,* p. 6.
2. Ibid, p. 12.
3. Ibid, p. 111.
4. Tilden, F., 1977, *Interpreting Our Heritage.*
5. Lewis, W., 1980, *Interpreting for Park Visitors.*
6. Ham, S., 1992, *Environmental Interpretation.*
7. Knudson, D., Cable, T. and & L. Beck, 2003, *Interpretation of Cultural and Natural Resources,* 2nd Edition.
8. Brochu, L. & T. Merriman, 2008, *Personal Interpretation,* 2nd edition.
9. Leftridge, A., 2006, *Interpretive Writing.*
10. Brochu, L., 2003, *Interpretive Planning.*
11. Merriman, T. & L. Brochu, 2005, *Management of Interpretive Sites.*
12. Caputo, P., Lewis, S., & L. Brochu, 2008, *Interpretation by Design.*
13. Knapp, D., 2007, *Applied Interpretation.*

Introduction

1. Leopold, A., 1949, *A Sand County Almanac.*
2. Tilden, F., 1977, *Interpreting Our Heritage.*
3. Mills, E., 1920, *Adventures of a Nature Guide and Essays in Interpretation,* p. 130.
4. Tilden, F., Undated, *The Fifth Essence,* pp. 56-7.
5. Mills, p. 128.
6. Mills, p. 128.
7. Cable, T. & L. Cadden, 2007, "The Common Roots of Environmental Education and Interpretation."
8. Tilden, 1977, p. 9.
9. Mills, p. 126.
10. Ibid, p. 158.
11. Tilden, 1977, p. 9.
12. Mills, p. 6.
13. Ibid, p. 130.
14. Tilden, 1977, p. 9.
15. Mills, p. 170.
16. Tilden, 1977, p. 9.
17. Mills, p. 170.
18. Tilden, 1977, p. 9.
19. Mills, p. 129.
20. Tilden, 1977, p. 9
21. Mills, p. 120.

22. Cable, T. & L. Beck, 2001, "The Need for Interpretation: Now More than Ever." This essay may also be found in a book by the authors, published in 2010, titled *Interpretive Perspectives: A Collection of Essays on Interpreting Nature and Culture.*
23. Carson, R., [1956], 1998, *The Sense of Wonder*, pp. 100-101.
24. Nash, R., 2001, *Wilderness and the American Mind.*
25. Jefferson, T., [1820], 1993, In: Baron, R., *Jefferson The Man: In His Own Words*, p. 18. (Letter to William Charles Jarvis, September 28, 1820.)

Chapter 1

1. Wurman, R.S., 1989, *Information Anxiety*, p. 138.
2. Tilden, F., 1977, *Interpreting Our Heritage.*
3. Beck, L., 2001, "What is the Essence of Our Professional Responsibility?" This essay may also be found in a book by the authors, published in 2010, titled *Interpretive Perspectives: A Collection of Essays on Interpreting Nature and Culture.*
4. Hammitt, W., 1981, "A Theoretical Foundation for Tilden's Interpretive Principles."
5. Knopf, R., 1981, "Cognitive Map Formation as a Tool for Facilitating Information Transfer in Interpretive Programming."
6. Hammitt, p. 10.
7. Sylwester, R. & Joo-yun Cho, 1992/1993, "What Brain Research Says About Paying Attention."
8. Ibid, p. 72.
9. Silverman, L.H., 1997, "Personalizing the Past: A Review of the Literature with Implications for Historical Interpretation."
10. Barrie, E., 2001, "Ingredients of Meaningful Interpretive Experiences."
11. Ham, S., 2009, "From Interpretation to Protection: Is There a Theoretical Basis?"
12. Anderson, J. & D. Blahna, 1995, "Who Are These People, and What do They Want? Assessment of Interpreters' Knowledge of Their Audience."
13. Ibid.
14. Hood, M., 1991, "Significant Issues in Museum Audience Research."
15. Loomis, R., 1996, "How Do We Know What the Visitor Knows? Learning From Interpretation."
16. Vance, C. & D. Schroeder, 1991, "Matching Visitor Learning Style with Exhibit Type: Implications for Learning in Informal Settings."
17. Bixler, R., Carlisle, C., Hammitt, W. & M. Floyd, 1994, "Observed Fears and Discomforts Among Urban Students on School Field Trips to Wildland Areas."
18. Csikszentmihalyi, M. & K. Hermanson, 1995, "Intrinsic Motivation in Museums: What Makes Visitors Want to Learn?"
19. Becker, C. L., 1932, "Everyman His Own Historian."
20. Thelen, D., 1991, "History Making in America."
21. Silverman.
22. Ibid.
23. Romey, W.D., 1968, *Inquiry Techniques for Teaching Science.*
24. Everhart, W., 1988, "Some Thoughts for Those Who Charm and Inform," p. T6.
25. France, A., quoted in Tilden, F., "Foreword to the Second Edition," by George Hartzog.

Chapter 2

1. Mills, E., 1920, *Adventures of a Nature Guide and Essays in Interpretation*, p. 180.
2. Ibid, p. 126.
3. Tilden, F., 1977, *Interpreting Our Heritage*.
4. Ibid, p. 18.
5. See Dahlen, D., et al., 2000, "The Process of Interpretation: A Five-Session Study of Effective Interpretation"
6. Larsen, D., Editor, 2003, *Meaningful Interpretation: How to Connect Hearts and Minds to Places, Objects, and Other Resources*.
7. Beck, L., 2001, "What is the Essence of Our Professional Responsibility?" This essay may also be found in a book by the authors, published in 2010, titled *Interpretive Perspectives: A Collection of Essays on Interpreting Nature and Culture*.
8. Dahlen, D., et al.
9. Beck, L., 2001, and McCullough, D., 2002, "The Power of Place."
10. Beck, L. & T. Cable, 2002, "The Meaning of Interpretation." This essay may also be found in a book by the authors, published in 2010, titled *Interpretive Perspectives: A Collection of Essays on Interpreting Nature and Culture*.
11. Brochu, L. & T. Merriman, 2008, *Personal Interpretation: Connecting Your Audience to Heritage Resources*.
12. Beck, L., 2001.
13. Larsen, D.
14. Tilden, F.
15. Adams, S., 1996, Dilbert, August 18, 1996.
16. Wurman, 1989, *Information Anxiety*, p. 201.
17. Lawler, A., 2010, *Tending the Garden of Technology*.
18. Kane, H., 2001, *Triumph of the Mundane*, p. 183.
19. The discussion is based on Sylwester, R. & Joo-yun Cho, 1992/1993, "What Brain Research Says About Paying Attention."
20. Dustin, D., 2006, *The Wilderness Within*.
21. Sylwester, R. & Joo-yun Cho, pp. 74-75.
22. Csikszentmihalyi, M., 1990, *Flow: The Psychology of Optimal Experience*, pp. 123-24.
23. Burroughs, J., 1912, Quoted in Cable, T., 1992, "To Enjoy Understandingly."
24. Mills, E., p. 126.
25. Knapp, D., 2007, *Applied Interpretation*.
26. Tulving, E., 1972, "Episodic and Semantic Memory," and Tulving, E., 1983, *Elements of Episodic Memory*.
27. Ham, S., 2007, Foreword, *Applied Interpretation*, p. ix.
28. Knapp, D.
29. Ham, S., p. x.
30. Dickinson, E., Quoted in Campbell, J., 1972, *In Touch with Students*.

Chapter 3

1. Danton, T., 1990, Foreword to Mills, E., *Adventures of a Nature Guide and Essays in Interpretation.*
2. Tilden, F., 1977, *Interpreting Our Heritage*, p. 26.
3. Ibid, p. 29.
4. Mills, p. 180 and Tilden, pp. 26-7.
5. Compiled from Ham, S., 1992, *Environmental Interpretation*, pp. 10, 11, 14; Kawasaki, G., 1991, *Selling the Dream*, p. 104; and Knudson, D., Cable, T., & L. Beck, 2003, *Interpretation of Cultural and Natural Resources.*
6. Sartre, J-P., 1965, *Nausea.*
7. Jackson, P.W., 1995, "On the Place of Narrative in Teaching."
8. Rifkin, J., 1991, *Biosphere Politics.*
9. Caduto, M. & J. Bruchac, 1988, *Teacher's Guide to Keepers of the Earth.*
10. Strauss, S., 1996, *The Passionate Fact.*
11. Tilden, p. 28.
12. Ibid.
13. Beck, L., 1989, "Conversation with a Tramp: Lee Stetson on Interpretation." This essay may also be found in a book by the authors, published in 2010, titled *Interpretive Perspectives: A Collection of Essays on Interpreting Nature and Culture.*
14. Ibid, p. 7
15. Kawasaki, G., 1991, *Selling the Dream.*
16. See Knudson, D., Cable, T., & L. Beck, 2003, *Interpretation of Cultural and Natural Resources, Arts in Interpretation.*
17. Coles, R., 1989, *The Call of Stories: Teaching and the Moral Imagination.*
18. Williams, T. T., 1984, *Pieces of White Shell.* Also see, 1996, "An Interview with Terry Tempest Williams."
19. McClelland, M. 2010. "Get a (Second) Life."
20. Sanders, S. 2000. *The Force of Spirit*, p. 84
21. Lopez, B., 1988, *Crossing Open Ground.*
22. Sanders, S., 2006, *A Private History of Awe.*

Chapter 4

1. McFague, S. 2001. *Life Abundant*, p. 202.
2. Beck, L., 1989, "Conversations with Barry Lopez: Musings on Interpretation." This essay may also be found in a book by the authors, published in 2010, titled *Interpretive Perspectives: A Collection of Essays on Interpreting Nature and Culture.*
3. Williams, T.T., 1996, "Make us Uncomfortable." p. 9.
4. Abbey, E., 1968, *Desert Solitaire*, p. 233.
5. Tilden, F., 1977, *Interpreting Our Heritage*, p. 38
6. Beck.
7. Zeufle, M., 1994, "The Interface of Religious Beliefs and Environmental Values with the Interpretative Profession."
8. Knapp, D., 2007, *Applied Interpretation.*
9. Ibid, p. 55.
10. Ibid.

11. Ibid.
12. Ibid, p. 65.
13. Ibid, pp. 66-70.
14. Leopold, A., 1949, *A Sand County Almanac*, pp.223-224.
15. Senge, P., 1990, *The Fifth Discipline*.
16. Kawasaki, G., 1991, *Selling the Dream*.
17. Olson, S., 1982, *Reflections From the North Country*.
18. McKibben, B., 1990, "The Courage to Look for Trouble." p. 15.
19. Ibid.
20. Wilson, E. O., 1992, *The Diversity of Life*. p. 351.
21. Whalley, N., 2005, "Conserving Efforts."
22. Sam Ham quoted in Whalley, N., 2005, "Conserving Efforts."
23. Cable, T., 2006, "The Role of Interpretation in International Tourism." This essay may also be found in a book by the authors, published in 2010, titled *Interpretive Perspectives: A Collection of Essays on Interpreting Nature and Culture*.
24. Beck, L., 2008, "Voluntourism: Seeing the World and Saving the World." This essay may also be found in a book by the authors, published in 2010, titled *Interpretive Perspectives: A Collection of Essays on Interpreting Nature and Culture*.

Chapter 5

1. Olson, S., 1982, *Reflections from the North Country*, p. 112.
2. Commoner, B., 1971, *The Closing Circle*, p. 29.
3. Miller, G., 1956, "The Magical Number Seven, Plus or Minus Two: Some Limits on Our Capacity for Processing Information."
4. Tilden, F., 1977, *Interpreting Our Heritage*, p. 40.
5. Ham, S., 1992, *Environmental Interpretation*. See this source for an excellent discussion of thematic interpretation.
6. For further discussion see Ham, S., 1992, *Environmental Interpretation*, p. 39, and Ham, S., 1983, "Cognitive Psychology and Interpretation: Synthesis and Application." Also, see Thorndyke, P.W., 1977, "Cognitive Structures in Comprehension and Memory of Narrative Discourse."
7. From Little Bighorn Battlefield National Monument Interpretive Prospectus, unpublished document.
8. Lundberg, A., 1997, "Toward a Thesis-Based Interpretation."
9. Ibid.
10. Ibid.
11. Maslow, A., 1987, *Motivation and Personality*.
12. Tilden, p. 46.
13. Borun, M., Massey, C. & T. Lutter, 1993, "Naive Knowledge and the Design of Science Museum Exhibits."
14. Ackerman, D., 1990, *A Natural History of the Senses*, xviii.
15. Werling, D., 1995, "Regional Model Heritage Education."
16. Frome, M., 1982, "To Sin by Silence . . ."
17. Ibid. Cited in Frome, p. 41.
18. Tilden, p. 40.

Chapter 6

1. Mills, 1920, *Adventures of a Nature Guide and Essays in Interpretation*, p. 233.
2. Ibid, p. 130.
3. Tilden, 1977, *Interpreting Our Heritage*, p. 47.
4. Machlis, G. & D. Field, 1992, *On Interpretation*, p. 66.
5. Ibid.
6. Knudson, D., Cable, T., & L. Beck, 2003, *Interpretation of Cultural and Natural Resources*.
7. Louv, R., 1991, *Childhood's Future*.
8. Louv, R., 2005, *Last Child in the Woods*.
9. Dubos, R., cited in Tanner, T., 1974, *Ecology, Environment, and Education*.
10. Chawla, L., 1988, "Children's Concern for the Natural Environment," p. 19.
11. Nabhan, G. & S. Trimble, 1994, *The Geography of Childhood*.
12. Louv, 1991, p. 178.
13. Williams, T., 1988, "Why Johnny Shoots Stop Signs," p. 120.
14. Kingsolver, B., 1995, *High Tide in Tucson*.
15. Williams, p. 120. Quote by Marshal Case, National Audubon's vice-president for education.
16. Bixler, R., Carlisle, C., Hammitt, W., & M. Floyd, 1994, "Observed Fears and Discomforts Among Urban Students on Field Trips to Wildland Areas."
17. Sobel, D., 1996, *Beyond Ecophobia*.
18. Weilbacher, M., Quoted in Leinbach, K. (2008), "It's Kind of Fun to do the Impossible: The Story of Milwaukee's Urban Ecology Center."
19. Sobel, p. 27.
20. Ibid, p. 35.
21. Fogg, C. & L. Hartmann, 1985, "Interpretation for the Very Young." The discussion concerning Austin Nature Center programs for children is derived from this article.
22. Ibid, p. 24.
23. Bixler, et al.
24. The discussion concerning "Babes in the Woods" was derived from a program outline of the same title from the Missouri Department of Conservation. (Unpublished Document)
25. Ibid.
26. Summarized from Tilden's Chapter 7 in *Interpreting Our Heritage* and Mills's *Adventures of a Nature Guide and Essays in Interpretation*.
27. The discussion is a summary of a section titled "Children and Social Groups" in Machlis, G. & D. Field, pp. 69-71.
28. The discussion is a summary of a section titled "Interpretive Approaches" in Machlis, G. & D. Field, pp. 71-73.
29. Machlis, G. & D. Field, p. 72.
30. Ibid.
31. Tilden, p. 48.
32. Mills, p. 236.
33. Compiled from Burr Oak Woods Conservation Nature Center, Blue Springs, Missouri, Program Schedules. (Unpublished Documents)

34. LaCombe, L. Nature Center Manager. Pers. Comm. 2010.
35. Baumer, M., 1996, "Youth Volunteer Naturalists—Something to Believe In," p. 7.
36. Ibid.
37. Ibid.
38. Bultena, G., Field, D, & R. Renninger, 1992, "Interpretation for the Elderly."

Chapter 7

1. Luzader, J. & J. Spellman, 1996, "Living History: Hobby or Profession?" p. 241.
2. Luzader, J. Personal Communication. 16 February 2011.
3. Luzader & Spellman. p. 241.
4. Anderson, J., 1984, *Time Machines: The World of Living History*, pp. 189-192.
5. Luzader, J. Personal Communication. 16 February 2011.
6. Golda, J., 1996, "The Conquistadors: The Best and Worst of Human Nature." p.3.
7. Doerner, J. & A. Heinlein, 1996, "American Battlefields: Compelling Stories and Interpretive Challenge."
8. Saxe, D., 2009, Living Heritage: An Experimental Model Mixing Heritage and Entertainment, p. 33.
9. Ibid. p. 34.
10. Ibid. p. 34.
11. Harrison, E., 1993, "Can Walt Disney Interpret History?"
12. Ibid, p. 2
13. Ibid, p. 2
14. Bigley, J.D., 1991, "Living History and Battle Reenactment -The Dilemma of Selective Interpretation."
15. Bigley, p. 16.
16. *Visitor's Guide*, United States Holocaust Memorial Museum.
17. Winks, R., Quoted in *The National Parks: America's Best Idea Untold Stories Discussion Guide*, 2009, "Sue Kunitomi Embrey and Manzanar National Historic Site," p. 4.
18. Leatherman, T., Quoted in *The National Parks: America's Best Idea Untold Stories Discussion Guide*, 2009, "Sue Kunitomi Embrey and Manzanar National Historic Site," p. 4.
19. National Park Service Park Brochure, Brown v. Board of Education National Historic Site.
20. Ibid.
21. Mellish, X., 1996, "For Someone Who Died in 1826, He Gives a Lifelike Performance."
22. Ibid.
23. McCullough, D., 2002, "The Power of Place," pp. 50-51

Chapter 8

1. Sydney Harris, quoted in Peter, L.J., 1977, *Peter's Quotations: Ideas for Our Time*, p. 64.
2. Beck, L., 2008, "WebQuests, Wikis, and Wilderness."
3. Nielsen Survey, 2011, and Kaiser Family Foundation Study, 2010.
4. Oparnica, S., 2011, "Technology is Becoming Our Worst Addiction."

5. Richtel, M., 2010, "Your Brain on Computers: Hooked on Gadgets and Paying a Mental Price."
6. Ibid.
7. Ibid.
8. Richtel, M., 2010, "Digital Devices Deprive Brain of Needed Downtime."
9. Dustin, D., 2006, *The Wilderness Within.*
10. Richtel, M., 2010, "Your Brain on Computers: Hooked on Gadgets and Paying a Mental Price."
11. Richtel, M., 2010, "Outdoors and Out of Reach, Studying the Brain."
12. Sternberg, E., 2009, *Healing Spaces: The Science of Place and Well-Being,* p. 10.
13. Dustin, D., et al., 2011, *Stewards of Access, Custodians of Choice.*
14. Myers, J., 2008, "The Health Benefits and Economics of Physical Activity."
15. Kaufman, L., 2010, "Technology Leads More Park Visitors Into Trouble."
16. Ibid.
17. Ibid.
18. Ibid.
19. Thoreau, H. D., quoted in Peter, p. 64.
20. Blehm, E., 2010, *Molly the Owl.*
21. Ibid.
22. Ibid.
23. Tilden, F., 1977, *Interpreting Our Heritage,* p. 95.
24. Beck, L., & T. Cable, 1998 and 2002, *Interpretation for the 21st Century.*
25. Bettles, C., Davies, T., & W. Davis, 2007, *The Future of WebRangers,* p. 1.
26. Olson, L., & M. Reynolds, 1991, "Geographic Information Systems Make Good Interpretive Signs."
27. Johnson, W. C., 1996, "Habitats and Satellites."
28. O'Meara, M., 2000, "Harnessing Information Technologies for the Environment." See also Hawken, P., 2007, *Blessed Unrest.*
29. Caputo, P., Lewis, S., & L. Brochu, 2008, *Interpretation by Design,* p. 6.
30. Routman, E. & R. Korn, 1993, "The Living World Revisited: Evaluation of High Tech Exhibits at the Saint Louis Zoo," p. 20.
31. Ibid.

Chapter 9

1. Tilden, F., 1977, *Interpreting Our Heritage,* p. 80.
2. Ibid, p. 78.
3. Ibid, p. 82.
4. For studies describing how the length of labels in museum exhibits negatively affects visitor attention see, for example: Bitgood, et al. (1986) and Thompson and Bitgood (1988). These studies have found that signs and labels with short texts typically are read more frequently than those with longer texts.
5. Miller, G., 1956, "The Magical Number Seven, Plus or Minus Two: Some limits on Our Capacity for Processing Information."
6. Patterson & Bitgood (1988) reviewed the satiation literature and presented several studies supporting the concept of object satiation and museum fatigue.
7. Bitgood, S., 1991, "The ABCs of label design."
8. Bitgood, S., Patterson, D. & A. Benefield, 1988, "Exhibit Design and Visitor Behavior—Emperical Relationships."

9. Serrell, B., & B. Becker, 1990, "Stuffed Birds on Sticks: Plans to Re-do the Animal Halls at Field Museum," p. 266-267.
10. Ibid.
11. Whitman, W., quoted in Mills, S. (Ed.), 1990, *In Praise of Nature*.
12. Cable, T. & V. Brack, 1985, "The Martin-Mosquito Myth: Interpretative Propaganda?"
13. The following information about myths from films and paintings is from personal communication with John Doerner, Chief of Interpretation, Little Bighorn Battlefield National Monument, 23 July 1996.
14. James Loewen keynoted the 2007 NAI National Workshop, November 7, 2007, in Wichita, Kansas. He has written extensively on historic misconceptions.
15. Zuefle, M. & L. Beck, 1996, "Are We Ministers of Misinformation?"
16. See: Rothenberg, D., 1999, "Will the Real Chief Seattle Please Speak Up? An Interview with Ted Perry," Hargrove, E., 1989, "The Gospel of Chief Seattle is a Hoax," Jones, M. & R. Sawhill, 1992, "Just Too Good to Be True: Another Reason to Beware of False Eco-prophets," Meredith, J. & W. Steele, 1993, "The Truth of Chief Seattle," and Suzuki, D. and P. Knudtson, 1992, *Wisdom of the Elders: Sacred Native Stories of Nature*.
17. Zuefle, M. & L. Beck, p. 6.
18. Dillon, C., 1994, "Interpreting Myths and Misconceptions of U.S. History."
19. Ibid.
20. Ibid.
21. Ibid.
22. Cyr, D., 2000, "How to Visit an Art Museum: Former Met Director Thomas Hoving Says to Look Closely, But Not to Think Too Hard."
23. Ibid.

Chapter 10

1. For further information see: Knudson, D., Cable, T., & L. Beck, *Interpretation of Cultural and Natural Resources*, 2003, Performance Interpretation; Veverka, J., 1994, *Interpretive Master Planning*, Chapter 6, Planning Conducted Interpretive Programs; Ham, S., 1992, *Environmental Interpretation*, Chapter 3, How to Prepare and Present a Talk; Lewis, W., 1980, *Interpreting for Park Visitors*, Chapter 3, Primary Elements of Interpretation and Chapter 5, Talks.
2. Dillard, A., 1989, *The Writing Life*.
3. Lewis, W., 1980, *Interpreting for Park Visitors*.
4. Beck, L., 1989, "Conversations with Barry Lopez: Musings on Interpretation." This essay may also be found in a book by the authors, published in 2010, titled *Interpretive Perspectives: A Collection of Essays on Interpreting Nature and Culture*.
5. Ibid.
6. Ibid.
7. National Association for Interpretation "Mission" in Legacy, 2010, 21(5):6.
8. As listed in *InterpNews* (Newsletter for the National Association for Interpretation).
9. Beck, L., 2001, "What is the Essence of Our Professional Responsibility?" This essay may also be found in a book by the authors, published in 2010, titled *Interpretive Perspectives: A Collection of Essays on Interpreting Nature and Culture*.

Chapter 11

1. Tilden, F., 1977, *Interpreting Our Heritage*, p. 59.
2. Ibid.
3. Ibid.
4. Kingsolver, B., 1995, *High Tide in Tucson*, p. 250.
5. Tilden, p. 60.
6. Johnson, S. quoted in Winokur, J., 1990, *WOW – Writers on Writing*, p. 281.
7. Johnson, S. quoted in Royal Bank of Canada, 1976, *The Communication of Ideas: A Collection of Monthly Letters*, p. 97.
8. Dillard, A., 1989, *The Writing Life*, p. 68.
9. Lopez, B., 1998, *About This Life*, pp. 13-14.
10. Ibid, p. 14.
11. Edison, T. quoted in Davidoff, H., 1952, *The Pocketbook of Quotations*, p. 110.
12. Tilden, p. 59.
13. Brown, C.D. quoted in Winokur, J., 1990, *WOW – Writers on Writing*, p. 314.
14. Tilden.
15. Tilden, p. 59.
16. Emerson, R.W., quoted in Winokur, p. 272.
17. Fadimn, C., quoted in Winokur, p. 272.
18. Montaigne, M., quoted in Winokur, p. 272.
19. Tilden, p. 60.
20. Lopez, p. 15.
21. Gerard, P., 1996, *Creative Nonfiction*, p. 181.
22. Ibid. p. 182.
23. Zinsser, W., 2001, *On Writing Well*, p. 88.
24. Leftridge, A., 2006, *Interpretive Writing*, p. 123.
25. Steinbeck, J., quoted in Winokur, p. 346.
26. Tilden, p. 62.

Chapter 12

1. Personal Communication with Jay Miller, 2010.
2. This and all subsequent references to the interpretation program at Johnson County Parks and Recreation Department are based on an interview with Bill McGowan, Interpretive Program Supervisor, 28 January 2011.
3. Strand, L. 2007. *Friendraising- Increase Your Supporters and Your Audience*
4. See the story of Tim Merriman's fundraising efforts in Knudson, et al. (2003) pp. 342-343.
5. Jolley, G., M. Towns, N. Stimson, & K. Vogelpohl. 2007. *Partnerships Sustaining Interpretation: The Ford Transportation Interpreter Program.*
6. Volunteer in Parks, FY08 Director's Annual Report, Department of the Interior, National Park Service; GPO, Washington D.C.; 2008
7. Tung, Y. & H.C. Zinn. 2004. *Motivations of Volunteers in Taiwan: A Survey of Natural Trails Society Volunteers.*
8. Brown, A. & C. Lee. 2003. Bibliography of interpretive resources.
9. Barry, J. P. 2008. Interpretation saves lives.
10. Sharpe, G. interviewed in Bevilacqua, S., 1993, "Milestones, Millstones, and Stumbling Blocks."

11. Personal Communication with Jay Miller, Shea Lewis, and John Morrow, Arkansas State Parks. March 2011.

Chapter 13

1. Tilden, F., 1977, *Interpreting Our Heritage.*
2. Ibid, p. 85.
3. Mills, E., 1920, *Adventures of a Nature Guide and Essays in Interpretation*, p. 236.
4. Marshall, quoted in Nash, R., 2001, *Wilderness and the American Mind*, p. 203.
5. Teale, E.W., 1954, *The Wilderness World of John Muir*, p. 312.
6. Lopez, B., 1986, *Arctic Dreams.* [Paperback frontispiece.]
7. Marshall, R., 1930, "The Problem of the Wilderness."
8. Ibid.
9. Olson, S., 1982, *Reflections From the North Country*, p. 84.
10. Ackerman, D., 1990, *A Natural History of the Senses*, xviii.
11. Marshall.
12. Runte, A., 1987, *National Parks: The American Experience.*
13. Lopez, B., quoted in Beck, L., 1989, "Conversations with Barry Lopez," p. 4.
14. Whitman, W., quoted in Heat-Moon, p. 22.
15. Muir, J. quoted in Runte.
16. Tilden, p. 108.
17. Emerson, R. W. quoted in Nash.
18. Leopold, A., 1949, *A Sand County Almanac.*
19. de Botton, 2002, *The Art of Travel*, p. 216.
20. Ibid, p. 218.
21. Lopez, B., 1988, *Crossing Open Ground*, p. 64.
22. Tuan, Y-F., 1993, *Passing Strange and Wonderful.*
23. Mills, p. 106.
24. J. Ruskin, quoted in de Botton, p. 217.
25. Tilden, p. 88.
26. Muir, J., quoted in Wolfe, L.M., *Son of the Wilderness: The Life of John Muir.*
27. Ibid.
28. Muir, J., quoted in Nash, p. 126.
29. Saint-Exupéry, A., 1943, *The Little Prince*, p. 87.

Chapter 14

1. Csikszentmihalyi, M., 1990, *Flow: The Psychology of Optimal Experience.*
2. Ibid, p. 3.
3. Dustin, D., McAvoy, L., & L. Beck, 1986, "Promoting Recreationist Self-Sufficiency."
4. Csikszentmihalyi, M. & Kleiber, D., 1991, "Leisure and Self-Actualization."
5. Hedge, A., 1995, "Human Factor Considerations in the Design of Museums to Optimize Their Impact on Learning."
6. Csikszentmihalyi.
7. Dustin, D., McAvoy, L., & L. Beck.
8. Csikszentmihalyi, M. & K. Hermanson, 1995, "Intrinsic Motivation in Museums: What Makes Visitors Want to Learn?"
9. Csikszentmihalyi.

10. Csikszentmihalyi, M. and K. Hermanson.
11. Csikszentmihalyi, p. 62.
12. Hedge.
13. Csikszentmihalyi.
14. Csikszentmihalyi.
15. Mills, E., 1920, *Adventures of a Nature Guide and Essays in Interpretation*.
16. Csikszentmihalyi, M., 1975, *Beyond Boredom and Anxiety*.
17. These qualities are derived from the following document: Chartering a Management Philosophy for the Forest Service, signed by F. Dale Robertson, Chief, December 19, 1989.

Chapter 15

1. Boyer, D., 1985, "Yosemite Forever?"
2. Tilden, F., 1977, Interpreting Our Heritage.
3. Meadows, D., Meadows, D. & J. Randers, 1992, *Beyond the Limits*.
4. Beck, L., 1989, "Conversations with Barry Lopez." This essay may also be found in a book by the authors, published in 2010, titled *Interpretive Perspectives: A Collection of Essays on Interpreting Nature and Culture*.
5. Lopez, B., 1988, *Crossing Open Ground*.
6. Tilden, p. 90.
7. Sax, J., 1980, *Mountains Without Handrails*.
8. Cable, T. & L. Beck, 2001, "The Need for Interpretation: Now More than Ever."
9. Beck, L., 1989, "Conversations with Barry Lopez."
10. Buscaglia, L., 1982, *Living, Loving and Learning*.
11. Jones, S., 1996, "Open Your Heart to More Love."
12. Holmes, E., 1996, "Love in Everyday Living."

Conclusion

1. Mills, E., 1920, *Adventures of a Nature Guide and Essays in Interpretation*, p. 180.
2. Hyde, L., 1983, *The Gift*.
3. Yeats, W. B., "Adam's Curse," in 1992, *W. B. Yeats: Selected Poems*.
4. Hyde, p. xii.
5. D. H. Lawrence, quoted in Hyde, p. xii.
6. Finch, R. In Trimble, S., 1989, *Words From the Land*. p. 23.
7. Snyder, G., quoted in Hyde, L., p. 149.
8. Hyde, p. xii.
9. Ibid.
10. Ibid, p. xiv.
11. Ibid, p. 16.
12. Ibid, p. 20.
13. The following section is drawn from an essay in the *Journal of Interpretation Research* titled "The Meaning of Interpretation" (Beck, L. & T. Cable 2002) and an expanded version of this essay included in the book *Interpretive Perspectives* (Beck, L. & T. Cable 2010).
14. King, M., 1968, "The Meaning of Hope." (Taped Sermon.)
15. Havel, V., quoted in Sanders, S., 1998, *Hunting for Hope*, p. 27.
16. King.

17. Collins, J., 2001, *Good to Great: Why Some Companies Make the Leap … and Others Don't.*
18. Ibid.
19. Ibid.
20. Chesterton, G.K. Quoted in Beck, L. & T. Cable (2010) *Interpretive Perspectives: A Collection of Essays on Interpreting Nature and Culture*, p. 60.
21. Mills, p. 125.

Epilogue

1. This paragraph was inspired by the writings of E.B. White and Barry Lopez.

BIBLIOGRAPHY

Abbey, E. (1968). *Desert solitaire.* New York: Simon & Schuster.

Ackerman, D. (1990). *A natural history of the senses.* New York: Random House.

Adams, S. (1996). *Dilbert.* August 18, 1996.

Anderson, J. (1984). *Time machines: The world of living history.* Nashville, TN: The American Association for State and Local History.

Anderson, J., & Blahna, D. (1995). "Who are these people, and what do they want?: Assessment of interpreters' knowledge of their audience." *Proceedings of the 1995 National Interpreters' Workshop*: 280-292.

Baron, R. (1993). *Jefferson the man: In his own words.* Golden, CO: Fulcrum.

Barrie, E. (2001). "Ingredients of meaningful interpretive experiences." *Proceedings of the 2001 National Interpreters' Workshop*: 191-192.

Barry, J. P. (2008). "Interpretation saves lives." *Proceedings of the 2008 National Interpreters' Workshop*: 36-37.

Barry, J. P. (1993). "Anchoring safely in current: An example of using interpretation to solve a management problem." *Legacy, 4*(4):22.

Beck, L. (2008). "Webquests, wikis, and wilderness." *The Interpreter.* May/June:16-17.

Beck, L. (2008). "Voluntourism: Seeing the world and saving the world." *Legacy, 19*(1):28-29.

Beck, L. (2001). "What is the essence of our professional responsibility?" *Legacy, 12*(4):29-32.

Beck, L. (1989). "Conversations with a tramp: Lee Stetson on interpretation." *Journal of Interpretation 13*(6):6-7.

Beck, L. (1989). "Conversations with Barry Lopez: Musings on interpretation." *Journal of Interpretation, 13*(3):4-7.

Beck, L., & Cable, T. (2010). *Interpretive perspectives: A collection of essays on interpreting nature and culture.* Fort Collins, CO: InterpPress.

Beck, L., & Cable, T. (2002). *Interpretation for the 21st Century* (2nd ed.). Urbana, IL: Sagamore.

Beck, L., & Cable, T. (2002). "The meaning of interpretation." *Journal of Interpretation Research 7*(1):7-10.

Beck, L., & Cable, T. (1995). "Resolving the interpreter's identity problem." *Legacy, 6*(5):28-29.

Becker, C. L. (1932). "Everyman his own historian." *The American Historical Review, 37*(2):221-236.

Bettles, C., Davies, T., & W. Davis. (2007). *The future of webrangers: A report from the 2007 visioning workshop.* National Park Service. Department of the Interior.

Bevilacqua, S. (1993). "Milestones, millstones, and stumbling blocks." *Legacy, 4*(4):24-26.

Bigley, J. D. (1991). "Living history and battle reenactment – The dilemma of selective interpretation." *History News, 46*(6):1218.

Bitgood, S. (1991). "The ABCs of label design." *Visitor Studies: Theory, Research and Practice, Volume 3. (Proceedings of the 1990 Visitors Studies Conference)*: 115-129.

Bitgood, S. (1991). "Bibliography: Hands-on, participatory, and interactive exhibits." *Visitor Behavior, 6*(4):14-17.

Bitgood, S., Nichols, G., Pierce, M., Conroy, P., & Patterson, D. (1986). *Effect of label characteristics on visitor behavior.* Center for Social Design Technical Report No. 86-55:Jacksonville, AL.

Bitgood, S., Patterson, D., & Benefield, A. (1988). "Exhibit design and visitor behavior-empirical relationships." *Environment and Behavior, 20*(4):474-491.

Bixler, R., Carlisle, C., Hammitt, W., & Floyd, M. (1994). "Observed fears and discomforts among urban students on field trips to wildland areas." *Journal of Environmental Education, 26*(1):24-33.

Blehm, E. (2010). *Molly the owl.* Cardiff by the Sea, CA: Molly the Owls Books.

Borun, M., Massey, C., & Lutter, T. (1993). "Naive knowledge and the design of science museum exhibits." *Curator, 36*(3):201-219.

Boyer, D. (1985). "Yosemite forever?" *National Geographic.* January.

Brochu, L. (2003). *Interpretive planning.* Fort Collins, CO: InterpPress.

Brochu, L., & T. Merriman. (2008). *Personal interpretation: Connecting your audience to heritage resources* (2nd ed.). Fort Collins, CO: InterpPress.

Brown, B. (1996). "Dollars and sense." *Proceedings of the 1996 National Interpreters' Workshop*: 83-85.

Brown, A., & Lee, C. (2003). "Bibliography of interpretive resources." *Journal of Interpretation Research, 8*(2):1-16.

Bultena, G., Field, D., & Renninger, R. (1992). "Interpretation for the elderly." In Machlis, G., & D. Field (Eds.), *On interpretation* (revised ed.). Corvallis, OR: Oregon State University Press.

Buscaglia, L. (1982). *Living, loving and learning.* Thorofare, New Jersey: Charles B. Slack.

Cable, T. (2006). "The role of interpretation in international tourism." Pp. 71-77. Chapter in T. Merriman and L. Brochu (Eds.), *The history of interpretation in the United States.* Fort Collins, CO: InterpPress.

Cable, T. (1992). "To enjoy understandingly." *Legacy, 3*(2):8-9.

Cable, T., & Beck, L. (2001). "The need for interpretation: Now more than ever." *Legacy, 12*(5):47.

Cable, T., & Cadden, L. (2007). "The common roots of environmental education and interpretation." *Journal of Interpretation Research, 12*(1):39-46.

Cable, T., & Brack, Jr., V. (1985). "The martin-mosquito myth: Interpretative propaganda?" *Journal of Interpretation*, 10:29-32.

Cable, T., Knudson, D., Udd, E., & Stewart, D. (1987). "Attitude changes as a result of exposure to interpretive messages." *Journal of Park and Recreation Administration,* 5(1):47-60.

Caduto, M., & Bruchac, J. (1988). *Teacher's guide to keepers of the earth.* Golden, CO: Fulcrum.

Campbell, J. (1972). *In touch with students: A philosophy for teachers.* Columbia, MO: Educational Affairs Publishers.

Caputo, P., Lewis, S., & Brochu, L. (2008). *Interpretation by design.* Fort Collins, CO: InterpPress.

Carley, T., Linn, J., & C. McAlear. (2000). "The virtual visitor center: Helping the visitors help themselves." *Proceeedings of the 2000 National Interpreters' Workshop*: 215-216.

Carson, R. (1998). [Text originally published in 1956]. *The sense of wonder.* New York: HarperCollins.

Chawla, L. (1988). "Children's concern for the natural environment." *Children's Environments Quarterly, 5*(3):13-20.

Cialdini, R. (1996). "Activating and aligning two kinds of norms in persuasive communications." *Journal of Interpretation Research, 1*(1):3-10.

Cokinos, C. (2000). *Hope is the thing with feathers.* Warner Books.

Coles, R. (1989). *The call of stories: Teaching and the moral imagination.* Boston: Houghton Mifflin.

Collins, J. (2001). *Good to great.* New York: HarperCollins Publishers.

Commoner, B. (1971). *The closing circle.* New York, NY: Knopf.

Covel, J. (1995). "Enhancing interpretive services and products: Lessons from successful businesses." *Proceedings of the 1995 National Interpreters' Workshop*: 167-169.

Csikszentmihalyi, M. (1975). *Beyond boredom and anxiety.* San Francisco: Jossey-Bass.

Csikszentmihalyi, M. (1990). *Flow: The psychology of optimal experience.* New York: Harper & Row.

Csikszentmihalyi, M., & Kleiber, D. (1991). "Leisure and self-actualization." In Driver, B., Brown, P., & Peterson, G. (Eds.), *Benefits of leisure.* State College, PA: Venture.

Csikszentmihalyi, M., & Hermanson, K. (1995). "Intrinsic motivation in museums: What makes visitors want to learn?" *Museum News*, May/June:35-37, 59-61.

Curran, M. (1992). "Let's interact: Developing an interactive video computer system to interpret your site." *Proceedings of the 1992 National Interpreters' Workshop*: 203-206.

Cyr, D. (2000). "How to visit an art museum." *Attache*, April:32-36.

Dahlen, D., Fudge, R., Lacome, B., Larsen, D., & Weber, S. (2000). "The process of interpretation: A five-session study of effective interpretation." *Proceedings of the 2000 National Interpreters' Workshop*: 159-161.

Davidoff, H. (Ed.). (1952). *The pocket book of quotations.* New York, NY: Simon and Schuster.

de Botton, A. (2002). *The art of travel.* Vintage International Books. New York.

Dillard, A. (1989). *The writing life.* New York: Harper & Row.

Dillon, C. (1994). "Interpreting myths and misconceptions of U.S. History." *Legacy, 5*(1):10-11.

Doerner, J., & Heinlein, A. (1996) "American battlefields: Compelling stories and interpretive challenge." *Proceedings of the 1996 National Interpreters' Workshop*: 223.

Dustin, D. (2006). *The wilderness within.* Urbana, IL: Sagamore.

Dustin, D., McAvoy, L, & Beck, L. (1986). "Promoting recreationist self-sufficiency." *Journal of Park and Recreation Administration, 4*(4):43-52.

Dustin, D., McAvoy, L., Schultz, J., Bricker, K., Rose, J., & Schwab, K. (2011). *Stewards of access: Custodians of choice* (4th ed.). Urbana, IL: Sagamore.

Erickson, D. (1993). "CD-1: Advancing interactive video systems." *Proceedings of the 1993 National Interpreters' Workshop*: 77-80.

Everhart, W. C. (1988). "Some thoughts for those who charm and inform." *Journal of Interpretation, 12*(1):T5-T7.

Flavin, C., & Topfer, K. (2001). *Vital signs 2001: The trends that are shaping our future.* New York: W.W. Norton.

Fogg, C., & Hartmann, L. (1985). "Interpretation for the very young." *Journal of Interpretation, 10*(1):21-27.

Frome, M. (1982). "To sin by silence." *Journal of Interpretation,7*(2):41-45.

Gerard, P. (1996). *Creative nonfiction—Researching and crafting stories of real life.* Cincinnati, OH: Story Press.

Golda, J. (1996). "The Conquistadors: The best and worst of human nature." *The Explorer, 4*(7):1-3.

Ham, S. (1983). "Cognitive psychology and interpretation: Synthesis and application." *Journal of Interpretation, 8*(1):11-27.

Ham, S. (1992). *Environmental interpretation: A practical guide for people with big ideas and small budgets.* Golden, CO: North American Press.

Ham, S. (2009). "From interpretation to protection: Is there a theoretical basis?" *Journal of Interpretation Research, 14*(2):49-57.

Ham, S., & Krumpe, E. (1996). "Identifying audiences and messages for nonformal environmental education: A theoretical framework for interpreters." *Journal of Interpretation Research, 1*(1):11-23.

Hammitt, W. (1981). "A theoretical foundation for Tilden's interpretive principles." *Journal of Environmental Education, 12*(3):13-16.

Hargrove, E. (1989). "The gospel of Chief Seattle is a hoax." *Environmental Ethics,* 11:195-196.

Harrison, E. (1993). "Can Walt Disney interpret history?" *INTERPR8* (National Association for Interpretation-Region VIII Newsletter). Holiday Edition:2-3.

Hawken, P. (2007). *Blessed unrest.* New York: Viking.

Heat-Moon, W. L. (1991). *PrairyErth.* Boston: Houghton Mifflin.

Hedge, A. (1995). "Human factor considerations in the design of museums to optimize their impact on learning." In Falk, J., & Dierking, L. (Eds.), *Public institutions for personal learning: Establishing a research agenda.* Washington, D.C.:American Association of Museums.

Holmes, E. (1996). "Love in everyday life." *Science of Mind, 69*(5):24-30.

Hood, M. (1991). "Significant issues in museum audience research." *Visitor Studies: Theory, Research, and Practice Volume 4. (Collected Papers from the Visitor Studies Conference)*:19-23.

Hooper, J., & Weiss, K. (1990). "Interpretation as a management tool: A national study of interpretive professionals' views." *Proceedings of the 1990 National Interpreters' Workshop*: 350-357.

Horovitz, B. (2001). "Marketers call on kids to help design web sites." *USA Today,* June 5, 2001, p. B-1.

Hyde, L. (1983). *The gift: Imagination and the erotic life of property.* New York: Vintage.

Jackson, P. W. (1995). "On the place of narrative in teaching." In McEwan, H., & Egan, K. (Eds.), *Narrative in teaching, learning, and research.* New York: Teachers College Press.

Johnson, W. (1996). "Habitats and satellites." *Legacy, 7*(3):13-14.

Jolley, G., M. Towns, N. Stimson, & Vogelpohl, K. (2007). "Partnerships sustaining interpretation: The Ford transportation interpreter program." *Proceedings of the 2007 National Interpreters' Workshop*: 32.

Jones, S. (1996). "Open your heart to more love." *Science of Mind, 69*(5):6-12.

Jones, M., & Sawhill, R. (1992). "Just too good to be true: Another reason to beware of false eco-prophets." *Newsweek,* May 4:68.

Kane, H. (2001). *Triumph of the mundane: The unseen trends that shape our lives and environment.* Washington, D.C.: Island Press.

Kaufman, L. (2010). "Technology leads more park visitors into trouble." *New York Times,* August 21.

Kawasaki, G. (1991). *Selling the dream.* New York: HarperBusiness.

Kilgore, D. (1978). *How did Davy die?* College Station, TX: Texas A&M University Press.

Kingsolver, B. (1995). *High tide in Tucson.* New York, NY: HarperCollins.

Klevans, M. (1990). "An evaluation of an interactive microcomputer exhibit in a museum setting." *Proceedings of the 1990 Visitor Studies Conference*, 3:237-254.

Knapp, D. (2007). *Applied interpretation.* Fort Collins, CO: InterpPress.

Knopf, R. (1981). "Cognitive map formation as a tool for facilitating information transfer in interpretive programming." *Journal of Leisure Research*, 13(3):232-242.

Knudson, D., Cable, T., & Beck, L. (2003). *Interpretation of cultural and natural resources* (2nd ed.). State College, PA: Venture.

LaCombe, L. (2010). Nature Center Manager. Personal Communication. 13 April 2010.

Larsen, D. (Ed.). (2003). *Meaningful interpretation.* Eastern National.

Lawler, A. (2010). "Tending the garden of technology." *Orion*, January/February: 36-41.

Leftridge, A. (2006). *Interpretive writing.* Fort Collins, CO: InterpPress.

Leinbach, K. (2008). "It's kind of fun to do the impossible: The story of Milwaukee's urban ecology center." *Children, Youth and Environments*, 18(2).

Leopold, A. (1949). *A Sand County almanac.* Oxford University Press.

Lewis, W. (1980). *Interpreting for park visitors.* Philadelphia, PA: Eastern Acorn Press.

Little, C. (1987). "Letting Leopold down." *Wilderness*, 50(177):45-48.

Loomis, R. (1996). "How do we know what the visitor knows?: Learning from interpretation." *Journal of Interpretation Research*, 1(1):39-45.

Lopez, B. (1986). *Arctic dreams.* New York: Charles Scribner's Sons.

Lopez, B. (1988). *Crossing open ground.* New York: Charles Scribner's Sons.

Lopez, B. (1990). *The rediscovery of North America.* Lexington, KY: The University Press of Kentucky.

Lopez, B. (1998). *About this life: Journeys on the threshold of memory.* New York: Knopf.

Louv, R. (2005). *Last child in the woods.* Chapel Hill: Algonquin Books of Chapel Hill.

Louv, R. (1991). *Childhood's future.* New York: Doubleday.

Lundberg, A. (1997). "Toward a thesis-based interpretation." *Legacy*, 8(2):14-17, 30-31.

Luzader, J. C. F., & Spellman, J. (1996). "Living history: Hobby or profession?" *Proceedings of the 1996 National Interpreters' Workshop*: 241-243.

Machlis, G., & Field, D. (Eds.). (1992). *On interpretation.* (Revised ed.). Corvallis, OR: Oregon State University Press.

Machlis, G., & Field, D. (1992). "Getting connected: An approach to children's interpretation." In *On interpretation* (Revised ed.). Corvallis, OR: Oregon State University Press.

Manfredo, M., & Bright, A. (1991). "A model for assessing the effects of communication on recreationists." *Journal of Leisure Research*, 23(1):1-20.

Marshall, R. (1930). "The problem of the wilderness." *The Scientific Monthly*. Reprinted in *The Living Wilderness*, 40:31-35.

Maslow, A. (1987). *Motivation and personality* (Third ed.). New York: Harper & Row.

McClelland, M. (2010). "Get a (second) life." *Orion*, March/April: 38-42.

McCullough, D. (2002). "The power of place." *National Parks*, 76(1-2):50-51.

McFague, S. (2001). *Life abundant.* Minneapolis, MN: Fortress Press.

McGuire, F., Boyd, R., & Tedrick, R. (1996). *Leisure and aging.* Champaign, IL: Sagamore Publishing.

McKibben, B. (1990). "The courage to look for trouble." *Courier*, March: 14-15.

Meadows, D., Meadows, D., & Randers, J. (1992). *Beyond the limits.* Post Mills, Vermont: Chelsea Green.

Mellish, X. (1996). "For someone who died in 1826, he gives a lifelike performance." *The Wall Street Journal*, Nov. 15, 1996. B1.

Meredith, J., & Steele, W. (1993). "The truth of Chief Seattle." *Legacy*, 4(2):30-31.

Merriman, T. (1996). "Working toward a customer-centered interpretive business-A paradigm sheet." *Proceedings of the 1996 National Interpreters' Workshop*: 112-115.

Merriman, T., & Brochu, L. (2006). *The history of heritage interpretation in the United States*. Fort Collins, CO: InterpPress.

Merriman, T., & Brochu, L. (2005). *Management of interpretive sites*. Fort Collins, CO: InterpPress.

Miles, R. (1989). "Audiovisuals, a suitable case for treatment." *Visitors studies: Theory, research, and practice, Volume two. (Proceedings of the 1989 Visitors Studies Conference)*:245-251.

Miller, G. (1956). "The magical number seven, plus or minus two: Some limits on our capacity for processing information." *Psychological Review, 63*(2):81-97.

Miller, M.J. (2001). "Forward thinking." *PC Magazine*, September 4, 2001, p. 8.

Mills, E. (1920). *Adventures of a nature guide and essays in interpretation.* Friendship, WI: New Past Press.

Mills, S. (Ed.). (1990). *In praise of nature.* Washington, D.C.:Island Press.

Moscardo, G. (1988). "Toward a cognitive model of visitor responses in interpretive centers." *The Journal of Environmental Education, 20*(1):29-37.

Murie, A. (1962). *Mammals of Denali.* Alaska Natural History Association.

Myers, J. (2008). "The health benefits and economics of physical activity." *Current Sports Medicine Reports, 7*(6):314-316.

Nabhan, G., & Trimble, S. (1994). *The geography of childhood.* Boston: Beacon Press.

Nash, R. (2001). *Wilderness and the American mind.* (4th ed.) New Haven: Yale University Press.

Norris, K. (1993). *Dakota.* New York: Houghton Mifflin.

Oliver, S., Roggenbuck, J., & A. Watson. (1985). "Education to reduce impacts in forest campgrounds." *Journal of Forestry, 83*:234-236.

Olson, S. (1982). *Reflections from the North Country.* New York: Knopf.

Olson, L., & M. Reynolds. (1991). "Geographic information systems make good interpretive signs." *Proceedings of the 1991 National Interpreters' Workshop*: 242-243.

O'Meara, M. (2000). "Harnessing information technologies for the environment." In: Brown, L., (2000). *State of the world 2000.* New York: W.W. Norton.

Oparnica, S. (2011). "Technology is becoming our worst addiction." *The Daily Aztec*, 24 January:4.

Osterbauer, R., & Martel, M. (1995). "High-tech magic: Satellites to schools." *Proceedings of the 1995 National Interpreters' Workshop*: 275-277.

Patterson, D., & Bitgood, S. (1988). "Some evolving principles of visitor behavior." *Proceedings of the First Annual Visitor Studies Conference.* Jackson State University, Jacksonville, AL. 40-50.

Person, J. E., Jr. (Ed.). (1993). *Statistical forecasts of the U. S.* Detroit: Gale Research, Inc.

Peter, L. (1977). *Peter's quotations: Ideas for our time.* New York: Wm. Morrow.

Quammen, D. (1985). *Natural acts: A side long view of science and nature.* New York: Avon Books.

Rasp, D. (1996). "Satellite technology brings millions to the edge of creation." *Legacy, 7*(4):30-31.

Richtel, M. (2010). "Your brain on computers: Hooked on gadgets and paying a mental price." *New York Times*, June 7.

Richtel, M. (2010). "Outdoors and out of reach, studying the brain." *New York Times*, August 15.

Richtel, M. (2010). "Digital devices deprive brain of needed downtime." *New York Times,* August 24.

Rifkin, J. (1991). *Biosphere politics.* New York: Crown.

Romey, W. (1968). *Inquiry techniques for teaching science.* Englewood Cliffs, NJ: Prentice-Hall.

Rothenberg, D. (1999). "Will the real Chief Seattle please speak up?: An interview with Ted Perry." In: Rothenberg, D., & Ulvaeus, M. (Ed.). *The new earth reader.* Cambridge: The MIT Press.

Routman, E. (1994). "Considering high-tech exhibits?" *Legacy,5*(6):19-22.

Routman, E., & Korn, R. (1993). "The living world revisited: Evaluation of high-tech exhibits at the Saint Louis Zoo." *Museumedia. 3*(4):2-5.

Runte, A. (1987). *National parks: The American experience.* Lincoln: University of Nebraska Press.

Saint-Exupéry, A. (1943). *The little prince.* New York: Harcourt Brace Jovanovich.

Sanders, S. (1998). *Hunting for hope.* Boston: Beacon Press.

Sanders, S. (2000). *The force of spirit.* Boston: Beacon Press.

Sartre, J-P. (1965). *Nausea.* Harmondsworth, UK: Penguin.

Sawhill, J. (1995). "The art of giving." *Nature Conservancy,* November/December:5.

Sax, J. (1980). *Mountains without handrails.* Ann Arbor: The University of Michigan Press.

Saxe, D. (2009). "Living heritage: An experimental model mixing heritage and entertainment. " *Journal of Interpretation Research, 14*(1):33-46.

Schaller, D.T., Allison-Bunnel, S. & Nagel, S.A. (Unpublished Document). "Developing goal-based scenarios for web education." Document distributed at the 2001 National Interpreters' Workshop, Des Moines, Iowa.

Screven, C. (1990). "Computers in exhibit settings." *Visitor Studies: Theory, Research, and Practice, Volume Three (Proceedings of the 1990 Visitor Studies Conference):*130-138.

Senge, P. (1990). *The fifth discipline.* New York: Doubleday.

Serrell, B., & Becker, B. (1990). "Stuffed birds on sticks: Plans to re-do the animal halls at field museum." *Visitor Studies: Theory, research, and practice, Volume three (Proceedings of the 1990 Visitor Studies Conference):* 263-267.

Silverman, L.H. (1997). "Personalizing the past: A review of literature with implications for historical interpretation." *Journal of Interpretation Research, 2*(1):1-12.

Sobel, D. (1996). *Beyond ecophobia.* Great Barrington, MA: The Orion Society.

Stalder, M., & Cahill, B. (1992). "Bears, bears and more bears – Interpretation as a resource management tool: A success story!" *Proceedings of the 1992 National Interpreters' Workshop:* 40-43.

Stegner, W. (1991). "The gift of wilderness." In Willers, B. (Ed.), *Learning to listen to the land.* Washington, D.C.: Island Press.

Sternberg, E. (2009). *Healing spaces.* Cambridge, MA: Harvard.

Stofan, J. (1995). "Crossing the sea: Sea World's distance education." *Proceedings of the 1995 National Interpreters' Workshop:* 264-266.

Strand, L. (2007). "Friendraising- Increase your supporters and your audience." *Proceedings of the 2007 National Interpreters' Workshop:* 19.

Strauss, S. (1996). *The passionate fact.* Golden, CO: North American Press.

Suzuki, D., & Knudtson, P. (1992). *Wisdom of the elders: Sacred native stories of nature.* New York: Bantam.

Sylwester, R., & Joo-Yun Cho. (1992/1993). "What brain research says about paying attention." *Educational Leadership, 50*(4):71-75.

Tanner, T. (1974). *Ecology, environment, and education.* Lincoln, Nebraska: Professional Educators Publications.

Teale, E. W. (1954). *The wilderness world of John Muir.* Boston: Houghton Mifflin.

The National Parks: America's Best Idea Untold Stories Discussion Guide. (2009). "Sue Kunitomi Embrey and Manzanar National Historic Site."

Thelen, D. (1991). "History making in America." *Historian, 53*(4):631.

Thorndyke, P. W. (1977). "Cognitive structures in comprehension and memory of narrative discourse." *Cognitive Psychology, 9*(1): 77-110.

Tilden, F. (Undated). *The fifth essence.* Washington, D.C.: The National Park Trust Fund Board.

Tilden, F. (1977). *Interpreting our heritage* (3rd ed.). Chapel Hill: The University of North Carolina Press.

Tilden, F. (1983). *The national parks.* New York: Knopf.

Trimble, S. (1989). *Words from the land.* Salt Lake City: Peregrine Smith.

Tuan, Y-F. (1993). *Passing strange and wonderful: Aesthetics, nature, and culture.* Washington, D.C.: Island Press.

Tung, Y. , & Zinn, H. C. (2004). "Motivations of volunteers in Taiwan: A survey of natural trails society volunteers. *Journal of Interpretation Research, 9*(1):27-39.

Vance, C., & Schroeder, D. (1991). "Matching visitor learning style with exhibit type: Implications for learning in informal settings." *Visitor Studies: Theory, Research, and Practice, Volume Four (Proceedings of the 1991 Visitor Studies Conference)*: 185-199.

Veverka, J. (1994). *Interpretive master planning.* Helena, Montana: Falcon Press.

Volunteer in Parks, FY08 Director's Annual Report. (2008). Department of the Interior, National Park Service; GPO, Washington D.C.; 2008.

Werling, D. (1995). "Regional model heritage education." *Legacy, 6*(5):16-17.

Whalley, N. (2005). "Conserving efforts." *Monash Magazine.* Monash Univeristy. October 2005.

Williams, T. (1988). "Why Johnny shoots stop signs." *Audubon, 90*(5):112-121.

Williams, T. T. (1984). *Pieces of white shell.* New York: Charles Scribner's Sons.

Williams, T. T. (1996). "Make us uncomfortable (Williams challenges park interpreters.)" *The Exchange, 13*(2):7-10.

Williams, T. T. (1996). "An interview with Terry Tempest Williams." *Timeline,* Issue 25, January/February: 10-14.

Wilson, E. O. (1992). *The diversity of life.* Cambridge: Harvard University Press.

Winokur, J. (1990). *WOW – Writers on writing.* Philadelphia, PA: Running Press.

Wolfe, L.M. (1973). *Son of the wilderness: The life of John Muir.* Madison: The University of Wisconsin Press.

Worts, D. (1990). "The computer as catalyst: Experiences at the Art Gallery of Ontario." *ILVS Review: A Journal of Visitor Behavior. 1*(2):91-108.

Wurman, R.S. (1989). *Information anxiety.* New York: Doubleday.

Yeats, W.B. (1992). *Selected poems.* New York: Random House.

Zinsser, W. (2001). *On writing well* (25th anniversary edition). New York: Harper Collins.

Zuefle, D. M., & Beck, L. (1996). "Are we ministers of misinformation?" *Legacy, 7*(1):4-6.

Zuefle, D. M. (1994). *The interface of religious beliefs and environmental values with the interpretive profession: A multimethodological exploratory study.* Ph.D. Dissertation. Texas A&M University, College Station.

INDEX

ACKNOWLEDGMENTS

The following individuals provided information, reviewed chapters, or in some other way helped us in writing this book: Michele Baumer, Adelle Beck, James Bigley, Stephen Bitgood, Rob Bixler, Mary Bonnell, Roxanne Brickell-Reardon, LuAnn Cadden, Christopher Cokinos, John Doerner, Dan Dustin, Susan Fowler, Robin Grumm, Shea Lewis, Bob Loudon, John Luzader, Elaine Marshall, Bill McGowan, Jay Miller, Mark Morgan, Andrea Saltzman Martin, Lois Silverman, Gerry Snyder, and Ron Zimmerman. We are also grateful for the editing expertise of Sarah Caldwell-Hancock.

ABOUT THE AUTHORS

Larry Beck, Ph.D., is a professor in the L. Robert Payne School of Hospitality and Tourism Management at San Diego State University. He has a B.S. in Natural Resource Planning and Interpretation from Humboldt State University, M.A. in Education from Azusa Pacific University, and a Ph.D. in Education from the University of Minnesota. He worked as an interpreter for the National Park Service at Denali National Park and Preserve (Alaska), Glen Canyon National Recreation Area (Arizona/Utah), and Cabrillo National Monument (California). Dr. Beck is the author/coauthor of four books and more than 100 articles on natural resource management, cultural and environmental interpretation, and higher education. He has received numerous awards for his teaching and scholarship, including the Meritorious Service Award and Fellow Award from the National Association for Interpretation.

Ted T. Cable, Ph.D., is a professor of Park Management and Conservation at Kansas State University. He has a B.S. in Biology from the University of Illinois- Chicago, and both a M.S. in Wildlife Ecology and Ph.D. in Forest Recreation from Purdue University. He worked as an interpreter for the Cook County Forest Preserve District (Illinois) and for Lake County Parks and Recreation Department (Indiana). Dr. Cable is the author/coauthor of 11 books and more than 150 articles on natural resource management, wildlife, and interpretation. He has consulted on conservation projects in more than 25 states, has designed several nature parks and preserves, and has worked on conservation projects in Latin America and Africa. In addition to having received numerous university awards, he is a Fellow of the National Association for Interpretation and has been honored by both the U.S. Environmental Protection Agency and the U.S. Department of Agriculture for outstanding teaching in the field of conservation and interpretation.